The Classic Hundred Poems

The Classic

EDITED BY

William Harmon

Hundred Poems

ALL-TIME FAVORITES

SECOND EDITION

COLUMBIA UNIVERSITY PRESS   NEW YORK

COLUMBIA UNIVERSITY PRESS
NEW YORK

Columbia University Press
Publishers Since 1893
New York   Chichester, West Sussex
Copyright © 1990, 1998 Columbia University Press
Pages 359–60 constitute an extension of this copyright page. This book was first
published in 1990 under the title *The Concise Columbia Book of Poetry*.
All rights reserved

Library of Congress Cataloging-in-Publication Data
The classic hundred poems : all-time favorites / edited by William
  Harmon. — 2nd ed.
    p. cm.
  Rev. ed. of: The concise Columbia book of poetry. c1990.
  Includes bibliographical references and index.
  ISBN 978–0–231–11259–8 (paperback : alk. paper). — ISBN 0–231–10974–1
  (CD-ROM)
    1. English poetry. 2. American poetry. I. Harmon, William, 1938– . II. Concise
  Columbia book of poetry.
  PR1175.C55 1998
  821.008—dc21

                                                                    97–43683

Casebound editions of Columbia University Press books are printed on permanent
and durable acid-free paper.
Printed in the United States of America

Designed by Linda Secondari

p 10 9 8 7

CONTENTS

Other Columbia University Press Poetry Publications

The Top 500 Poems
  William Harmon, ed. (1992)

The Classic Hundred Poems CD-ROM: A Multimedia Anthology
  William Harmon, Alice Quinn, and Cindy Scott, eds. (1988)

The Columbia Anthology of American Poetry
  Jay Parini, ed. (1995)

The Columbia Anthology of British Poetry
  Carl Woodring and James Shapiro, eds. (1995)

The Columbia Book of Civil War Poetry
  Richard Marius, ed. (1994)

Poetry of the American West
  Alison Hawthorne Deming, ed. (1996)

The Columbia History of American Poetry
  Jay Parini, ed. (1995)

The Columbia History of British Poetry
  Carl Woodring and James Shapiro, eds. (1995)

The Columbia Granger's® World of Poetry CD-ROM, 2nd release (1995)

The Columbia Granger's® Index to Poetry in Anthologies, 11th ed.
  Nicholas Frankovich, ed. (1997)

The Columbia Granger's® Index to Poetry in Collected and Selected Works
  Nicholas Frankovich, ed. (1996)

The Columbia Granger's® Dictionary of Poetry Quotations
  Edith P. Hazen, ed. (1992)

PREFACE TO THE SECOND EDITION

THE FIRST EDITION of this anthology presented the hundred poems most frequently reprinted in anthologies, according to the ninth edition of *The Columbia Granger's® Index to Poetry in Anthologies*. This second edition presents a slightly different hundred poems, based as it now is on the eighth, ninth, and tenth edition of *Granger's*. According to this new tally, nineteen poems have gained in popularity, replacing nineteen that have slipped, and the number one spot that had belonged to William Blake's "The Tyger" now belongs to John Keats's "To Autumn."

The arrangement of the poems in this edition is no longer in order of popularity, but chronological with the listing according to popularity given in a table at the back to the book. The biographies, introductions, and notes have been considerably expanded, in order to explain all proper names, allusions, and unfamiliar terms. And now there is a glossary of technical terms. My hope is that nothing remains to puzzle readers or stand in the way of their appreciation of the beauty and interest of the poems.

Editors of anthologies, almost by definition, choose the works to be included. I did no such thing. The poems in this book were selected for me by the thousands of poets, critics, and editors who had made choices for their hundreds of anthologies. The resulting consensus selection is a straightforward objective statistical record. My job, a huge pleasure, consisted of exploring what has made these poems so popular. Why are these poems classics? My way of answering these questions has been to provide what most anthology editors, even anthology textbook editors, do not provide, namely detailed comments on all the poems individually. These hundred poems, even if they do not absolutely represent my personal choice, are a superb collection, illustrating much of what is best in the whole history of poetry in English for more than five hundred years.

For the record, we have here a hundred poems by forty-six named and three anonymous poets. Eighty-eight of the poems are English, Scottish, Welsh, and Irish; twelve are American. One expects disproportion here, since British literary history—as far as the English language is concerned, at any rate—has been going on for several centuries longer. The breakdown by historical period is illuminating:

Before 1550	4
1551–1650	35
1651–1750	2
1751–1850 (British)	27
1751–1850 (American)	2
1851–present (British)	20
1851–present (American)	10

Both poems in the 1651–1750 period are by Thomas Gray. He was not by any means the only poet active during those hundred years, but fashion during much of the period favored the sorts of long didactic and satiric poems that have not been favored by anthologists. Similar sorts of reasons no doubt account for the absence of some of the greatest poets of the language from this collection, such as Chaucer, Pope, and Whitman.

More than half of the poets in the book are represented by only one poem. Representation among the rest is as follows:

Shakespeare	7
Donne	7
Blake	5
Wordsworth	5
Keats	4
Yeats	4
Robert Browning	3
Dickinson	3
Herbert	3
Herrick	3
Hopkins	3
Jonson	3
Shelley	3
Tennyson	3
Thomas	3

I have included notes on the verse form of each poem at the end of the commentary on the poem. It may be of interest to note here that not one poem in the book is in free verse: all follow some measure of rhythm (overwhelmingly iambic) and meter, and ninety-seven involve rhyme in some pattern (the remaining three are in blank verse, which obeys dictates of rhythm and meter). Sixteen of these poems are conventional sonnets of fourteen lines; Hopkins called "Pied Beauty" a curtal sonnet, which has ten-and-a-fraction lines. Ten poems rhyme in couplets, two in triplets. Twenty-six employ some species of quatrain; there are six five-line stanzas and seven six-line stanzas. Seventeen poems, including those called odes, use various other stanzaic patterns. One poem is in rhyme royal, one in terza rima, one in ottava rima, and one is a villanelle. (Again, all terms are explained in the notes or the glossary.) Seven poems are zoned into irregular patterns of meter and rhyme, and Owen's unique "Strange Meeting" experimentally replaces rhyme with a combination of alliteration and consonance whereby, for example, "years" is mated not with "tears" but with "yours."

As the tally changes, new lines of perspective open up in ways that I still find exciting. As I read and re-read these poems, I became more and more convinced that they are very far from a loose assembly chosen at haphazard from an unruly democracy always threatening to lapse into anarchy. True, they are splendidly varied, but in my commentaries I have suggested many linkages and kinships, demonstrating that poetry is the work of a community, even of a family of artists extended over thousands of years and thousands of square miles. Christopher Marlowe writes a parody of a popular pastoral fad, and Sir Walter Ralegh soon parodies Marlowe's parody. George Herbert's "Love III" contains the phrase "ah my dear," which returns 250 years later in Gerard Manley Hopkins's "The Windhover" (Hopkins made a special trip to Salisbury Cathedral to honor the place where Herbert had been ordained). Then another passage from "The Windhover," containing "mastery," "brute," and "air," furnishes the substance of a line in William Butler Yeats's "Leda and the

Swan": "So mastered by the brute blood of the air" (Yeats and Hopkins met briefly toward the end of Hopkins's life). With few exceptions, the poems in this collection talk to one another and to many other great poems as well as to other great writings and works of art in other media.

A lyric poem is the supremely precious artwork: you can have it with you in its authentic form with very little trouble or expense. A painting or sonata may be, in the abstract, as great and as precious as a poem, but you have to go to some trouble to visit a museum or recital hall, or else settle for a reproduction or a recording. Accordingly, many people spend almost all of their lives with no direct experience of any primary human art. Some of those arts call for special training or special travel. For certain supreme experiences of music and architecture, one has to go to Bayreuth, Germany, and Bear Run, Pennsylvania. With poetry, however, any decent printed version just *is* the real thing, the thing itself, or as close to it as one can come. A penniless reader, who could conceivably be quite illiterate, may possess a lyric poem as fully and as authentically as anybody can. And that fact makes a poem the greatest bargain in the world: a poem is the cheapest and quickest means of making your life better in ways that deserve to be called noble.

The Classic Hundred Poems

Anonymous

Sir Patrick Spens

I. The Sailing

The king sits in Dunfermline town,
    Drinking the blude-red wine;
"O whare will I get a skeely skipper
    To sail this new ship o' mine?"

O up and spak an eldern knight,
    Sat at the king's right knee;
"Sir Patrick Spens is the best sailor
    That ever sail'd the sea."

Our king has written a braid letter,
    And seal'd it with his hand,
And sent it to Sir Patrick Spens,
    Was walking on the strand.

"To Noroway, to Noroway,
    To Noroway o'er the faem;
The king's daughter o' Noroway,
    'Tis thou must bring her hame."

The first word that Sir Patrick read
    So loud, loud laugh'd he;
The neist word that Sir Patrick read
    The tear blinded his e'e.

"O wha is this has done this deed
    And tauld the king o' me,
To send us out, at this time o' year,
    To sail upon the sea?

"Be it wind, be it weet, be it hail, be it sleet,
    Our ship must sail the faem;
The king's daughter o' Noroway,
    'Tis we must fetch her hame."

They hoysed their sails on Monenday morn
    Wi' a' the speed they may;
They hae landed in Noroway
    Upon a Wodensday.

II. The Return

"Mak ready, mak ready, my merry men a'!
    Our gude ship sails the morn."
"Now ever alack, my master dear,
    I fear a deadly storm.

"I saw the new moon late yestreen
    Wi' the auld moon in her arm;
And if we gang to sea, master,
    I fear we'll come to harm."

They hadna sail'd a league, a league,
    A league but barely three,
When the lift grew dark, and the wind blew loud,
    And gurly grew the sea.

The ankers brak, and the topmast lap,
    It was sic a deadly storm:
And the waves cam owre the broken ship
    Till a' her sides were torn.

"Go fetch a web o' the silken claith,
    Another o' the twine,
And wap them into our ship's side,
    And let nae the sea come in."

They fetch'd a web o' the silken claith,
    Another o' the twine,
And they wapp'd them round that guide ship's side,
    But still the sea came in.

O laith, laith were our gude Scots lords
    To wet their cork-heel'd shoon;
But lang or a' the play was play'd
    They wat their hats aboon.

And mony was the feather bed
    That flatter'd on the faem;
And mony was the gude lord's son
    That never mair cam hame.

O lang, lang may the ladies sit,
    Wi' their fans into their hand,
Before they see Sir Patrick Spens
    Come sailing to the strand!

And lang, lang may the maidens sit
    Wi' their gowd kames in their hair,
A-waiting for their ain dear loves!
    For them they'll see nae mair.

Half-owre, half-owre to Aberdour,
    'Tis fifty fathoms deep;
And there lies gude Sir Patrick Spens,
    Wi' the Scots lords at his feet!

COMPOSED AROUND 1325; PUBLISHED 1765. This kind of poem, a ballad, comes from Scotland and the border between Scotland and England. These regions, much farther north than any place in the United States, are relatively cold and wild. For hundreds of years they have been the setting of bloody conflicts. Such recent movies as *Rob Roy* and *Braveheart*, along with the *Highlander* movies and the related television series, show that Scotland still fascinates us with its rough country and violent history. (Of the first five Scottish kings named James, none died a peaceful death.)

In "Sir Patrick Spens" the exact details are missing, but the general situation is clear enough. No words are wasted in descriptions or explanations. A troubled king is drinking (and the color of the blood-red wine is a preview of what's to come) and talking alone to himself. He needs a good sailor to take a new ship on a round trip to Norway, which is four hundred miles away and even farther north than the north of Scotland. Sailors in the Middle Ages seldom went to sea in the winter, but there seems to be a political motive here: bringing back a king's daughter, maybe as part of an arranged marriage. The king announces his need, an advisor suggests Sir Patrick, the king writes a letter, Sir Patrick reads the letter, and very soon the exploit is underway. To make a trip of four hundred miles in forty-eight hours calls for a speed of eight knots, about ten miles per hour: not very fast by today's standards but most impressive given the notoriously rough conditions in the North Sea, especially in winter. In the days before radar and satellites, sailors had to depend on signs and traditions, some of which were superstitions, some of which were accurate (and some were both). Storms at sea tend to be worse in September and March, at the times of the equinoxes, and tides are both higher and lower with the new moon and the full moon. Displays at a museum in Penzance, Cornwall, suggest that there have been 250,000 significant shipwrecks in human history. Modern sailors say that there is a newsworthy marine disaster somewhere in the world about once per week.

Coleridge's "Rime of the Ancient Mariner" is another poem about a disaster at sea. Coleridge was familiar with "Sir Patrick Spens": his "Dejection: An Ode" begins, "Well! If the Bard was weather-wise, who made / The grand old ballad of Sir Patrick Spence. . . ." ("Spens" and "Spence" are two spellings of the same name.)

FORM: Ballad measure: quatrains alternating tetrameter and trimeter lines rhyming *abcb*.

Edward, Edward

"Why does your brand so drop with blood,
　　　Edward, Edward?
Why does your brand so drop with blood,
　　And why so sad go ye, O?"
"O I have killed my hawk so good,
　　　Mother, mother;
O I have killed my hawk so good,
　　And I have no more but he, O."

"Your hawk's blood was never so red,
　　　Edward, Edward;
Your hawk's blood was never so red,
　　My dear son, I tell thee, O."
"O I have killed my red-roan steed,
　　　Mother, mother;
O I have killed my red-roan steed,
　　That went so fair and free, O."

"Your steed was old, and ye have more,
　　　Edward, Edward;
Your steed was old, and ye have more,
　　Some other dole ye dree, O."
"O I have killed my father dear,
　　　Mother, mother;
O I have killed my father dear,
　　Alas, and woe is me, O!"

"And what penance will ye dree for that,
　　　Edward, Edward?
What penance will ye dree for that,
　　My dear son, now tell me, O."
"I'll set my foot in yonder boat,
　　　Mother, mother,
I'll set my foot in yonder boat,
　　And I'll fare o'er the sea, O."

"And what will ye do with your towers and your hall,
    Edward, Edward?
And what will ye do with your towers and your hall,
    That were so fair to see, O?"
"I'll let them stand till down they fall,
    Mother, mother;
I'll let them stand till down they fall,
    For here never more must I be, O."

"And what will ye leave to your bairns and your wife,
    Edward, Edward?
And what will ye leave to your bairns and your wife,
    When ye go o'er the sea, O?"
"The world's room: let them beg through life,
    Mother, mother;
The world's room: let them beg through life,
    For them never more will I see, O."

"And what will you leave to your own mother dear,
    Edward, Edward?
And what will ye leave to your own mother dear,
    My dear son, now tell me, O?"
"The curse of hell from me shall ye bear,
    Mother, mother;
The curse of hell from me shall ye bear,
    Such counsels ye gave to me, O!"

PROBABLY DEVELOPED IN ORAL TRADITION BEFORE 1500; PUB-
LISHED 1765. This rugged little drama comes out of the same bloody time and
place that produced *Macbeth* and "Sir Patrick Spens." With their landscape of
wild highlands and lochs of otherworldly beauty and with a terrible winter cli-
mate, the Scots have developed a literature of matchless severity.

    But that literature is not primitive in concept or in execution. This poem is
extremely sophisticated in the way it compresses an entire domestic catastrophe
into speeches without introduction or context. There are no fillers such as "She
asked anxiously." The reader is plunged right into the middle of things: a man

who has just killed his own father answers questions from his mother. We do not know why, but we do know that such things happen every day: MAN SLAYS DAD, BLAMES MOM. We have to admire the artistry that compresses whole personalities and lifetimes into a few words.

FORM: Eight-line stanza with the first and third lines the same, as also the fifth and seventh. The second and sixth lines, consisting of repeated terms of address, are the same in each stanza. The first and third lines rhyme with the fifth and seventh, and the fourth and eighth line rhyme, always on the same sound. The second and sixth do not rhyme. The metrical scheme is tetrameter, dimeter, tetrameter, trimeter, tetrameter, dimeter, tetrameter, trimeter.

Western Wind

Western wind, when wilt thou blow?
The small rain down can rain.
Christ, that my love were in my arms,
And I in my bed again.

PROBABLY COMPOSED AROUND 1500 BUT NOT PUBLISHED UNTIL
1792. An eighteenth-century antiquarian found this splendid verse, with a
musical setting, in a handwritten book of songs dating from the early sixteenth
century. The first publication was in Joseph Ritson's *Ancient Songs*.

Nothing is known about the poet, except that he or she created a memorable
speaker who, at a time of separation from a lover, expresses frustration in con-
crete terms. Instead of talking *about* something abstract, the poem talks *to* some-
thing concrete and familiar: the wind that blows from the west and is known in
Europe for its gentleness. This may be an autumn poem, like Shelley's "Ode to
the West Wind," or a spring poem, calling out for the west wind to bring the
light rains that will promote spring growth, ending a time of drought, both
meteorological and personal.

Here is the poem as spelled five hundred years ago:

Westron wynde when wyll thow blow
the smalle rayne downe can rayne
Chryst yf my love were in my armys
and I yn my bed a gayne.

Only one word is no longer used: *thou*. With a very slight modernizing of
word order, the poem would still be something that many people feel and say.

FORM: Ballad measure (quatrain of alternating tetrameter and trimeter lines
rhyming *abcb*, with noteworthy alliteration on the first three stressed syllables of
the first line ("West-," "wind," "will").

Sir Thomas Wyatt
(1503–1542)

WYATT, THE EARLIEST of the named poets in this collection, was born into a noble family in Kent, educated at Cambridge, and employed as a courtier and diplomat by Henry VIII. Thought to have been involved with Anne Boleyn before her marriage to the king, Wyatt was imprisoned briefly after her downfall in 1536, but he soon found his way back into the king's favor. He served as an ambassador, but was later accused of treason. He died a natural death at an early age, although his son, also called Sir Thomas Wyatt, was hanged for treason twelve years after his father's death.

Wyatt was witty, learned, and passionate. He was an excellent translator and an effective writer of satirical verse epistles. In technical terms, he was perhaps the most original and inventive of English poets, since he was the first to use terza rima, ottava rima, and the sonnet (all imported from Italy) as well as one of the best practitioners of the rhyme royal stanza that had been imported from France somewhat earlier. As the pioneer in these most important verse forms, Wyatt has had followers in the thousands and possibly even in the millions.

In friendship and in literary relations, Wyatt is commonly linked with Henry Howard, Earl of Surrey.

Further Reading

The Complete Works. Ronald A. Rebholz, ed. New Haven: Yale University Press, 1981.

Greenblatt, Steven. *Renaissance Self-Fashioning*. Chicago: University of Chicago Press, 1980.

Thompson, Patricia. *Sir Thomas Wyatt and His Background*. Stanford: Stanford University Press, 1964.

🗡 *They Flee from Me That Sometime Did Me Seek*

They flee from me that sometime did me seek
With naked foot stalking in my chamber.
I have seen them gentle, tame, and meek
That now are wild and do not remember
That sometime they put themselves in danger
To take bread at my hand; and now they range
Busily seeking with a continual change.

Thanked be fortune, it hath been otherwise
Twenty times better, but once in special,
In thin array after a pleasant guise,
When her loose gown from her shoulders did fall
And she me caught in her arms long and small,
Therewithal sweetly did me kiss
And softly said, "Dear heart, how like you this?"

It was no dream: I lay broad waking.
But all is turned thorough my gentleness
Into a strange fashion of forsaking.
And I have leave to go of her goodness
And she also to use newfangleness.
But since that I so kindly am served
I fain would know what she hath deserved.

COMPOSED AROUND 1535; PUBLISHED 1557. This is the oldest poem here by a known author, Sir Thomas Wyatt, who was born almost five hundred years ago. He was one of those astonishingly versatile Renaissance figures: soldier, courtier, diplomat, scholar, translator, and possibly the greatest English poet between Chaucer and Shakespeare. None of his poems were published in his lifetime in any book or collection that has survived. A few may have appeared in a collection entitled *The Court of Venus*, published a few years before his death in 1542. The first widespread publication of Wyatt did not come until 1557, in a collection entitled *Songs and Sonnets*, edited by Richard Tottel, now generally known as "Tottel's *Miscellany*." A few years before 1557, Wyatt's son Thomas, Junior, had been executed for treason, and the family name may have been somewhat clouded, so that Tottel paid more attention to poems by Wyatt's colleague Henry Howard, the Earl of Surrey, and also saw fit to tidy up Wyatt's poems.

Scholars are still at work on the problems of Wyatt's style, but it is clear that he was not writing consistently regular iambic verses. Many of his lines can be scanned quite easily, and most of his rhyme words still rhyme; but many lines are eccentric, and some rhymes seem to involve unstressed syllables of a sort not usually considered fit for rhyme. "Seek" and "meek" have been rhyming perfectly for many centuries, but "danger" and "chamber" have never rhymed in any conventional way. Wyatt's line "Into a strange fashion of forsaking" contains ten syllables by modern accounting, maybe eleven by Wyatt's habits, with "strange" sounded as two. Tottel (or a subeditor) altered Wyatt's line to "Into a bitter fashion of forsaking," which may be smoother but distorts Wyatt's meaning and weakens his music. "Strange" echoes "range" and "change" from an earlier stanza, and the whole phrase shows a fascinating pattern of initial consonants: *strange fashion of forsaking*. Such multiple alliteration on more than one sound is relatively unusual. Wyatt's "kindly" is ironic, as when someone hurts you and you say, "Very kind of you." But the Tottel agent seems to have missed the point and shifted to "unkindly."

The text is Wyatt's, in modernized spelling. As far as anybody knows, Wyatt did not give the poem a title. Tottel thought it needed thirteen words: "The Lover Showeth How He Is Forsaken of Such as He Sometime Enjoyed."

FORM: Three stanzas of rhyme royal (seven pentameter lines rhyming *ababbcc*).

Sir Walter Ralegh
(1554?–1618)

RALEGH WAS CHIEFLY KNOWN as a military, political, and diplomatic genius, and also as an inspiring adventurer. He was born in South Devon and, after a short stay at Oxford, left in 1569 to serve in the Huguenot army. Thereafter he engaged in various adventures and enterprises involving the New World. He was in and out of favor with Queen Elizabeth over the years, being knighted in 1585 but committed to the Tower in 1592. For the next eight or nine years he was involved in an incredible array of exploits. He seems to have been the kind of magnetic and charismatic genius about whom many legends spring up. Most of them are false or at least exaggerated, but they continue to emphasize how extraordinary Ralegh must have been, even in a Golden Age that, after 400 years, remains unsurpassed in the brilliance of its writers and adventurers.

When King James I came to the throne in 1603, Ralegh was again charged with crimes against the state (conspiracy among them) and sent to the Tower. He was released briefly in 1616 to go to the Orinoco in search of gold, but, after that expedition fizzled, he was arrested again, this time to be executed (October 29, 1618).

He wrote history and poetry of a most distinguished order. Much of what he wrote has been lost, but a few short pieces remain. Among his prose writings are *A Report of the Truth of the Fight about the Isles of the Azores* (1591) and the first volume of a *History of the World* (1614).

Ralegh is the first important English writer to have a significant interest in America, especially in the colony that was to become North Carolina. The capital of that state is named in his honor ("Raleigh" is one of dozens of variant spellings of the name).

Further Reading

The Poems. Agnes M. C. Latham, ed. London: Athlone, 1965.
Greenblatt, Stephen J. *Sir Walter Ralegh: The Renaissance Man and His Roles*.
    New Haven: Yale University Press, 1973.
May, Steven. *Sir Walter Ralegh*. Boston: Twayne, 1989.

✴ The Nymph's Reply to the Shepherd

If all the world and love were young,
And truth in every shepherd's tongue,
These pretty pleasures might me move
To live with thee and be thy Love.

But Time drives flocks from field to fold;
When rivers rage and rocks grow cold;
And Philomel becometh dumb;
The rest complains of cares to come.

The flowers do fade, and wanton fields
To wayward Winter reckoning yields:
A honey tongue, a heart of gall,
Is fancy's spring, but sorrow's fall.

Thy gowns, thy shoes, thy beds of roses,
Thy cap, thy kirtle, and thy posies,
Soon break, soon wither—soon forgotten,
In folly ripe, in reason rotten.

Thy belt of straw and ivy-buds,
Thy coral clasps and amber studs,—
All these in me no means can move
To come to thee and be thy Love.

But could youth last, and love still breed,
Had joys no date, nor age no need,
Then these delights my mind might move
To live with thee and be thy Love.

COMPOSED AROUND 1595; PUBLISHED 1600. No poem says it all or tells the whole story, and no poem stands alone. Sometimes a single poet, like Blake with "The Tyger" and "The Lamb," will write complementary poems—two works that mutually complete each other; Milton and Browning did the same. Sometimes one poet will answer another poet's work, as seems to be the case with this poem, which wittily answers Marlowe's "The Passionate Shepherd to His Love." It is likely that Marlowe's original poem is a joke, making fun of the pastoral conventions popular toward the end of the sixteenth century. A shepherd makes ludicrous claims in his wooing and promises rewards no shepherd could ever deliver. Here, the woman addressed by the shepherd calls his bluff.

FORM: Tetrameter quatrains rhyming *aabb*.

Sir Philip Sidney
(1554–1586)

It is hard not to admire Sidney. Like Sir Walter Ralegh, he exemplifies what is meant by "Renaissance hero": he was brilliant, versatile, patriotic, courageous, and witty. He was learned in the arts of antiquity but his thinking was also ahead of his time. He argued for the values of the ancients but experimented restlessly with ideas and styles.

He attended Oxford briefly during his mid-teens and then traveled as a courtier, soldier, and diplomat. He belonged to a most distinguished family of public servants and was himself an up-and-coming member of Queen Elizabeth's court until a religious difference of opinion in 1580 resulted in his temporary banishment from the royal circle. In a brief but concentrated burst of creativity, he wrote many poems, the first important critical text in English (*Defense of Poesy*), and a celebrated pastoral romance that mixes prose and poetry, the *Arcadia*. At about the same time he was engaged to Penelope Devereux, who became the model for "Stella" in the sonnet sequence *Astrophil and Stella*. She married another in 1581, and in 1583 he married Frances Walsingham. By this time he was back in royal favor, enough to be sent to the continent as governor of Flushing in the Low Countries. He was wounded in battle and died of gangrene, aged thirty-two.

As hard as it is to say bad things about someone so heroic, T. S. Eliot managed in some ways to disparage Sidney, whom he regarded as overrated. One stanza of Eliot's "A Cooking Egg" reads:

> I shall not want Honour in Heaven
> For I shall meet Sir Philip Sidney
> And have talk with Coriolanus
> And other heroes of that kidney.

Further Reading

Complete Poems. William A. Ringler, ed. Oxford: Clarendon, 1962.

Kalstone, David. *Sidney's Poetry: Contexts and Interpretations*. Cambridge: Harvard University Press, 1965.

McCoy, Richard. *Sir Philip Sidney: Rebellion in Arcadia*. New Brunswick, NJ: Rutgers University Press, 1979.

⚘ *With How Sad Steps, O Moon, Thou Climb'st the Skies!*

With how sad steps, O moon, thou climb'st the skies,
    How silently, and with how wan a face.
    What, may it be that even in heavenly place
    That busy archer his sharp arrows tries?
Sure, if that long-with-love-acquainted eyes
    Can judge of love, thou feel'st a lover's case;
    I read it in thy looks; thy languished grace
    To me, that feel the like, thy state descries.
Then, even of fellowship, O moon, tell me,
    Is constant love deemed there but want of wit?
    Are beauties there as proud as here they be?
Do they above love to be loved, and yet
    Those lovers scorn whom that love doth possess?
    Do they call virtue there ungratefulness?

COMPOSED 1582; PUBLISHED 1591. This is number 31 in Sidney's sonnet sequence called *Astrophil and Stella*. "Stella" means "star" in Latin; "Astrophil" combines Greek roots meaning "star" and "lover." Sidney's Astrophil is a frustrated lover, complaining sometimes directly to Stella about her treatment of him and sometimes indirectly to friends, muses, or, as in this poem, the moon.

You can be so burdened by love that the pains have to be downloaded onto everything around. When you are sad, the world seems sad too. When you are hurt by somebody too changeful, then you notice other changeful things, like the moon, which is never the same from one day to the next. Fidelity and constancy—or their absence—are also at issue in Arnold's "Dover Beach" (also to the accompaniment of moonlight), Shakespeare's "Let Me Not to the Marriage of True Minds," Suckling's "Why So Pale and Wan, Fond Lover?" Dowson's "Non Sum Qualis Eram Bonae Sub Regno Cynarae," Donne's "Go and Catch a Falling Star," and Wyatt's "They Flee from Me That Sometime Did Me Seek." A formal poem—in effect a working model of strict regularity—is a good means of showing up irregular behavior. The contrast between the consistency of the text and the inconsistency of someone fickle, hypocritical, disorderly, or crooked creates vivid drama.

FORM: Italian sonnet rhyming *abbaabbacdcdee*.

CHRISTOPHER MARLOWE
(1564–1593)

CHRISTOPHER MARLOWE WAS BORN at Canterbury, educated at Cambridge, and murdered at Deptford, presumably in a quarrel over the "reckoning" or bill at a tavern. In the swift blaze of his career, Marlowe produced a half-dozen tragedies, including *Tamburlaine*, *Doctor Faustus*, *The Jew of Malta*, and *Edward II*, as well as translations from the Latin of Ovid. In an age of unsurpassed greatness in literature, only Shakespeare was greater than Marlowe. Blank verse was introduced into English by the Earl of Surrey a half-century before Marlowe's plays; Marlowe revived the measure and gave it new strength in the form of "Marlowe's mighty line," with persistent exaggeration of rhetoric and image, along with maximal stress on long syllables (as in his best-known lines, "Was this the face that launched a thousand ships/And burnt the topless towers of Ilium?").

Marlowe was spectacularly brilliant and led a spectacularly varied life. Tales persist about his being involved in criminal activity in the Netherlands, from which he was expelled for forging false money; and about his being a kind of secret agent for Queen Elizabeth. According to that scenario, his death was not a violent accident during a tavern brawl but an assassination to get rid of a dangerous political operative. It has also been suggested that Marlowe was a homosexual and an atheist. Whatever he did, he did to extremes, and his story remains probably the most exciting of all the lives of the poets in this collection.

Further Reading

The Complete Works. Fredson Bowers, ed. Cambridge: Cambridge University Press, 1981.

Boas, Frederick S. *Marlowe and His Circle: A Biographical Survey*. Oxford: Clarendon, 1953.

Kocher, Frederick S. *Christopher Marlowe: A Study of His Thought, Learning, and Character*. New York: Russell, 1962.

Levin, Harry. *The Overreacher: A Study of Christopher Marlowe*. Cambridge: Harvard University Press, 1952.

The Passionate Shepherd to His Love

Come live with me and be my love,
And we will all the pleasures prove
That valleys, groves, hills, and fields,
Woods, or steepy mountain yields.

And we will sit upon the rocks,
Seeing the shepherds feed their flocks
By shallow rivers, to whose falls
Melodious birds sing madrigals.

And I will make thee beds of roses
And a thousand fragrant posies,
A cap of flowers and a kirtle
Embroidered all with leaves of myrtle;

A gown made of the finest wool
Which from our pretty lambs we pull;
Fair-linèd slippers for the cold,
With buckles of the purest gold;

A belt of straw and ivy buds,
With coral clasps and amber studs.
And if these pleasures may thee move,
Come live with me and be my Love.

The shepherds' swains shall dance and sing
For thy delight each May morning.
If these delights thy mind may move,
Then live with me and be my Love.

COMPOSED AROUND 1590; PUBLISHED 1599. Marlowe had been dead for six years when this poem was first published.

Sheep, which give us food and clothing, need a lot of care. The world of sheep and sheepherders (or shepherds) also gives us food for thought: "Little Bo Beep" and "Mary Had a Little Lamb" are the most familiar nursery rhymes; and the most familiar psalm in the Bible, sung by the shepherd boy David, begins, "The Lord is my shepherd." The word "pastor" literally means "shepherd," and the form "pastoral" can mean the work of a preacher ("pastoral care") as well the work and play of a shepherd. So-called pastoral poetry has been around for centuries in serious forms like David's psalms but also in comic forms that stress the fact that shepherds, like other agricultural workers, may be ridiculously rustic.

A shepherd invites his love to join him in the pleasures of pastoral life, giving her a familiar inventory or catalogue of the recreational benefits of the country. Many details of the offer have to be exaggerated, since a real shepherd would hardly be in a position to offer someone "beds of roses," let alone "buckles of purest gold" for her slippers. This shepherd's style may also fall into the class of hick verse, since you have to wrench a syllable to make "morning" rhyme with "sing."

One can guess that Marlowe was mocking a set of corny conventions by writing a vivid caricature—so vivid in fact that Sir Walter Ralegh was inspired to produce "The Nymph's Reply to the Shepherd." Other related poems are Donne's "The Bait," William Carlos Williams's "Raleigh Was Right," and C. Day-Lewis's "Two Songs." The modern Americans Delmore Schwartz and Paul Engle each wrote a poem beginning "Come live with me and be my wife," and yet another takeoff appears in Peter DeVries's comic novel *The Tents of Wickedness* (1959).

FORM: Tetrameter quatrains rhyming *aabb*.

William Shakespeare
(1564–1616)

IN SPITE OF his eminence as the greatest English poet—and perhaps the greatest poet anywhere, ever—we know relatively little about Shakespeare's life. He came from Stratford-upon-Avon, where his father was a prominent citizen, working as butcher, glover, and wool-merchant. At eighteen Shakespeare married a somewhat older woman, Anne Hathaway, who gave birth to their daughter Susannah six months after the wedding. The twins Hamnet and Judith were born two years later, in 1585.

During the 1590s Shakespeare worked in the London theater as actor and playwright. He seems to have been successful and even prosperous, eventually buying a comfortable house in his native Stratford and dividing his time between that town and London. He wrote some long poems, including *Venus and Adonis* and *The Rape of Lucrece*, early in his career, and it is probable that most of the sonnets that make up half of his poems in this collection were done during the 1590s. The three dozen plays for which he is most celebrated are grouped as histories or chronicle plays (which Ezra Pound called "the true English epos"), comedies, romances, and tragedies. It is customary to speak of his "four great tragedies" (*Hamlet, King Lear, Macbeth,* and *Othello*), but their stature is in many ways rivaled by that of *Romeo and Juliet* and some of the so-called Roman plays, particularly *Julius Caesar, Antony and Cleopatra,* and *Coriolanus.*

Shakespeare has never been entirely out of fashion. Many of his plays are in production somewhere in the world at any given time, and, more than works by any other English writer, they have inspired artists in other media. Painters such as J. M. W. Turner have illustrated Shakespeare dramas; and musicians from the sixteenth century right through the present have provided songs, incidental music, and other such treatments. Millions of weddings have ended with a march from Felix Mendelson's music for *A Midsummer Night's Dream.* Three of Giuseppe Verdi's operas are Shakespearean: *Falstaff, Otello,* and *Macbeth. Romeo and Juliet* has inspired a dramatic symphony by Hector Berlioz, a fantasy overture by Pyotr Tchaikovsky, and a ballet by Sergey Prokofiev. For *King Lear,*

Dmitry Shostakovich composed incidental music (Opus 58a, 1940) and a film score (Opus 137, 1970); in the former, one of the Fool's songs sounds just like "Jingle Bells." The Bernstein-Sondheim musical *West Side Story* is a variation on the theme of *Romeo and Juliet*. The first American feature film was a production of Shakespeare's *Richard III*, and many of the great film directors have made adaptations: Orson Welles's *Othello, Macbeth,* and *Chimes at Midnight* stand out as classics, as do Laurence Olivier's *Henry V, Hamlet,* and *Richard III*. More recently, Kenneth Branagh has seemed to be recapitulating Olivier's achievements, with a *Henry V* and *Hamlet* of his own, along with *Much Ado About Nothing*. Akira Kurosawa's *Throne of Blood* and *Ran* are based on Shakespeare's *Macbeth* and *King Lear*. And every season sees yet new productions in every medium of entertainment.

Further Reading

The Poems. John Roe, ed. Cambridge: Cambridge University Press, 1992.

Booth, Stephen. *Shakespeare's Sonnets*. New Haven: Yale University Press, 1977.

Fineman, Joel. *Shakespeare's Perjured Eye: The Invention of Poetic Subjectivity in the Sonnets*. Berkeley: University of California Press, 1986.

Schoenbaum, Samuel. *Shakespeare: His Life, His English, His Theater*. New York: Signet, 1990.

Vendler, Helen. *The Art of Shakespeare's Sonnets*. Cambridge, MA: Harvard University Press, 1997.

Fear no more the heat o' the sun
    Nor the furious winter's rages;
Thou thy worldly task hast done,
    Home art gone, and ta'en thy wages:
Golden lads and girls all must,
As chimney-sweepers, come to dust.

Fear no more the frown o' the great;
    Thou art past the tyrant's stroke;
Care no more to clothe and eat;
    To thee the reed is as the oak:
The scepter, learning, physic, must
All follow this, and come to dust.

Fear no more the lightning flash,
    Nor the all-dreaded thunder stone;
Fear not slander, censure rash;
    Thou hast finished joy and moan:
All lovers young, all lovers must
Consign to thee, and come to dust.

No exorciser harm thee!
Nor no witchcraft charm thee!
Ghost unlaid forbear thee!
Nothing ill come near thee!
Quiet consummation have;
And renownèd be thy grave!

COMPOSED AROUND 1619; PUBLISHED 1623. This song comes from Shakespeare's romantic comedy *Cymbeline*. In the fourth act, two princes named Guiderius and Arviragus say this funeral song over the supposedly dead body of the supposedly male Fidele—really the live body of the female Imogen. The Elizabethan theater had no actresses. With all the roles being played by men or boys, there were plenty of plots involving change or confusion of gender. There were also plenty of make-believe deaths, in comedies and tragedies alike.

FORM: Three tetrameter stanzas rhyming *ababcc* with a final stanza of four trimeter and two tetrameter lines rhyming *aabbcc*.

When to the sessions of sweet silent thought
I summon up remembrance of things past,
I sigh the lack of many a thing I sought,
And with old woes new wail my dear time's waste.
Then can I drown an eye, unus'd to flow,
For precious friends hid in death's dateless night,
And weep afresh love's long since cancell'd woe,
And moan th' expense of many a vanish'd sight.
Then can I grieve at grievances foregone,
And heavily from woe to woe tell o'er
The sad account of fore-bemoaned moan,
Which I new pay as if not paid before.
    But if the while I think on thee, dear friend,
    All losses are restor'd and sorrows end.

COMPOSED ABOUT 1595; PUBLISHED 1609. Here we see an outer skeleton as distinct as a grasshopper's. The utterly clear structure has a frame built on "When . . . Then . . . Then . . . But. . . ." Many of the words come from law ("sessions" and "summon") and commerce. This sonnet belongs in a general group called "complaint," a favorite with English poets for many hundreds of years. Here, as in famous speeches in *Macbeth* and *Hamlet*, Shakespeare seems to relish the chance to make a long list of troubles. This problem, he seems to say, is but one of many problems that I have, and I am but one of many people with problems—as though the world were nothing but one big problem. However, the "But" at the end brings in a new note of happiness.

FORM: Shakespearean or English sonnet, fourteen pentameter lines rhyming *ababcdcdefefgg*.

Let Me Not to the Marriage of True Minds

Let me not to the marriage of true minds
Admit impediments. Love is not love
Which alters when it alteration finds,
Or bends with the remover to remove.
O, no! it is an ever-fixèd mark
That looks on tempests and is never shaken;
It is the star to every wand'ring bark,
Whose worth's unknown, although his height be taken.
Love's not Time's fool, though rosy lips and cheeks
Within his bending sickle's compass come;
Love alters not with his brief hours and weeks,
But bears it out even to the edge of doom.
    If this be error and upon me proved,
    I never writ, nor no man ever loved.

COMPOSED ABOUT 1595; PUBLISHED 1609. Faithfulness in love has been a favorite theme of poets, who usually bemoan the fickle (see "Go and Catch a Falling Star"). Dowson's "Non Sum Qualis Eram Bonae Sub Regno Cynarae," on the other hand, seems to gloat over the speaker's faithlessness. Shakespeare's Julius Caesar claims to be as "constant as the northern star"—that is, the Pole Star that seems to remain still while all the others revolve around it.

FORM: English or Shakespearean sonnet, fourteen pentameter lines rhyming *ababcdcdefefgg*.

⚔ *Shall I Compare Thee to a Summer's Day?*

Shall I compare thee to a summer's day?
Thou art more lovely and more temperate:
Rough winds do shake the darling buds of May,
And summer's lease hath all too short a date;
Sometime too hot the eye of heaven shines,
And often is his gold complexion dimm'd;
And every fair from fair sometime declines,
By chance or nature's changing course untrimm'd:
But thy eternal summer shall not fade
Nor lose possession of that fair thou ow'st;
Nor shall Death brag thou wand'rest in his shade,
When in eternal lines to time thou grow'st;
    So long as men can breathe or eyes can see,
    So long lives this, and this gives life to thee.

COMPOSED ABOUT 1595; PUBLISHED 1609. "Shall I Compare Thee to a Summer's Day?" plays with some of the tricks that had been used by earlier sonnet writers. Saying outlandish things like "Thou art like a day in summer, warm and bright" got to be so conventional that it became a mindless cliché. Shakespeare begins by denying the terms of the comparison, or simile. After a lighthearted opening, the poem settles down with the exaggerated claim of "eternal summer" for the person to whom the poem is addressed. It may have seemed conceited to claim that one's poem would endure, but this poet is right so far: the poem has been going strong for four hundred years.

FORM: English or Shakespearean sonnet, fourteen pentameter lines rhyming *ababcdcdefefgg*.

⚶ *The Expense of Spirit in a Waste of Shame*

The expense of spirit in a waste of shame
Is lust in action; and, till action, lust
Is perjured, murderous, bloody, full of blame,
Savage, extreme, rude, cruel, not to trust,
Enjoy'd no sooner but despisèd straight;
Past reason hunted, and no sooner had,
Past reason hated as a swallowed bait
On purpose laid to make the taker mad;
Mad in pursuit, and in possession so;
Had, having, and in quest to have, extreme;
A bliss in proof, and proved, a very woe,
Before, a joy proposed; behind, a dream.
    All this the world well knows, yet none knows well
    To shun the heaven that leads men to this hell.

COMPOSED ABOUT 1595; PUBLISHED 1609. In one of his darkest moods, Shakespeare looks here at an old human problem: you want something so much that you go crazy, but as soon as you get what you want, you hate it and yourself. Before lust is satisfied, it is the worst of masters; after, it is the airiest of vapors. And yet we never seem to learn.

FORM: English or Shakespearean sonnet, fourteen pentameter lines rhyming *ababcdcdefefgg*.

❧ *That Time of Year Thou Mayst in Me Behold*

That time of year thou mayst in me behold
When yellow leaves, or none, or few, do hang
Upon those boughs which shake against the cold,
Bare ruin'd choirs where late the sweet birds sang.
In me thou see'st the twilight of such day
As after sunset fadeth in the west,
Which by and by black night doth take away,
Death's second self, that seals up all in rest.
In me thou see'st the glowing of such fire
That on the ashes of his youth doth lie,
As the death-bed whereon it must expire,
Consum'd with that which it was nourish'd by.
    This thou perceiv'st, which makes thy love more strong,
    To love that well which thou must leave ere long.

COMPOSED ABOUT 1595; PUBLISHED 1609. This poem, which is usually counted as the seventy-third of Shakespeare's sonnets, belongs in a huge group with the same message: time is passing; here today, gone tomorrow; seize the day. This is an apt thing for poetry to present, since poetry itself has an unmistakable pulsating rhythm that matches the beating of a heart and the ticking of a clock. The running meter of a measured poem says, "Listen: the meter is running." Here, in keeping with a well-established tradition, Shakespeare argues the resemblance between the course of human life and the courses of a day and a year. When your life is in its third quarter, the situation is comparable to evening and autumn, and also to the life cycle of a fire that is past its time of full blazing and is now dying out.

The poem represents the speech of one person addressing a younger person. (The poet was not very old at the time, but he was probably within twenty years of his death, at age fifty-two; furthermore, given the average life expectancy four hundred years ago, he was justified in regarding himself, aged thirty, as being over the hill.) In typical sonnet style, the poem presents three examples of how earthly things grow old and die, with a final summing up. The phrase "in me" appears three times along with acts of seeing or beholding, as though to say, "You see before you such and such a sight."

FORM: English or Shakespearean sonnet, fourteen pentameter lines rhyming *ababcdcdefefgg*.

When icicles hang by the wall,
    And Dick the shepherd blows his nail
And Tom bears logs into the hall,
    And milk comes frozen home in pail,
When blood is nipp'd and ways be foul,
Then nightly sings the staring owl,
To-whit!
To-who!—a merry note,
While greasy Joan doth keel the pot.

When all aloud the wind doth blow,
    And coughing drowns the parson's saw,
And birds sit brooding in the snow,
    And Marian's nose looks red and raw,
When roasted crabs hiss in the bowl,
Then nightly sings the staring owl,
To-whit!
To-who!—a merry note,
While greasy Joan doth keel the pot.

COMPOSED AROUND 1595; PUBLISHED 1598. This is one of two songs sung at the end of Shakespeare's romantic comedy *Love's Labour's Lost*. The other song, associated with "Ver, the Spring" symbolized by the cuckoo, is matched by this song of "Hiems, Winter" symbolized by the owl.

FORM: Irregular six-line stanza rhyming *ababcc* with couplet as refrain.

John Donne
(1572–1631)

DONNE BEGAN as a Roman Catholic but later, while studying law, joined the Church of England. He grew up in an age that took religion very seriously indeed, and among his contemporaries are two poets who maintained their Catholic allegiance and were put to death for it: Saint Robert Southwell (1561?–1595) and Chidiock Tichborne (1568?–1586). Donne was a traveler, diplomat, and courtier. Rather late in life, he became a preacher, and was soon famous for his sermons; he was made Dean of St. Paul's in 1621. One of his meditations contains a passage so celebrated that it is a platitude: "No man is an island, entire of itself; every man is a piece of the continent, a part of the main. If a clod be washed away by the sea, Europe is the less, as well as if a promontory were, as well as if a manor of thy friend's or of thine own were. Any man's death diminishes me, because I am involved in mankind; and therefore never send to know for whom the bell tolls; it tolls for thee." (This is the source of the title of Ernest Hemingway's novel about the Spanish Civil War, *For Whom the Bell Tolls*.)

Donne's personality was marked by extraordinary passion and extraordinary ingenuity. He had the soul of a lover, the tongue of a wit, and the mind of a lawyer-preacher accustomed to analyzing complex problems. As the poems in this collection demonstrate, Donne could write, with equal facility and depth, passionate poems of secular love and passionate poems of sacred love, both sorts informed by large-minded wit.

Further Reading

The Complete Poetry. John T. Shawcross, ed. Garden City, NY: Doubleday, 1967.

Alvarez, A. *The School of Donne*. London: Chatto, 1961.

Bald, R. C. *John Donne: A Life*. London: Oxford University Press, 1970.

Death, be not proud, though some have callèd thee
Mighty and dreadful, for thou art not so;
For those whom thou think'st thou dost overthrow
Die not, poor Death, nor yet canst thou kill me.
From rest and sleep, which but thy pictures be,
Much pleasure; then from thee much more must flow,
And soonest our best men with thee do go,
Rest of their bones, and soul's delivery.
Thou'rt slave to fate, chance, kings, and desperate men,
And dost with poison, war, and sickness dwell;
And poppy or charms can make us sleep as well
And better than thy stroke; why swell'st thou then?
One short sleep past, we wake eternally,
And death shall be no more; Death, thou shalt die.

COMPOSED AROUND 1609; PUBLISHED 1633. Of the nineteen poems by Donne called "Holy Sonnets," three have made it into the elite company of the present selection: this one (which scholars count as either the sixth or the tenth) as well as "Batter My Heart, Three-Personed God" and "At the Round Earth's Imagined Corners." After a youth devoted to the life of a lawyer, diplomat, soldier, courtier, and hell-raiser, Donne became in his mid-forties a famous preacher. His poetry also became much more serious and pious, although he kept up some of the same practices as a writer. What had worked for secular love poems could work as effectively for sacred love poems. The same imperative commands that began worldly poems — such as "Go and Catch a Falling Star" — could also sound the keynote of otherworldly poems. In fact, all three of the Holy Sonnets here begin with imperatives: "be not proud, batter my heart, blow your trumpets."

In this poem death is no remote abstraction. No: it is Death, to whom a person can talk. The poem begins with a stern warning and then passes on to subtle faked sympathy for "poor" Death. The tone then changes again to a hush, with talk of rest and sleep. The climax comes in a jam-packed line: "Thou art slave to fate, chance, kings, and desperate men."

FORM: Italian sonnet rhyming *abbaabbacddcee*.

Batter my heart, three-personed God; for, you
As yet but knock, breathe, shine, and seek to mend;
That I may rise, and stand, o'erthrow me, and bend
Your force, to break, blow, burn, and make me new.
I, like an usurped town, to another due,
Labor to admit you, but oh, to no end,
Reason your viceroy in me, me should defend,
But is captived, and proves weak or untrue,
Yet dearly I love you, and would be loved fain,
But am betrothed unto your enemy,
Divorce me, untie, or break that knot again,
Take me to you, imprison me, for I
Except you enthrall me, never shall be free,
Nor ever chaste, except you ravish me.

COMPOSED AROUND 1609; PUBLISHED 1633. Donne wrote in an age of great preaching and also of great theater and political drama. In this poem God is no far-off abstraction but a physical presence. As with many other poems of Donne's, this one opens with a dramatic imperative.

The sonnet form that was such a big hit in the sixteenth century was employed mostly for worldly love poems, with all the exaggeration and paradox that one can still hear in love songs. Writing a little after the sonnet fad had passed, Donne lifted the level from worldly to divine, although he kept the dramatic emphasis on paradox. He also kept much of the erotic imagery and feeling from worldly love poems. Some readers may find these paradoxes outlandish, for they seem to ask God to divorce, imprison, and ravish a worshipper: "I / Except you enthrall me, never shall be free, / Nor ever chaste, except you ravish me."

According to some accounts, this poem was on J. Robert Oppenheimer's mind when he gave the name "Trinity" to atomic bomb tests in 1945 (a nucleus was bombarded—"battered"—with electrons from three directions).

FORM: Italian sonnet rhyming *abbaabbacdcdee.*

At the round earth's imagined corners, blow
Your trumpets, angels, and arise, arise
From death, you numberless infinities
Of souls, and to your scattered bodies go,
All whom the flood did, and fire shall o'erthrow,
All whom war, dearth, age, agues, tyrannies,
Despair, law, chance, hath slain, and you whose eyes,
Shall behold God, and never taste death's woe.
But let them sleep, Lord, and me mourn a space,
For, if above all these, my sins abound,
'Tis late to ask abundance of thy grace,
When we are there; here on this lowly ground,
Teach me how to repent; for that's as good
As if thou hadst sealed my pardon, with thy blood.

COMPOSED AROUND 1609; PUBLISHED 1633. Like "Death, Be Not Proud" and "Batter My Heart, Three-Personed God," this is one of Donne's "Holy Sonnets"; all are sinewy physical expressions of metaphysical theology. All three, in fact, combine direct address with strong imperative verbs, devices that add immediacy and concreteness.

This poem calls on the vivid drama of the end of the world as prophesied in the New Testament, with angels sounding forth trumpet-calls to wake the dead and gather the living for final judgment.

We can glimpse here something of the Metaphysical poets' fondness for paradox and education: this poet knows that the earth is round and its "corners" are merely imaginary; he also knows that angels are not bound by literal laws of physics. They, like the vernacular today, still observe "the four corners of the world."

FORM: Italian sonnet rhyming *abbaabbacdcdee*.

I wonder by my troth, what thou, and I
    Did, till we loved? were we not weaned till then,
But sucked on country pleasures, childishly?
    Or snorted we in the seven sleepers' den?
'Twas so; but this, all pleasures fancies be.
If every any beauty I did see,
Which I desired, and got, 'twas but a dream of thee.

And now good-morrow to our waking souls,
    Which watch not one another out of fear;
For love, all love of other sights controls,
    And makes one little room, an every where.
Let sea-discoverers to new worlds have gone,
Let maps to others, worlds on worlds have shown,
Let us possess one world, each hath one, and is one.

My face in thine eye, thine in mine appears,
    And true plain hearts do in the faces rest,
Where can we find two better hemispheres
    Without sharp north, without declining west?
Whatever dies, was not mixed equally;
If our two loves be one, or, thou and I
Love so alike, that none do slacken, none can die.

COMPOSED AROUND 1605; PUBLISHED 1633. Some love poems sound satisfied with the way things are, although repeating "I love you" over and over generates little drama or excitement. Other love poems express dissatisfaction with the way things are, although repeating "You did me wrong and I'm so blue" may generate so much melodrama that we believe that the mistreatment was deserved. Donne here produced a poem that falls between those two extremes: a poem of love accomplished, but without smug self-congratulation.

Donne was very learned and very good at using what he knew—of history, geography, philosophy, mapmaking—to write about the private lives of people in love. Some powerful critics have doubted the sincerity of such mixing of things of the mind and things of the heart. Samuel Johnson said of Donne and other members of the Metaphysical School, "Their wish was only to say what they hoped had never been said before." More recently, T. S. Eliot has praised the Metaphysicals for keeping all the parts of life together and for achieving a consistent personality. For Donne, mind and heart are one; and love, which takes over a whole person, can use the language of science, just as science might use the language of emotion. In modern particle physics, one technical term is "charm." A gene involved in the production of a mutation in fruit flies is called "bride-of-sevenless" (Lubert Stryer, *Biochemistry*, 4th ed., p. 356). If Donne were writing today, he would be in the thick of science, data processing, space travel, and international finance, raiding their vocabularies for new ways to say "I love you."

Technically, this poem is a variant of the aubade: a morning song, or morning-after song, of lovers who have parted. But here they are still together.

FORM: Seven-line pentameter stanza (with hexameter in last line) rhyming *ababccc*. Possibly a variant of the rhyme royal pattern *(ababbcc)*.

The Sun Rising

Busy old fool, unruly sun,
    Why dost thou thus,
Through windows, and through curtains call on us?
Must to thy motions lovers' seasons run?
    Saucy pedantic wretch, go chide
    Late school-boys, and sour prentices,
  Go tell court-huntsmen that the King will ride,
  Call country ants to harvest offices;
Love, all alike, no season knows, nor clime,
Nor hours, days, months, which are the rags of time.

    Thy beams, so reverend, and strong
    Why shouldst thou think?
I could eclipse and cloud them with a wink,
But that I would not lose her sight so long:
    If her eyes have not blinded thine,
    Look, and tomorrow late, tell me,
  Whether both th'Indias of spice and mine
  Be where thou left'st them, or lie here with me.
Ask for those kings whom thou saw'st yesterday,
And thou shalt hear, All here in one bed lay.

    She's all states, and all princes, I,
    Nothing else is.
Princes do but play us; compared to this,
All honor's mimic; all wealth alchemy.
    Thou sun art half as happy as we,
    In that the world's contracted thus;
  Thine age asks ease, and since thy duties be
  To warm the world, that's done in warming us.
Shine here to us, and thou art everywhere;
This bed thy center is, these walls, thy sphere.

COMPOSED AROUND 1605; PUBLISHED 1633. Donne wrote devotional sonnets so fine that three are in this collection: "Death, Be Not Proud," "Batter My Heart, Three-Personed God," and "At the Round Earth's Imagined Corners." But the same poet, using many of the same resources of rhetoric and versification, also wrote witty secular love poems included here: "The Good Morrow," "A Valediction: Forbidding Mourning," and "Go and Catch a Falling Star." The dramatic energy of both kinds of poetry is generated by tense situations in which a believable voice is heard talking most emphatically to an addressee. This poem, like "Go and Catch a Falling Star" and all three Holy Sonnets in this collection, is imperative: it gives directions to someone or something. Such a thing might be an abstraction like death or a heavenly body like the sun, which symbolizes time. For writers, Donne's best lesson could be summarized as "Don't speculate *about* something general: talk *to* something specific."

If you read this poem carefully, you may see that it does not really have much to do with the sun at all. By seeming to talk to the sun and give it orders and call it names, the poet most vividly records how exceedingly great his love is.

FORM: Ten-line stanza rhyming *abbacdcdee,* meter variable: tetrameter, dimeter, pentameter, pentameter, tetrameter, tetrameter, pentameter, pentameter, pentameter, pentameter.

A Valediction: Forbidding Mourning

As virtuous men pass mildly away,
    And whisper to their souls to go,
Whilst some of their sad friends do say,
    The breath goes now, and some say, no:

So let us melt, and make no noise,
    No tear-floods, nor sigh-tempests move,
'Twere profanation of our joys
    To tell the laity our love.

Moving of the earth brings harms and fears,
    Men reckon what it did and meant,
But trepidation of the spheres,
    Though greater far, is innocent.

Dull sublunary lovers' love,
    Whose soul is sense, cannot admit
Absence, because it doth remove
    Those things which elemented it.

But we by a love so much refined
    That our selves know not what it is,
Interassurèd of the mind,
    Care less eyes, lips, and hands to miss.

Our two souls therefore, which are one,
    Though I must go, endure not yet
A breach, but an expansion,
    Like gold to airy thinness beat.

If they be two, they are two so
    As stiff twin compasses are two,
Thy soul, the fixed foot, makes no show
    To move, but doth if th' other do.

And though it in the center sit,
    Yet when the other far doth roam,
It leans, and hearkens after it,
    And grows erect as that comes home.

Such wilt thou be to me, who must
    Like th' other foot, obliquely run;
Thy firmness makes my circle just,
    And makes me end where I begun.

COMPOSED AROUND 1611; PUBLISHED 1633. Donne wrote five valedictions, or poems of farewell. In all of them, the necessity of being apart tests the strength of love. The lover finds various ingenious ways to express his love and put his beloved at peace. Some readers reject Donne's rhetoric as too conceited to be taken seriously. Surely one can find a less outlandish way to express feelings. And yet, according to other readers, what else could the poet do? No strictly rational argument will do a better job of saying goodbye, and the stoical attitude of acquiescing in necessity is not much more appealing. Donne's approach may ultimately be more convincing, since it seems to say, "Dear, nothing I can say will adequately express either my love for you or my sadness at having to be away from you, and that's really all there is to it. However, I do want you to know that my feelings here are extremely powerful—so much so, indeed, that my imagination is driven to discover some means of telling you what's in my heart: Rather than resorting to one more meaningless cliché, I shall send my agitated spirit in search of a new figure of speech, and its outlandishness— although obviously inadequate—will at least show the strength of my love." With something of a sacramental imagination, then, the poet finds in all sorts of objects—metal foil, a drafting instrument—an outward and visible sign of his inward and invisible state. Once the imagination goes to work, propelled by passion, all sorts of extra meanings start to build up: The compass turns out to be especially appropriate. The speaker must go on a long trip (as Donne had to, between July 1611 and September 1612, accompanying Sir Robert Drury on travels in France and the Low Countries), and compasses are used in planning such trips and in measuring distances and computing routes on maps. A perfect circle can be drawn only if the fixed foot or leg of the compass is stable and constant: together, they create the symbol of perfection as well as an ancient symbol for gold (a circle around a central point).

FORM: Tetrameter quatrains rhyming *abab*.

Go and Catch a Falling Star

Go and catch a falling star,
    Get with child a mandrake root,
Tell me where all past years are,
    Or who cleft the Devil's foot,
Teach me to hear mermaids singing,
    Or to keep off envy's stinging,
        And find
        What wind
Serves to advance an honest mind.

I thou beest borne to strange sights,
    Things invisible to see,
Ride ten thousand days and nights,
    Till age snow white hairs on thee.
Thou, when thou return'st, wilt tell me
    All strange wonders that befell thee,
        And swear
        Nowhere
Lives a woman true, and fair.

If thou find'st one, let me know,
    Such a pilgrimage were sweet;
Yet do not, I would not go,
    Though at next door we might meet;
Though she were true, when you met her,
    And last till you write your letter,
        Yet she
        Will be
False, ere I come, to two, or three.

COMPOSED AROUND 1605; PUBLISHED 1633. With the same energy and ingenuity that animate his religious poems, Donne here indulges in a light-hearted joke about women's manners. By means of paradoxes, the speaker advances a set of impossible conditions, and then remarks that, when these conditions are met, a woman will be both fair (in appearance) and faithful (in conduct). The first five lines contain flatly impossible challenges (and use the same vigorous imperatives that Donne uses in many of his religious poems). From lines six to nine, however, the focus shifts to include matters of conduct: how to avoid envy and how to be honest without suffering for your honesty.

The impossible tasks are fairly conventional matters, like saying "When hell freezes over"—which isn't going to happen. They may be joined, however, by an underlying pattern of similarity. The devil (Lucifer, once the brightest angel in heaven) is a sort of falling star, the mandrake root supposedly looks like a human figure, mermaids' singing (as also at the end of T. S. Eliot's "The Love Song of J. Alfred Prufrock") is said to portend disaster and death. And it may be that the condition of the world, with so many people envious, dishonest, and inconstant, was caused by the Fall of Man in the Garden of Eden.

FORM: Three nine-line stanzas rhyming *ababccddd,* feminine rhymes in fifth and sixth lines throughout, all lines tetrameter except seventh and eighth, which are monometer.

BEN JONSON
(1572–1637)

BEN JONSON WAS BORN in London and remained very much a Londoner for most of his full and active life. Early in life we was a bricklayer and soldier, but he soon settled down to a theatrical career. His first important comedy, *Every Man in His Humour*, was staged in 1598, with William Shakespeare among the players. Jonson went on to turn out comedies, tragedies, satires, and masques for the stage as well as songs, epigrams, and translations for the printed page. He was one of the most intelligent people of his age, and he brought to the popular theater an unusual degree of classical learning. A given comedy or song may look simple, but in Jonson's hands it may take on depth and dimension from classical antiquity.

Jonson seems to have been rather hard to get along with, and he was in trouble with the law on more than one occasion: he killed another actor in a duel in 1598, and a few years later he was imprisoned for his share in a play that was thought to insult the Scots (at a time when the new king had come from Scotland). Even so, Jonson came to enjoy an extraordinary measure of royal favor, becoming in effect the first Poet Laureate (although John Dryden, later in the seventeenth century, was the first to hold that title officially). His friends included some of the greatest writers of the time, or any time, including John Donne and William Shakespeare. Some of his younger followers were given nicknames that wittily refer to the Old Testament: the Sons of Ben or the Tribe of Ben. The group included Robert Herrick and Sir John Suckling.

Jonson is the earliest English writer who is routinely called by a nickname, a familiarity that seems justified by Jonson's vigor and good humor. He seems to have enjoyed life immensely, and there is some evidence that he weighed as much as twenty stone: 280 pounds. If that is true, he is probably the heaviest poet in this collection.

Further Reading

The Complete Poetry. William B. Hunter, Jr., ed. New York: Norton, 1968.

Peterson, Richard S. *Imitation and Praise in the Poems of Ben Jonson*. New Haven: Yale University Press, 1981.

Riggs, David. *Ben Jonson: A Life*. Cambridge: Harvard University Press, 1989.

𝕏 *On My First Son*

Farewell, thou child of my right hand, and joy;
 My sin was too much hope of thee, loved boy.
Seven years thou wert lent to me, and I thee pay,
 Exacted by thy fate, on the just day.
Oh, could I lose all father now! For why
 Will man lament the state he should envy?
To have so soon 'scaped world's and flesh's rage,
 And, if no other misery, yet age?
Rest in soft peace, and, asked, say here doth lie
 Ben Jonson his best piece of poetry;
For whose sake, henceforth, all his vows be such,
 As what he loves may never like too much.

COMPOSED AROUND 1603; PUBLISHED 1616. Jonson was a classical scholar, and his epitaph on his first-born son, also called Benjamin, who died on his seventh birthday ("on the just day") in 1603, displays learning as well as a species of classical stoicism uncommon in English verse.

The boy was a junior, and, as Jonson knew, the name "Benjamin" means "son of the right hand," or "favorite." Jonson also knew that "poetry" means "things made" or "products," so that, by a reversible conceit, one may speak of one's poems as children and of one's children as poems. Although an epitaph, the poem is addressed to the boy.

FORM: Pentameter couplets rhyming *aabbcc* etc.

✎ Song: To Celia

Drink to me only with thine eyes,
    And I will pledge with mine;
Or leave a kiss but in the cup,
    And I'll not look for wine.
The thirst that from the soul doth rise
    Doth ask a drink divine;
But might I of Jove's nectar sup,
    I would not change for thine.
I sent thee late a rosy wreath,
    Not so much honoring thee
As giving it a hope that there
    It could not withered be.
But thou thereon didst only breathe,
    And sent'st it back to me;
Since when it grows, and smells, I swear,
    Not of itself, but thee.

COMPOSED AROUND 1615; PUBLISHED 1616. Three of Jonson's poems are called "To Celia." Two of them have to do with the play *Volpone*, in which the virtuous wife is named Celia. Volpone's song to her echoes Marlowe's "The Passionate Shepherd to His Love": "Come my Celia, let us prove / While we may, the sports of love."

This "Song: To Celia," which is not from a play, closely imitates a clever exercise in a poem by Philostratus. A set of *Epistles* by the Greek poet challenge themselves to see how far they can take outlandish comparisons and exaggerations without collapsing into nonsense. A modern counterpart would be something like Cole Porter's "You're the Top" or "I Get a Kick out of You."

Many poems in this collection began as songs, and many others have been set to music. But this song (set to a traditional tune possibly not known in Jonson's time), Blake's "And Did Those Feet," and Howe's "The Battle Hymn of the Republic" are the only works here with melodies that many people know well.

FORM: Two eight-line stanzas joined, each alternating tetrameter and trimeter lines and rhyming *abcbabcb*.

Still to be neat, still to be dressed,
As you were going to a feast;
Still to be powdered, still perfumed:
Lady, it is to be presumed,
Though art's hid causes are not found,
All is not sweet, all is not sound.

Give me a look, give me a face,
That makes simplicity a grace;
Robes loosely flowing, hair as free:
Such sweet neglect more taketh me
Than all the adulteries of art;
They strike mine eyes, but not my heart.

COMPOSED AROUND 1608; ACTED 1609; PUBLISHED 1640. This song comes early in Jonson's play *Epicène, or The Silent Woman*. A modern equivalent is Carly Simon's "You're So Vain." Robert Herrick, who called Jonson "Saint Ben" (because he wrote like an angel, not because he lived piously), helped himself to parts of this song: "sweet" and "neglect" are used also in Herrick's "Delight in Disorder," and the vivid word "taketh" reappears in Herrick's "Upon Julia's Clothes."

FORM: Two six-line tetrameter stanzas rhyming *aabbcc*.

Robert Herrick
(1591–1674)

Herrick was superficially a good deal like his near-contemporary George Herbert: a poet and clergyman educated at Cambridge. But, markedly unlike the pious and saintly Herbert, Herrick was much better at secular poetry than at the sacred. In his marvelously constructed lyrics, there is an appreciation of nature and the physical— including the body, with and without clothes.

And, unlike Herbert, Herrick lived a very long life amid most complicated times in which he enjoyed himself among the urban sophisticates in London, then was sent to a country vicarage at Dean Prior, in Devonshire, then found himself ejected during the Civil War by a Parliament that disapproved of Herrick's Royalist sympathies, then spent fifteen years without a job, then returned to his old vicarage in the west, having been reinstated in the Restoration. The title of his single volume, *Hesperides*, is a tribute to his time in Devonshire. Although at times he regarded his stay in the west country as exile and deprivation, he also recognized the power and charm of country life, especially for his verse, which benefited from the exposure to folk customs and a bountiful world of nature and agriculture. By means of the title, Herrick is advertising his situation, in somewhat the way that the title of Thomas Hardy's first book of poetry, *Wessex Poems*, advertised his situation in Wessex, which includes Devonshire. In fact, the first element of "Hesperides" and the first element of "Wessex" can be traced back to a common Indo-European root that means "evening" or "west" (where the sun goes in the evening).

Further Reading

The Complete Poetry. J. Max Patrick, ed. New York: Norton, 1968.

Patrick, Roger B. and Roger Rollin, eds. *"Trust to Good Verses": Herrick Tercentenary Essays*. Pittsburgh: University of Pittsburgh Press, 1978.

Rollin, Roger B. *Robert Herrick*. New York: Twayne, 1992.

⚘ *To the Virgins, to Make Much of Time*

Gather ye rose-buds while ye may,
    Old Time is still a-flying;
And this same flower that smiles today,
    Tomorrow will be dying.

The glorious lamp of heaven, the sun,
    The higher he's a-getting,
The sooner will his race be run,
    And nearer he's to setting.

That age is best which is the first,
    When youth and blood are warmer;
But being spent, the worse, and worst
    Times, still succeed the former.

Then be not coy, but use your time,
    And while ye may, go marry;
For having lost but once your prime,
    You may for ever tarry.

COMPOSED AROUND 1630; PUBLISHED 1648. Herrick must have written poems all the time, but he published only one collection in his lifetime, *Hesperides* (1648), consisting of some 1200 poems, most of them short. This poem addresses a straightforward appeal to young women. The rhythmic pulsation of measured verse is an emphatic reminder of the rhythmic pulsation of passing time. As time flees (*tempus fugit*) one must try to seize the day (*carpe diem*) for whatever enjoyment can be had. The speaker exploits two old figures, the life cycle of a plant and the life cycle of a solar day.

    Other *carpe diem* poems in this collection are "That Time of Year Thou Mayst in Me Behold," "To His Coy Mistress," "The Passionate Shepherd to His Love," and "Go, Lovely Rose."

FORM: Ballad measure with feminine rhymes in lines 2 and 4 throughout.

✺ Upon Julia's Clothes

Whenas in silks my Julia goes,
Then, then, methinks, how sweetly flows
That liquefaction of her clothes.

Next, when I cast mine eyes and see
That brave vibration each way free,
O how that glittering taketh me!

COMPOSED AROUND 1630; PUBLISHED 1648. Among Herrick's many poems are several addressed to "Julia": "Julia's Petticoat," "The Night-Piece, to Julia," "Upon His Julia," "Upon Julia Washing Herself in the River," "Upon Julia's Breasts," "Upon Julia's Ribband," "Upon Julia's Voice," two or three called just "To Julia," and this magnificent snapshot. The highlights of the poem are the surprisingly technical "liquefaction" and the brilliant stroke (underscored by alliteration) of "brave vibration."

FORM: Tetrameter triplets rhyming *aaa*.

Delight in Disorder

A sweet disorder in the dress
Kindles in clothes a wantonness.
A lawn about the shoulders thrown
Into a fine distractión;
An erring lace, which here and there
Enthralls the crimson stomacher;
A cuff neglectful, and thereby
Ribbons to flow confusèdly;
A winning wave, deserving note,
In the tempestuous petticoat;
A careless shoestring, in whose tie
I see a wild civility;
Do more bewitch me than when art
Is too precise in every part.

COMPOSED AROUND 1630; PUBLISHED 1648. Most poems are highly organized, and their good order shows up the bad order of the stupid and the wicked. Both tragedy and comedy work to establish order, whether the ritual be a funeral or a wedding. It was clever of Herrick, accordingly, to use a poem to praise disorder and, along the way, indulge himself in a certain amount of disorder of grammar and rhyme. The poem owes something to Jonson's "Still to Be Neat," as does another Herrick poem in this company, "Upon Julia's Clothes."

FORM: Tetrameter couplets rhyming *aabbcc* etc. The first couplet is a sentence; then the next twelve lines make up a single rather messy sentence.

GEORGE HERBERT
(1593–1633)

THE YOUNGER BROTHER of Edward, Lord Herbert of Cherbury, George Herbert spent his early maturity as an apprentice courtier, but in his thirties he took orders and spent the remaining few years of his life (he died at thirty-nine) as a most devout clergyman and as a religious poet of great intellect and passion. His poetry, mostly contained in *The Temple; or, Sacred Poems and Private Ejaculations*, was not published until 1633, after his death. The book has remained a favorite for three and a half centuries.

On the one hand, his poems are almost monotonous in their choice of subject (almost always scriptural) and the way they handle those subjects. On the other hand, the poems display a breathtaking variety of moods and versatility of technique. Sometimes the diction is ornate and exotic, but at other times it seems a transcription of daily conversation. The effect of this common touch is so strong and durable that the phrase "Ah my dear" from Herbert's "Love III" reappeared after 250 years in Gerard Manley Hopkins's "The Windhover," as fresh as it was on the first day it was uttered. Herbert enjoyed the advantage of being a religious poet at a time when religious poetry was flourishing, and he designed his whole book to be a place of worship, with porch, altar, window, and so forth.

The end of the seventeenth century was very nearly also the end of religious poetry, since what followed tended to be either secular or pagan. A renewal of interest in religious poetry came about during the nineteenth century, and with it came a refurbishing of the reputations of poets like Herbert.

Further Reading

The Works. F. E. Hutchinson, ed. Oxford: Clarendon, 1945.

Charles, Amy M. *A Life of George Herbert*. Ithaca: Cornell University Press, 1977.

Vendler, Helen. *The Poetry of George Herbert*. Cambridge: Harvard University Press, 1975.

Love III

Love bade me welcome; yet my soul drew back,
    Guilty of dust and sin.
But quick-eyed Love, observing me grow slack
    From my first entrance in,
Drew nearer to me, sweetly questioning
    If I lacked any thing.

"A guest," I answered, "worthy to be here";
    Love said, "You shall be he."
"I, the unkind, ungrateful? Ah my dear,
    I cannot look on Thee."
Love took my hand, and smiling did reply,
    "Who made the eyes but I?"

"Truth Lord, but I have marred them; let my shame
    Go where it doth deserve."
"And know you not," says Love, "who bore the blame?"
    "My dear, then I will serve."
"You must sit down," says Love, "and taste My meat."
    So I did sit and eat.

COMPOSED AROUND 1630; PUBLISHED 1633. Herbert was ordained as deacon in 1624 and as priest in 1630. This poem was written sometime during the last nine or ten years of his short life. *The Temple*, published shortly after Herbert's death, has something of the design of a sacred building, with poems like "The Church-Porch" and "The Altar" (which is actually *shaped* like an altar). "Love III" comes at the end of the very large subdivision called "The Church." That it is the third of Herbert's poems bearing the title "Love" shows how much the subject meant to him.

"Love III," closely following apocalyptic poems "Death," "Doomsday," "Judgement," and "Heaven," records the experience of a soul brought into the presence of the God who is Love. As throughout *The Temple*, the speaker presents himself as unworthy: dusty, sinful, unkind, ungrateful, guilty of wastefulness and shame. With each protest, Love offers forgiveness and redemption.

The poem personifies Love as a "quick-eyed" figure on a stage almost like that of a theater ("my first entrance") where a little drama is quickly enacted.

FORM: Six-line stanza rhyming *ababcc* with alternating pentameter and trimeter lines.

When God at first made man,
Having a glass of blessings standing by,
"Let us," said He, "pour on him all we can:
Let the world's riches, which dispersed lie,
 Contract into a span."

So strength first made a way;
Then Beauty flowed, then Wisdom, Honor, Pleasure:
When almost all was out, God made a stay,
Perceiving that alone of all His treasure
 Rest in the bottom lay.

"For if I should," said He,
"Bestow this jewel also on My creature,
He would adore My gifts instead of Me,
And rest in Nature, not the God of Nature:
 So both should losers be.

"Yet let him keep the rest,
But keep them with repining restlessness:
Let him be rich and weary, that at least,
If goodness lead him not, yet weariness
 May toss him to My breast."

COMPOSED AROUND 1630; PUBLISHED 1633. Here is a little poem that amounts to a sermon on the question, "Why Are We So Restless?" The point is that God gave us many great gifts, but why did he not just go ahead and give us everything? The answer cleverly exploits a metaphor from the world of simple machines: our restlessness acts as God's pulley. The poem also involves a number of explanatory creation myths, including the Hebrew and the Greek. The "glass of blessings" here resembles the box of Pandora, whose name means "All Gifts" (although Pandora brought evils and not blessings).

FORM: Five-line stanza rhyming *ababa,* first and last lines trimeter, all others pentameter.

Sweet day, so cool, so calm, so bright,
The bridal of the earth and sky:
The dew shall weep thy fall tonight; ·
    For thou must die.

Sweet rose, whose hue angry and brave
Bids the rash gazer wipe his eye:
Thy root is ever in its grave,
    And thou must die.

Sweet spring, full of sweet days and roses,
A box where sweets compacted lie;
My music shows ye have your closes,
    And all must die.

Only a sweet and virtuous soul,
Like seasoned timber, never gives;
But though the whole world turn to coal,
    Then chiefly lives.

COMPOSED AROUND 1630; PUBLISHED 1633. A number of Herbert's poems sound like sermons on a given text or a certain key word. Here the key, as Louis Martz has observed, is "sweet" in many senses, progressing from the sensual to the spiritual. The emphasis on passing time, symbolized by a rose, makes the poem resemble such *carpe diem* lyrics as Herrick's "To the Virgins, to Make Much of Time" and Waller's "Go, Lovely Rose." But, when urging one to seize the day, Herbert means to do so in taking care of one's immortal soul, not of one's carnal body.

Herbert wrote other poems involving sweetness: "Church-music" begins, "Sweetest of sweets, I thank you"; "The Odour" begins, "How sweetly doth *My Master* sound!"

FORM: Four quatrains of three tetrameter lines followed by one dimeter, rhyming *abab* with same rhyme in even-numbered lines of the first three stanzas, which all end with the same word.

THOMAS CAREW
(1595–1639?)

CAREW, WHOSE NAME is pronounced "Carey," was a lawyer's son. He was educated in the law at Oxford and the Middle Temple and spent several years in the diplomatic service, including tours in Venice, Holland, and France. Later, in recognition of his standing as an official of the court, he was given an estate by King Charles I. Although he died about three years before the outbreak of the Civil War in 1642, he qualifies as a Cavalier lyricist and is included among the "Courtly" poets who specialized in lighthearted (but not lightheaded) lyrics in praise of love. Carew's poems show the influence of his two most-admired precursors, Donne and Jonson. One can see the spirit of Donne at work in some of the Metaphysical conceits in "Ask Me No More Where Jove Bestows," but the spirit of Jonson is also unmistakable in the phrasing and the allusions to classical mythology. Like Jonson, Carew wrote masques. "The Rapture" remains one of the most extraordinary poems of the first half of the seventeenth century.

Further Reading

The Poems of Thomas Carew with His Masque Coelum Britannicum. Rhodes Dunlap, ed. Oxford: Clarendon, 1949.
Sadler, Lynn. *Thomas Carew*. Boston: Twayne, 1979.
Selig, Edward I. *The Flourishing Wreath*. Hamden, Conn.: Archon Books, 1970.

Ask Me No More Where Jove Bestows

Ask me no more where Jove bestows,
When June is past, the fading rose;
For in your beauty's orient deep
These flowers, as in their causes, sleep.

Ask me no more whither do stray
The golden atoms of the day;
For in pure love heaven did prepare
Those powders to enrich your hair.

Ask me no more whither doth haste
The nightingale when May is past,
For in your sweet dividing throat
She winters, and keeps warm her note.

Ask me no more where those stars light
That downwards fall in dead of night,
For in your eyes they sit, and there
Fixed become, as in their sphere.

Ask me no more if east or west
The phoenix builds her spicy nest,
For unto you at last she flies
And in your fragrant bosom dies.

COMPOSED AROUND 1630; PUBLISHED 1640. Carew, a Cavalier poet much influenced by Ben Jonson and John Donne, produced this gallant and extravagant trifle in praise of a beloved woman. Such an itemized inventory of attractions, called a *blason* or blazon, is found in many other poems: Marvell's "To His Coy Mistress," Byron's "She Walks in Beauty," and Poe's "To Helen" are among the best examples in this collection.

The poem is addressed to the woman with a repetition of "Ask me no more" (a device called anaphora) at the beginning of each stanza. The rather amusing implication is that she has been asking these serious questions—What becomes of the beauty of the rose when the rose dies?—although it is hard to imagine such a conversation between actual people.

FORM: Tetrameter quatrains rhyming *aabb*.

EDMUND WALLER
(1606–1687)

A COMPLEX MAN surviving in most complex times, Waller was a politician in the good and bad senses. By the age of sixteen, having spent a while at Eton and Cambridge, he became a member of Parliament. Early in his career he was in the opposition, as an advocate of the rights of Parliament against the king, but in time he switched to the Royalist side and was active in the Civil Wars. Captured and imprisoned in 1643, he informed on his associates and was given lenient treatment. This episode has been interpreted as a bad example of treachery, cowardice, faithlessness, and hypocrisy.

Waller spent years on the Continent until 1651, when he was allowed to come home. At the time he professed support for Cromwell, but, at the Restoration in 1660, he regained his seat in Parliament, having switched once again to the party supporting the king. Thereafter, no further opportunities for advantageous switching presented themselves, and Waller lived out his days in relative consistency of mind and conscience. He survived through a dangerous period when many lost their fortunes, positions, and lives by supporting one or another side in a baffling conflict. His troublesome political and religious character fades into nothingness when one considers that Waller gave the world, whether Parliamentarian or Royalist or neutral, some really beautiful and abiding poetry.

Further Reading

The Poems. G. Thorn Drury, ed. 1893; reprint, New York: Scribner's, 1968.

Chernaik, Warren L. *The Poetry of Limitation: A Study of Edmund Waller*. New Haven: Yale University Press, 1968.

Gilbert, Jack Glenn. *Edmund Waller*. Boston: Twayne, 1979.

Go, Lovely Rose

Go, lovely rose!
Tell her that wastes her time and me
     That now she knows,
When I resemble her to thee,
     How sweet and fair she seems to be.

Tell her that's young
And shuns to have her graces spied,
     That, hadst thou sprung
In deserts where no men abide,
     Thou must have uncommended died.

Small is the worth
Of beauty from the light retired:
     Bid her come forth,
Suffer herself to be desired,
     And not blush so to be admired.

Then die, that she
The common fate of all things rare
     May read in thee,
How small a part of time they share
     That are so wondrous sweet and fair.

Composed around 1635; published 1645. A diplomatic envoy is somebody *sent* (French *envoye*, ultimately derived from *en voie*, "on the way") to a foreign government on a mission; an invoice (originally a plural form of the same French word) is a list of things *sent*. Correspondingly, this poem is an envoy: a work or part of a work that is sent to someone.

Here, as in Jonson's "Song: To Celia," the thing sent as an envoy is a rose; as in Herrick's "To the Virgins, to Make Much of Time," the message of the rose is that flowers fade and die, as do all living things, including beautiful young people.

The original music for Milton's masque *Comus* was composed by Waller's great contemporary Henry Lawes, to whom both Milton and Herrick addressed poems of friendly praise. Lawes also set Waller's "Go, Lovely Rose" to music, and both artists survive in modern poetry in the *Envoi* of Ezra Pound's *Hugh Selwyn Mauberley*:

> Go, dumb-born book,
> Tell her that sang me once that song of Lawes
> When our two dusts with Waller's shall be laid,
> Siftings on siftings in oblivion,
> Till change hath broken down
> All things save Beauty alone.

It is also worth noting that Waller's image of the rose blooming unseen in the desert returns in Gray's "Elegy Written in a Country Churchyard": "Full many a flower is born to blush unseen / And waste its sweetness on the desert air."

Form: Five-line stanza (dimeter, tetrameter, dimeter, tetrameter, tetrameter) rhyming *ababb*.

JOHN MILTON
(1608–1674)

MILTON IS CUSTOMARILY RANKED as the second-greatest poet in English, surpassed only by Shakespeare. There have been attacks—most notably by Samuel Johnson in the eighteenth century and by Ezra Pound and T. S. Eliot in the twentieth—but Milton's place seems secure.

He was born in London, the son of a scrivener (that is, someone in the business of handling legal and financial documents, often involving investments and real estate). After several years at Cambridge, he spent several years in retirement, studying and preparing himself for great things. In his thirtieth year he traveled on the Continent and met, among many notables, Galileo Galilei.

The period from 1642 and 1660—a time of two civil wars and an experimental commonwealth—was perhaps the most difficult and turbulent in English history, and Milton was in the thick of it. Although he did not take part in military actions, he was a bold and resourceful warrior of controversy, producing many pamphlets on religious, political, and social topics. He was among the first to advocate freedom of the press (in the pamphlet "Areopagitica"). He was notorious for his liberal views on divorce—three centuries ahead of his time in this matter. He was never divorced, himself; his first wife died in 1652, after ten years of marriage, his second in 1658, after two years of marriage. His third wife, whom he married in 1662, survived him.

For about the middle twenty years of his life, he took on some unpoetic chores as Latin Secretary to Cromwell's Council of State (Andrew Marvell was his assistant for part of this time), and it was not until the Restoration in 1660 that he was free to return to poetry. He was arrested and fined for his part in the Commonwealth, and he lost a fortune; but he got off with lighter punishment than many others of his party. His sight was failing during his State service, and by 1663 he was totally blind.

His greatest work, *Paradise Lost*, was published in 1667, and *Paradise Regained* and *Samson Agonistes* followed four years later. His reputation seems to have hibernated for about a hundred years after his death, but he made a strong comeback with the Romantic poets who flourished between 1800 and 1832. Early in the nineteenth century, William Blake published *Milton: A Poem in 2 Books to Justify the Ways of God to Man*, from which we get "And did those feet in ancient time." William Wordsworth, inspired by Milton's prose and poetry, in 1802 started writing sonnets, including "London, 1802," which begins, "Milton! Thou shouldst be living at this hour" and ends with an image of Milton the extraordinary genius who also took on the most ordinary chores:

> Thy soul was like a Star, and dwelt apart;
> Thou hadst a voice whose sound was like the sea:
> Pure as the naked heavens, majestic, free,
> So didst thou travel on life's common way,
> In cheerful godliness; and yet thy heart
> The lowliest duties on herself did lay.

Byron's pantheon included "Milton, Dryden, Pope," and Keats wrote a touching poem called "On Seeing a Lock of Milton's Hair."

Further Reading

Complete Poems and Major Prose. Merritt Y. Hughes, ed. New York: Macmillan, 1957.

Bloom, Harold, ed. *Modern Critical Views: John Milton*. New York: Chelsea House, 1986.

Hanford, James Holly. *John Milton, Englishman*. New York: Crown, 1949.

Lycidas

In this Monody the Author bewails a learned Friend, unfortunately drown'd in his Passage from Chester *on the Irish Seas, 1637. And by occasion foretells the ruin of our corrupted Clergy then in their height.*

Yet once more, O ye laurels, and once more,
Ye myrtles brown, with ivy never-sere,
I come to pluck your berries harsh and crude,
And with forc'd fingers rude
Shatter your leaves before the mellowing year.
Bitter constraint and sad occasion dear
Compels me to disturb your season due:
For Lycidas is dead, dead ere his prime
Young Lycidas, and hath not left his peer.
Who would not sing for Lycidas? he well knew
Himself to sing, and build the lofty rhyme.
He must not float upon his watery bier
Unwept, and welter to the parching wind
Without the meed of some melodious tear.

Begin then, Sisters of the sacred well
That from beneath the seat of Jove doth spring;
Begin, and somewhat loudly sweep the string:
Hence with denial vain, and coy excuse.
So may some gentle Muse
With lucky words favor my destin'd urn,
And as he passes, turn
And bid fair peace be to my sable shroud.
For we were nurs'd upon the self-same hill,
Fed the same flock, by fountain, shade and rill.

Together both, ere the high lawns appear'd
Under the glimmering eyelids of the morn,
We drove afield, and both together heard
What time the gray-fly winds her sultry horn,
Battening our flocks with the fresh dews of night,
Oft till the ev'n-star bright
Toward heav'n's descent had slop'd his burnish'd wheel.

Meanwhile the rural ditties were not mute
Temper'd to th'oaten flute:
Rough Satyrs danc'd, and Fauns with cloven heel
From the glad sound would not be absent long,
And old Dametas lov'd to hear our song.

    But O the heavy change, now thou art gone,
Now thou art gone, and never must return!
Thee shepherd, thee the woods and desert caves
With wilde thyme and the gadding vine o'ergrown
And all their echoes mourn.
The willows and the hazel copses green
Shall now no more be seen
Fanning their joyous leaves to thy soft lays.
As killing as the canker to the rose,
Or taint-worm to the weanling herds that graze,
Or frost to flowers that their gay wardrobe wear
When first the whitethorn blows,
Such, Lycidas, thy loss to shepherd's ear.

    Where were ye Nymphs when the remorseless deep
Clos'd o'er the head of your lov'd Lycidas?
For neither were ye playing on the steep,
Where your old bards the famous Druids lie,
Nor on the shaggy top of Mona high,
Nor yet where Deva spreads her wizard stream.
Ay me, I fondly dream!
Had ye been there . . . for what could that have done?
What could the Muse herself that Orpheus bore,
The Muse herself, for her enchanting son?
Whom universal nature did lament,
When by the rout that made the hideous roar
His gory visage down the stream was sent,
Down the swift Hebrus to the Lesbian shore.

    Alas! What boots it with uncessant care
To tend the homely slighted shepherd's trade,
And strictly meditate the thankless Muse?
Were it not better done as others use,
To sport with Amaryllis in the shade,
Hid with the tangles of Neaera's hair?

Fame is the spur that the clear spirit doth raise
(That last infirmity of noble mind)
To scorn delights and live laborious days;
But the fair guerdon where we hope to find,
And think to burst out into sudden blaze,
Comes the blind Fury with th'abhorred shears
And slits the thin-spun life. "But not the praise,"
Phoebus repli'd, and touch'd my trembling ears.
"Fame is no plant that grows on mortal soil,
Nor in the glistering foil
Set off to th' world, nor in broad rumor lies;
But lives, and spreads aloft by those pure eyes
And perfect witness of all-judging Jove:
As he pronounces lastly on each deed,
Of so much fame in Heav'n expect thy meed."
        O fountain Arethuse, and thou honor'd flood,
Smooth-sliding Mincius, crown'd with vocal reeds,
That strain I heard was of a higher mood.
But now my oat proceeds,
And listens to the herald of the sea
That came in Neptune's plea.
He ask'd the waves, and ask'd the felon winds,
"What hard mishap hath doom'd this gentle swain?"
And question'd every gust of rugged wings
That blows from off each beaked promontory.
They knew not of his story,
And sage Hippotades their answer brings
That not a blast was from his dungeon stray'd;
The air was calm, and on the level brine
Sleek Panope with all her sisters play'd.
It was that fatal and perfidious bark,
Built in th'eclipse, and rigg'd with curses dark,
That sunk so low that sacred head of thine.
        Next Camus (reverend sire) went footing slow,
His mantle hairy and his bonnet sedge
Inwrought with figures dim, and on the edge
Like to that sanguine flower inscrib'd with woe.
"Ah! Who hath reft" (quoth he) "my dearest pledge?"

Last came, and last did go,
The pilot of the Galilean lake.
Two massy keys he bore of metals twain
(The golden opes, the iron shuts amain).
He shook his mitr'd locks, and stern bespake:
"How well could I have spar'd for thee, young swain,
Enough of such as for their bellies' sake
Creep and intrude and climb into the fold?
Of other care they little reckoning make
Than how to scramble at the shearers' feast
And shove away the worthy bidden guest.
Blind mouths! that scarce themselves know how to hold
A sheephook, or have learn'd aught else the least
That to the faithful herdman's art belongs!
What recks it them? What need they? They are sped.
And when they list their lean and flashy songs
Grate on their scrannel pipes of wretched straw,
The hungry sheep look up, and are not fed,
But swoll'n with wind and the rank mist they draw,
Rot inwardly, and foul contagion spread:
Besides what the grim wolf with privy paw
Daily devours apace, and little said.
But that two-handed engine at the door
Stands ready to smite once, and smites no more."
    Return, Alpheus, the dread voice is pass'd
That shrunk thy streams; return, Sicilian Muse,
And call the vales and bid them hither cast
Their bells and flowerets of a thousand hues.
Ye valleys low, where the mild whispers use
Of shades and wanton winds and gushing brooks,
On whose fresh lap the swart star sparely looks,
Throw hither all your quaint enamel'd eyes
That on the green turf suck the honey'd showers,
And purple all the ground with vernal flowers.
Bring the rathe primrose that forsaken dies,
The tufted crow-toe and pale jessamine,
The white pink, and the pansy freak'd with jet,
The glowing violet,

The musk-rose and the well-attir'd woodbine,
With cowslips wan that hang the pensive head,
And every flower that sad embroidery wears;
Bid amaranthus all his beauty shed,
And daffodillies fill their cups with tears
To strew the laureate hearse where Lycid lies.
For so, to interpose a little ease,
Let our frail thoughts dally with false surmise;
Ay me! whilst thee the shores and sounding seas
Wash far away, where e'er thy bones are hurl'd,
Whether beyond the stormy Hebrides,
Where thou perhaps under the whelming tide
Visit'st the bottom of the monstrous world,
Or whether thou, to our moist vows deni'd,
Sleep'st by the fable of Bellerus old,
Where the great vision of the guarded Mount
Looks toward Namancos and Bayona's hold.
Look homeward Angel now, and melt with ruth,
And O ye dolphins, waft the hapless youth.

    Weep no more, woeful shepherds, weep no more;
For Lycidas your sorrow is not dead,
Sunk though he be beneath the watery floor:
So sinks the daystar in the ocean bed,
And yet anon repairs his drooping head
And tricks his beams and with new-spangl'd ore
Flames in the forehead of the morning sky;
So Lycidas sunk low, but mounted high
Through the dear might of him that walk'd the waves,
Where other groves and other streams along
With nectar pure his oozy locks he laves
And hears the unexpressive nuptial song
In the bless'd kingdoms meek of joy and love.
There entertain him all the saints above
In solemn troops and sweet societies,
That sing, and singing in their glory move,
And wipe the tears for ever from his eyes.
Now, Lycidas, the shepherds weep no more.
Henceforth thou art the genius of the shore

In thy large recompense, and shalt be good
To all that wander in that perilous flood.

    Thus sang the uncouth swain to th'oaks and rills,
While the still morn went out with sandals gray;
He touch'd the tender stops of various quills,
With eager thought warbling his Doric lay.
And now the sun had stretch'd out all the hills,
And now was dropp'd into the western bay;
At last he rose, and twitch'd his mantle blue,
Tomorrow to fresh woods and pastures new.

COMPOSED LATE 1637; PUBLISHED 1638. Edward King drowned in a shipwreck off the west coast of England in August 1637. Milton's "Lycidas" was one item in a memorial volume put out in 1638 by a group of King's friends and relatives. Just about every word in Milton's headnote has stirred up debate, and, despite the passage of 360 years, "Lycidas" remains controversial and problematic.

Like a general moving armies around in complex maneuvers, Milton deploys his lament in a number of directions. The basis of all these movements is the word "pastor," meaning "shepherd." The work of caring for herds has furnished our most familiar model of guidance, protection, and devotion. Shepherds are exposed to bad weather and dangerous predators. Their chief implements—the hook and the sling—remain very important symbols. In literature, whether of biblical or classical antiquity, the shepherd represents the ideal of gentleness and strength. The most famous psalm begins, "The Lord is my shepherd." God is both a shepherd and a sacrificial lamb.

No single figure has so stirred our imagination as the person associated with livestock, whether the shepherd of pastoral literature or the horseman ("cavalryman," "cavalier," and "chevalier") or the cowboy. The movie *Babe*, about a pig that learns to do the job of a sheepdog, provides a most interesting variation on a complex theme.

The lamb as religious symbol appears vividly in Blake's "The Lamb." Literary shepherds appear in Marlowe's "The Passionate Shepherd to His Love" and Ralegh's witty response, "The Nymph's Reply to the Shepherd." The tradition, dating back to antiquity, gives the shepherds Greek-sounding names and lets them engage in singing contests and other amusements. (The name "Lycidas," which may be related to the Greek for "wolf," was used long before Milton in pastoral poems by Theocritus and Virgil.) The pastoral elegy was especially used when one poet mourned the death of another. This tradition continued through the nineteenth century in poems like Shelley's "Adonais" on the death of Keats and Arnold's "Thyrsis" on the death of Clough.

Since Edward King had been something of a poet, Milton was justified in adopting the pastoral elegy as a convention, although some literal-minded critics persist in thinking that the transformation of well-to-do university students into hard-working shepherds is ridiculous. (Norman Maclean, author of *A River Runs Through It*, who grew up among sheep farmers in Montana, liked to say that the more you know about real sheep the less you care for pastoral art.)

It would be pointless to ask whether King's poetry is any good and whether King or Milton ever actually dealt with unsymbolic sheep except as the remote source of wool and mutton. (Anyone interested in what shepherds really do can look at Shakespeare's "When Icicles Hang by the Wall," where "Dick the shepherd blows his nail" in the bitter cold; if that is not enough, Hardy's novel *Far from the Madding Crowd* presents a convincing portrait of Gabriel Oak, a professional shepherd.)

After moving some of his forces in the direction of pastoral elegy, Milton exploits a newer meaning of "pastor": a member of the clergy (especially in such nonepiscopal churches as the Lutheran but widespread in other denominations). The same Edward King who had written poems was also preparing for a career in the church, so that he becomes doubly pastoral. In this second deployment, Milton creates a poem that lives in three distinct dimensions: a personal foreground that concerns himself and a friend; a political and ecclesiastic middle distance that concerns the state of the English church, which was and is part of the government; and a mythical background that invests present, local, personal experience with the form of myth that involves ancient Celtic Britain, with its landscape full of spirits, as well as the ancient world of Greeks, Romans, and Hebrews. The multiple exposures can focus on scenes in close-up, or in the middle distance, or in a panoramic long shot.

Lines 1–102 constitute a conventional elegy with all the trappings of pastoral lament, invoking mythical figures of the rural landscape (since Lycidas was a shepherd), the sea (since he drowned), and England (since that is the immediate scene). Some read lines 64–84 as a digression on fame. Lines 103–131, also sometimes regarded as a digression, represent the movement toward the state of the clergy in Milton's day. From line 132 to the end (line 193) the poem returns to the mode of pastoral elegy and, in a gesture familiar in both classical and Christian funeral poems, denies that Lycidas's mortal death was his end, since his soul is immortal. The last eight lines—a distinct stanza of ottava rima recalling

Italian models in particular—act as a finale that suggests that all the foregoing has been the song of an "uncouth Swain"—an uneducated rustic youth. A similar maneuver occurs at the end of Gray's "Elegy Written in a Country Churchyard," with the introduction of another "swain" (a word that hardly occurs outside the confines of literature). The next-to-last word is "pastures," which repeats the same element as the keyword "pastor."

Note that all of these matters of detail and design, having been debated for almost four centuries, are not to be taken as gospel: they are nothing more than suggestions and guideposts.

FORM: Irregular meter and rhyme, occasional interludes of ottava rima, as in the final eight lines.

SIR JOHN SUCKLING
(1609–1642)

SUCKLING, BORN IN MIDDLESEX, was the son of a knight who served as Secretary of State and Comptroller of the Household under James I. Suckling was educated at Cambridge and Gray's Inn, and devoted some years to government service as a diplomat and soldier. A loyal supporter of Charles I, who knighted him in 1630, Suckling took part as a Royalist in various military actions early in the Civil Wars, including the unsuccessful Scottish campaign of 1639 and the Army Plot of 1641, which was even more unsuccessful. Thereupon he fled to the Continent and soon, reduced to poverty and misery, died in Paris, purportedly a suicide.

In his early youth Suckling was one of the most brilliant among a brilliant company of hell-raising wits. He wrote most of his poems and plays during the 1630s, and was famous and successful for a short while. A gambler and a sportsman, Suckling is said to have invented the game of cribbage, which is still played by thousands.

Further Reading

The Works. Thomas Clayton, ed. Oxford: Clarendon, 1971.
Squier, Charles L. *Sir John Suckling*. Boston: Twayne, 1978.

Why So Pale and Wan, Fond Lover?

> Why so pale and wan, fond lover?
>   Prithee, why so pale?
> Will, when looking well can't move her,
>   Looking ill prevail?
>   Prithee, why so pale?

Why so dull and mute, young sinner?
　　Prithee, why so mute?
Will, when speaking well can't win her,
　　Saying nothing do't?
　　Prithee, why so mute?

Quit, quit, for shame; this will not move,
　　This cannot take her.
If of herself she will not love,
　　Nothing can make her:
　　The devil take her!

COMPOSED BY 1637; PUBLISHED 1638. Like "Fear No More the Heat o'
the Sun" and "When Icicles Hang by the Wall" by Shakespeare, and "Still to Be
Neat" by Jonson, this little piece is a song from a play. The difference is that
Suckling's play *Aglaura* has been largely forgotten while Shakespeare's and
Jonson's plays are not only remembered but performed regularly. The situation
may be like that of modern songs that long survive the movies or stage shows
they come from. The musical setting of Suckling's poem used in the first per-
formance of *Aglaura* may have been composed by Henry Lawes, who has been
praised by poets through the years all the way from Milton to Pound.

The poem is in the form of an interview with someone about his lover. The
two persons of the drama may be one person talking to himself. All the questions
here are rhetorical: the answers are already implied, and most of the time they
are negative. "Why so mute?" means "You should not be mute." After ten lines
of questions, the final stanza shifts to repeated orders—"Quit, quit" and then
concludes with a piece of advice amounting to "Let her go to hell."

FORM: Five-line stanza arranged tetrameter, trimeter, tetrameter, trimeter,
trimeter, rhyming *ababb* with feminine rhymes in each stanza. The second and
fifth lines of each stanza end with the same word.

RICHARD LOVELACE
(1618–1658)

LOVELACE (PRONOUNCED "LOVELESS") began as gifted, handsome, amiable, and wealthy, but lost everything in supporting the Royalist cause. The eldest son of a wealthy knight living in Kent, in the southeast of England, Lovelace spent some of his teenage years at Oxford and then entered the fashionable literary and courtly world in London. He fought twice for his king: in the Scottish expeditions of 1639 and again, alongside the King of France, in 1646. And he was imprisoned twice in punishment for his service to his king. His most durable poems reflect the circumstances of his turbulent life; he really was in prison and he really did go to the wars, fighting and being wounded. During one period of confinement, he prepared a volume of poems entitled *Lucasta; Epodes, Odes, Sonnets, Songs, etc*. It has been thought that the name in that title and in the poem "To Lucasta, Going to the Wars" was a reference to one Lucy Sacheverell, who was Lovelace's fiancée who, on receiving an erroneous report of his death in battle, married someone else.

With the victory of Parliament over the king, Lovelace lost everything and died before reaching the age of forty.

Further Reading

The Poems. C. H. Wilkinson, ed. Oxford: Clarendon, 1963.

Hartmann, Cyril H. *The Cavalier Spirit and Its Influence on the Life and Work of Richard Lovelace*. Folcroft, Pa.: Folcroft Press, 1970.

Weidhorn, Manfred. *Richard Lovelace*. New York: Twayne, 1970.

⚔ *To Lucasta, Going to the Wars*

Tell me not, Sweet, I am unkind
    That from the nunnery
Of thy chaste breast and quiet mind,
    To war and arms I fly.

True, a new mistress now I chase,
    The first foe in the field;
And with a stronger faith embrace
    A sword, a horse, a shield.

Yet this inconstancy is such
    As you too shall adore;
I could not love thee, Dear, so much,
    Loved I not Honor more.

COMPOSED AROUND 1645; PUBLISHED 1649. This poem is addressed to the woman to whom (according to some accounts) Lovelace was engaged. "Lucasta" elevates the real name "Lucy" into what looks like "chaste light" in Latin: *lux casta.*

The reader joins the episode in the midst of an exchange. Lucasta has evidently said that the speaker is unkind to leave her and go off to war. The poem is the speaker's defense of himself in ingenious terms that transform what looks like inconstancy into greater devotion.

We can witness here some of the outlandish comparisons or conceits that were a vogue in the early seventeenth century. "The first foe in the field" becomes a most improbable "new mistress," and instead of literally embracing Lucasta, he figuratively embraces the equipment of battle. Lovelace was a cavalier: a horseman; and he was a Cavalier as well: a Royalist supporter of King Charles I in the Civil Wars. "Cavalier" is related to other words containing the Latin for "pack-horse" (*caballus*): "cavalry" and "chivalry." Lovelace may sound quaint, but his name still gleams with honor.

Form: Ballad measure.

✎ *To Althea, from Prison*

When Love with unconfinèd wings
   Hovers within my gates,
And my divine Althea brings
   To whisper at the grates;
When I lie tangled in her hair
   And fetter'd to her eye,
The birds that wanton in the air
   Know no such liberty.

When flowing cups run swiftly round
   With no allaying Thames,
Our careless heads with roses bound,
   Our hearts with loyal flames;
When thirsty grief in wine we steep,
   When healths and draughts go free—
Fishes that tipple in the deep
   Know no such liberty.

When, like committed linnets, I
   With shriller throat shall sing
The sweetness, mercy, majesty,
   And glories of my King;
When I shall voice aloud how good
   He is, how great should be,
Enlargèd winds, that curl the flood,
   Know no such liberty.

Stone walls do not a prison make,
   Nor iron bars a cage;
Minds innocent and quiet take
   That for an hermitage;
If I have freedom in my love
   And in my soul am free,
Angels alone, that soar above,
   Enjoy such liberty.

Composed around 1645; published 1649. Lovelace served faithfully on the Royalist side in the Civil Wars, for which service he was twice imprisoned. Many of the best seventeenth-century writers did time; at one point both John Milton and John Bunyan were in the same jail. Lovelace wrote this poem in 1642, during his first imprisonment.

The poem, supposedly addressed to a woman whose name is derived from the Greek *althein*, "to heal," seems to be *about* her but not spoken *to* her—unless he is using a kind of lover's code. "Has my sweetheart come to see me? I am happy to see her!"

Whatever the direction of the address, the poem plays on all sorts of paradoxes involving freedom and constraint. Many still repeat, "Stone walls do not a prison make"—without knowing that the sentiment comes from a poem by Lovelace.

FORM: Eight-line stanza alternating tetrameter and trimeter, rhyming *ababcdcd*, with each stanza ending "such liberty."

Andrew Marvell
(1621–1678)

MARVELL WAS BORN in Yorkshire and educated at Cambridge. Like Edmund Waller, he was a Member of Parliament, and a busy political career saw him serving both and the Cromwellians and the court of Charles II.

In 1650 he served as tutor to the daughter of Lord Fairfax. His time in rural Yorkshire gave him the inspiration for much of his loveliest poetry. In 1653 he became the tutor of Oliver Cromwell's ward, and in 1657 he assisted John Milton for a time in the Latin Secretaryship to the Council of State. (It is improbable that two poets of such great stature have been employed together so prosaically. But the work was vitally important in a Europe in which Latin still served as the language of diplomacy and political administration.) In the funeral of Cromwell in November 1658, the procession included three poets of the first rank: Marvell, Milton, and John Dryden.

Marvell survived into the Restoration and continued his life of public service and also public controversy. He was a formidably witty opponent, and his satire could reduce an enemy to ashes. Some of this energy and ingenuity can be seen, put to more benign use, in his poems in this collection.

Further Reading

Complete Poems. Elizabeth Story Donno, ed. Harmondsworth: Penguin, 1972.
Colie, Rosalie. *"My Echoing Song": Andrew Marvell's Poetry of Criticism*.
    Princeton: Princeton University Press, 1970.
Hunt, John Dixon. *Andrew Marvell: His Life and Writings*. Ithaca: Cornell
    University Press, 1978.

To His Coy Mistress

Had we but world enough and time,
This coyness, Lady, were no crime.
We would sit down and think which way
To walk, and pass our long love's day.
Thou by the Indian Ganges' side
Should'st rubies find; I by the tide
Of Humber would complain. I would
Love you ten years before the Flood,
And you should, if you please, refuse
Till the Conversion of the Jews.
My vegetable love should grow
Vaster than empires, and more slow.
An hundred years should go to praise
Thine eyes, and on thy forehead gaze,
Two hundred to adore each breast,
But thirty thousand to the rest.
An age at least to every part,
And the last age should show your heart.
For, Lady, you deserve this state,
Nor would I love at lower rate.
　　But at my back I always hear
Time's winged chariot hurrying near,
And yonder all before us lie
Deserts of vast eternity.
Thy beauty shall no more be found,
Nor in thy marble vault shall sound
My echoing song; then worms shall try
That long preserved virginity,
And your quaint honor turn to dust,
And into ashes all my lust.
The grave's a fine and private place,
But none, I think, do there embrace.
　　Now therefore, while the youthful hue
Sits on thy skin like morning glew
And while thy willing soul transpires

At every pore with instant fires,
Now let us sport us while we may;
And now, like amorous birds of prey,
Rather at once our time devour
Than languish in his slow-chapped power.
Let us roll all our strength and all
Our sweetness up into one ball
And tear our pleasures with rough strife
Thorough the iron gates of life.
Thus, though we cannot make our sun
Stand still, yet we will make him run.

COMPOSED AROUND 1650; PUBLISHED 1681. The poem is cast in the form of a lover's address to a woman who does not return his love. It belongs in a number of conventional categories. Like "To the Virgins, to Make Much of Time" it combines *tempus fugit* ("time flees") with *carpe diem* ("seize the day"), for both arguments furnishing vividly dramatic examples, such as "Time's winged chariot." The presence of "birds of prey" as symbols of right action connects this poem to both "The Windhover" and "The Eagle." Marvell's poem is also a *blason* or blazon: a poem of praise or encomium that considers attractions one by one (eyes, forehead, breasts, the rest, every part).

But, while it may be all of these emotional expressions, the poem is also a logical construction:

1. If we had time, you could hold out.
2. We don't have time.
3. "Now therefore . . ."

In truth, the poem may be just a fantastic exaggeration of *carpe diem* in order to praise someone, as though to say, "You are so beautiful and I love you so much that I can think of a really silly argument, thus. . . . Look what you have done to me!"

FORM: Tetrameter couplets.

The Garden

How vainly men themselves amaze
To win the palm, the oak, or bays,
And their incessant labors see
Crown'd from some single herb or tree,
Whose short and narrow-vergèd shade
Does prudently their toils upbraid;
While all flowers and all trees do close
To weave the garlands of repose!

Fair Quiet, have I found thee here,
And Innocence, thy sister dear?
Mistaken long, I sought you then
In busy companies of men:
Your sacred plants, if here below,
Only among the plants will grow:
Society is all but rude
To this delicious solitude.

No white nor red was ever seen
So amorous as this lovely green.
Fond lovers, cruel as their flame,
Cut in these trees their mistress' name:
Little, alas! they know or heed
How far these beauties hers exceed!
Fair trees, wheresoe'er your barks I wound,
No name shall but your own be found.

When we have run our passion's heat,
Love hither makes his best retreat:
The gods, that mortal beauty chase,
Still in a tree did end their race;
Apollo hunted Daphne so
Only that she might laurel grow;
And Pan did after Syrinx speed
Not as a nymph, but for a reed.

What wondrous life is this I lead!
Ripe apples drop about my head;
The luscious clusters of the vine
Upon my mouth do crush their wine;
The nectarine and curious peach
Into my hands themselves do reach;
Stumbling on melons, as I pass,
Ensnared with flowers, I fall on grass.

Meanwhile the mind from pleasure less
Withdraws into its happiness;
The mind, that ocean where each kind
Does straight its own resemblance find;
Yet it creates, transcending these,
Far other worlds, and other seas;
Annihilating all that's made
To a green thought in a green shade,

Here at the fountain's sliding foot,
Or at some fruit-tree's mossy root,
Casting the body's vest aside,
My soul into the boughs does glide;
There, like a bird, it sits and sings,
Then whets and combs its silver wings,
And, till prepared for longer flight,
Waves in its plumes the various light.

Such was that happy Garden-state
While man there walk'd without a mate:
After a place so pure and sweet,
What other help could yet be meet!
But 'twas beyond a mortal's share
To wander solitary there:
Two paradises 'twere in one,
To live in Paradise alone.

How well the skillful gard'ner drew
Of flowers and herbs, this dial new!

Where, from above, the milder sun
Does through a fragrant zodiac run:
And, as it works, th' industrious bee
Computes its time as well as we.
How could such sweet and wholesome hours
Be reckon'd but with herbs and flowers!

COMPOSED AROUND 1650; PUBLISHED 1681. This is Marvell's contribution to the age-old discussion of the meaning of flowers, trees, and gardens. We enjoy plants for themselves and also for their value as food and as symbol. The original Paradise was a garden, and all sorts of vegetation have been given such symbolic value that no one is surprised that a flower could be called "forget-me-not."

This poem could be the inner meditation of someone in a flourishing garden thinking about all the meanings that humankind has given to such places, whether in scriptural and classical myth or in practical affairs. "The Garden" works as a plea for the protection of the natural environment and also a realistic denial of symbolism.

FORM: Eight-line tetrameter stanza rhyming *aabbccdd*.

Henry Vaughan
(1622–1695)

HENRY VAUGHAN and his twin brother Thomas were born in a part of south-east Wales once inhabited by a tribe called the Silures (hence the geological "Silurian Age"); Henry Vaughan styled himself a "Silurist." He studied both law and medicine, and it is possible that he fought on the Royalist side in the Civil Wars. He returned to Wales during the 1640s and took up the practice of medicine.

His earliest poems concern worldly matters, but his third collection, *Silex Scintillans* (1655), represents an unmistakable turn toward religious devotion, stimulated in a large way, as Vaughan readily admitted, by the example of George Herbert, who was a generation older. Vaughan deliberately modeled many of his poems on Herbert's. The piety and passion affected Wordsworth a century after Vaughan's death.

Further Reading

The Complete Poems. Alan Rudrum, ed. Baltimore: Penguin, 1976.
Fridenreich, Kenneth. *Henry Vaughan*. Boston: Twayne, 1978.
Post, Jonathan F. S. *Henry Vaughan: The Unfolding Vision*. Princeton: Princeton University Press, 1982.

The Retreat

Happy those early days! when I
Shined in my angel-infancy.
Before I understood this place
Appointed for my second race,
Or taught my soul to fancy aught
But a white, celestial thought,
When yet I had not walked above
A mile or two, from my first love,
And looking back (at that short space)
Could see a glimpse of his bright face;
When on some *gilded cloud* or *flower*
My gazing soul would dwell an hour,
And in those weaker glories spy
Some shadows of eternity;
Before I taught my tongue to wound
My conscience with a sinful sound,
Or had the black art to dispense
A sev'ral sin to ev'ry sense,
But felt through all this fleshly dress
Bright *shoots* of everlastingness.
   O how I long to travel back
And tread again that ancient track!
That I might once more reach that plain,
Where first I left my glorious train,
From whence th' inlightened spirit sees
That shady city of palm trees;
But (ah!) my soul with too much stay
Is drunk, and staggers in the way.
Some men a forward motion love,
But I by backward steps would move,
And when this dust falls to the urn
In that state I came, return.

COMPOSED AROUND 1648; PUBLISHED 1650. Most of Vaughan's poems are devotional, but it is hard to pin them down to a specific doctrine of Christian faith. "The Retreat" takes traditional Christian images from the Old and New Testaments and boldly combines them with images of reincarnation that resemble beliefs held by Hindus and by various Pythagorean and Platonic schools in antiquity. At least, the poet argues that our life resembles a succession of births or incarnations and that, if we can be born again, maybe we were born before. We labor to regain the innocence of childhood, when we were closer to God.

FORM: Tetrameter couplets rhyming *aabbcc,* etc.

Thomas Gray

(1716–1771)

Like John Milton, Thomas Gray was the son of a scrivener (that is, some-one involved in the legal and financial care of documents and investments). Gray was born in London and educated at Eton and Cambridge. Although he had a law degree, he never practiced, choosing instead to devote his life to the study of literature and antiquities. Toward the end of his life he was awarded the Professorship of Modern History at Cambridge.

Gray was a wonderfully versatile poet, and though he may not rank among the top superstars, his "Elegy" is probably better known than poems by more celebrated figures. We could call Gray a bridge, or at least a bridge-builder: between the neoclassical values of the Augustan Age and the romantic values of the late eighteenth century, and also between the interest of scholarly learning and the fascination of great popularity. One of his closest friends was Horace Walpole, son of Sir Robert Walpole, who had been Prime Minister at various times in the first half of the eighteenth century. Horace Walpole's pampered pet is the central figure in Gray's "Ode on the Death of a Favorite Cat, Drowned in a Tub of Gold Fishes."

Further Reading

Complete Poems. J. R. Hendrickson and H. W. Starr, eds. Oxford: Clarendon, 1966.

Downey, James and Ben Jones, eds. *Fearful Joy: Papers from the Thomas Gray Bicentenary Conference at Carleton University*. Montreal: McGill-Queen's University Press, 1974.

Ketton-Cremer, R. W. *Thomas Gray*. Cambridge: Cambridge University Press, 1955.

The curfew tolls the knell of parting day,
    The lowing herd wind slowly o'er the lea,
The plowman homeward plods his weary way,
    And leaves the world to darkness and to me.

Now fades the glimmering landscape on the sight,
    And all the air a solemn stillness holds,
Save where the beetle wheels his droning flight,
    And drowsy tinklings lull the distant folds;

Save that from yonder ivy-mantled tower
    The moping owl does to the moon complain
Of such as, wand'ring near her secret bower,
    Molest her ancient solitary reign.

Beneath those rugged elms, that yew tree's shade,
    Where heaves the turf in many a mold'ring heap,
Each in his narrow cell for ever laid,
    The rude forefathers of the hamlet sleep.

The breezy call of incense-breathing morn,
    The swallow twitt'ring from the straw-built shed,
The cock's shrill clarion, or the echoing horn,
    No more shall rouse them from their lowly bed.

For them no more the blazing hearth shall burn,
    Or busy houswife ply her evening care;
No children run to lisp their sire's return,
    Or climb his knees the envied kiss to share.

Oft did the harvest to their sickle yield,
    Their furrow oft the stubborn glebe has broke;
How jocund did they drive their team afield!
    How bowed the woods beneath their sturdy stroke!

Let not Ambition mock their useful toil,
    Their homely joys, and destiny obscure;
Nor Grandeur hear with a disdainful smile
    The short and simple annals of the poor.

The boast of heraldry, the pomp of pow'r,
    And all that beauty, all that wealth e'er gave,
Awaits alike th' inevitable hour.
    The paths of glory lead but to the grave.

Nor you, ye Proud, impute to these the fault,
    If Mem'ry o'er their tomb no trophies raise,
Where through the long-drawn aisle and fretted vault
    The pealing anthem swells the note of praise.

Can storied urn or animated bust
    Back to its mansion call the fleeting breath?
Can Honor's voice provoke the silent dust,
    Or Flatt'ry soothe the dull cold ear of Death?

Perhaps in this neglected spot is laid
    Some heart once pregnant with celestial fire;
Hands that the rod of empire might have swayed,
    Or waked to ecstasy the living lyre.

But Knowledge to their eyes her ample page
    Rich with the spoils of time did ne'er unroll;
Chill Penury repressed their noble rage,
    And froze the genial current of the soul.

Full many a gem of purest ray serene,
    The dark unfathomed caves of ocean bear:
Full many a flower is born to blush unseen,
    And waste its sweetness on the desert air.

Some village Hampden, that with dauntless breast
    The little tyrant of his fields withstood;
Some mute inglorious Milton here may rest,
    Some Cromwell, guiltless of his country's blood.

Th' applause of list'ning senates to command,
    The threats of pain and ruin to despise,
To scatter plenty o'er a smiling land,
    And read their hist'ry in a nation's eyes,

Their lot forbade; nor circumscribed alone
    Their glowing virtues, but their crimes confined;
Forbade to wade through slaughter to a throne,
    And shut the gates of mercy on mankind,

The struggling pangs of conscious truth to hide,
    To quench the blushes of ingenuous shame,
Or heap the shrine of Luxury and Pride
    With incense kindled at the Muse's flame.

Far from the madding crowd's ignoble strife,
    Their sober wishes never learned to stray;
Along the cool sequestered vale of life
    They kept the noiseless tenor of their way.

Yet ev'n these bones from insult to protect
    Some frail memorial still erected nigh,
With uncouth rhymes and shapeless sculpture decked,
    Implores the passing tribute of a sigh.

Their name, their years, spelt by th' unlettered Muse,
    The place of fame and elegy supply:
And many a holy text around she strews,
    That teach the rustic moralist to die.

For who to dumb Forgetfulness a prey,
    This pleasing anxious being e'er resigned,
Left the warm precincts of the cheerful day,
    Nor cast one longing ling'ring look behind?

On some fond breast the parting soul relies,
    Some pious drops the closing eye requires;
Ev'n from the tomb the voice of Nature cries,
    Ev'n in our ashes live their wonted fires.

For thee, who mindful of th' unhonor'd dead
    Dost in these lines their artless tale relate;
If chance, by lonely contemplation led,
    Some kindred spirit shall inquire thy fate,

Haply some hoary-headed swain may say,
    "Oft have we seen him at the peep of dawn
Brushing with hasty steps the dews away
    To meet the sun upon the upland lawn.

"There at the foot of yonder nodding beech
    That wreathes its old fantastic roots so high,
His listless length at noontide would he stretch,
    And pore upon the brook that babbles by.

"Hard by yon wood, now smiling as in scorn,
    Mutt'ring his wayward fancies he would rove,
Now dropping, woeful wan, like one forlorn,
    Or crazed with care, or crossed in hopeless love.

"One morn I missed him, on the customed hill,
    Along the heath and near his fav'rite tree;
Another came; nor yet beside the rill,
    Nor up the lawn, nor at the wood was he;

"The next with dirges due in sad array
    Slow though the churchway path we saw him borne.
Approach and read (for thou can'st read) the lay,
    Graved on the stone beneath yon aged thorn."

The Epitaph

Here rests his head upon the lap of Earth
    A youth to Fortune and to Fame unknown.
Fair Science frowned not on his humble birth,
    And Melancholy marked him for her own.

Large was his bounty, and his soul sincere,
    Heav'n did a recompence as largely send:

He gave to Mis'ry all he had, a tear,
    He gained from Heav'n ('twas all he wished) a friend.

No farther seek his merits to disclose,
    Or draw his frailties from their dread abode,
(There they alike in trembling hope repose),
    The bosom of his Father and his God.

COMPOSED AROUND 1741–1750; PUBLISHED 1751, SUBSTANTIALLY REVISED 1768. Gray's "Elegy Written in a Country Churchyard" is the best and most important work to come out of the eighteenth-century movement called "the Graveyard School." Such poems are solemn meditations on mortality and death, and many are set in graveyards.

Like Hardy's "The Darkling Thrush," this elegy presents an isolated figure in a rural setting at evening twilight; but Gray's present-tense poem seems to be spoken in the spring, while Hardy's past-tense poem is set in winter. This elegy concerns the deaths of a whole class of people, who have been just the sort that nobody bothers to write elegies about. More specific elegies are Shakespeare's "Fear No More the Heat o' the Sun," Wordsworth's "She Dwelt Among the Untrodden Ways," Jarrell's "The Death of the Ball Turret Gunner," Thomas's "A Refusal to Mourn the Death, by Fire, of a Child in London," and Milton's "Lycidas." Gray's other poem in this collection, "Ode on the Death of a Favorite Cat, Drowned in a Tub of Gold Fishes," could also be called an elegy, but of a different sort.

For such a famous poem, Gray's "Elegy Written in a Country Churchyard" presents some difficulties. Since we know that Gray worked on the poem on and off for a quarter-century, it could never have been literally "written in a country churchyard." That fiction of its composition suggests that it may really be an inward meditation, so that the "me" in line 4, the "thee" in line 93, and the "him" in line 98 refer to the same speaker, who is talking to himself; likewise the "youth" in the concluding Epitaph also seems to be one with the "me" and "thee" earlier in the poem. The church of St. Giles's in Stoke Poges, in Buckinghamshire, is still rural, with even now a country churchyard. Gray is buried inside the church.

FORM: Heroic quatrain (pentameter rhyming *abab*).

Ode on the Death of a Favorite Cat, Drowned in a Tub of Gold Fishes

'Twas on a lofty vase's side,
Where China's gayest art had dyed
   The azure flowers that blow;
Demurest of the tabby kind,
The pensive Selima reclined,
   Gazed on the lake below.

Her conscious tail her joy declared;
The fair round face, the snowy beard,
   The velvet of her paws,
Her coat, that with the tortoise vies,
Her ears of jet, and emerald eyes,
   She saw; and purr'd applause.

Still had she gazed; but 'midst the tide
Two angel forms were seen to glide,
   The Genii of the stream:
Their scaly armor's Tyrian hue
Thro' richest purple to the view
   Betray'd a golden gleam.

The hapless Nymph with wonder saw:
A whisker first and then a claw,
   With many an ardent wish,
She stretch'd in vain to reach the prize.
What female heart can gold despise?
   What Cat's averse to fish?

Presumptuous Maid! with looks intent
Again she stretch'd, again she bent,
   Nor knew the gulf between.
(Malignant Fate sat by, and smil'd)
The slipp'ry verge her feet beguil'd,
   She tumbled headlong in.

Eight times emerging from the flood
She mew'd to ev'ry watry God,
   Some speedy aid to send.
No Dolphin came, no Nereid stirr'd:
Nor cruel *Tom*, nor *Susan* heard.
   A Fav'rite has no friend!

From hence, ye Beauties, undeceiv'd,
Know, one false step is ne'er retriev'd,
   And be with caution bold.
Not all that tempts your wand'ring eyes
And heedless hearts, is lawful prize;
   Nor all, that glisters, gold.

COMPOSED 1747; PUBLISHED 1748, REVISED 1768. Gray's "Ode" and his "Elegy Written in a Country Churchyard" display perhaps a greater range of styles than any other set of poems by the same poet in this collection. The "Elegy" is somber, dark, and earnest; this poem is flippant and airy.

It belongs to the family of animal fables whose pedigree goes back to Aesop and, beyond that, to the Pleistocene (and—who knows?—comes forward to the bestiary preserved in cartoons of every sort).

There are pedants whose chief recreation lies in pointing out, ever so patronizingly and disdainfully, that the Bible does not say "sweat of your brow" or "gild the lily" or "spare the rod and spoil the child" or whatever; even in their sleep they murmur "Under *a* spreading chestnut tree" and "'Twas the night before Christmas *when* all through," etc. This poem is a favorite of theirs (and, blush, mine) on account of the "glisters" in the last line (not "glitters," you ninny).

Gray's good friend Horace Walpole had a favorite cat named Selima. When Selima drowned in a china vase, Gray produced this mock elegy.

FORM: Six-line stanzas rhyming *aabccb*, tetrameter, tetrameter, trimeter, tetrameter, tetrameter, trimeter.

WILLIAM BLAKE
(1757–1827)

A LONDONER, BLAKE was a poet, painter, engraver, and visionary. *Songs of Innocence* and *Songs of Experience*, words and designs alike, were engraved on copper by Blake himself. Blake designed and executed illustrations for most of the poems of Thomas Gray. After an early period of relatively simple lyrics, Blake turned to the production of visionary poems of great originality and scope; his last works were *Jerusalem* and *Milton*. Of the poets in this collection, few can match Blake's tremendous scope in writing verses that a three-year-old can learn and verses that still baffle the most intelligent critics. Through it all, Blake kept up a splendid sense of humor and an equally splendid sense of indignation and exasperation. Anyone can recognize the force and wisdom of some of Blake's utterances, such as some "Proverbs of Hell" that ought to be flown on large banners above schools: "The tygers of wrath are wiser than the horses of instruction" and "Damn braces. Bless relaxes."

Blake's unique combination of sophistication, naiveté, sublimity, piety, and coarseness impresses many as peculiarly English; his influence continues today among painters and writers on both sides of the Atlantic, and there is something that can be called authentically Blakean in the poetry of the American Allen Ginsberg as well as in the prose of the Irishman Joyce Cary (especially the character Gulley Jimson in *The Horse's Mouth* and other novels).

Further Reading

The Complete Poetry and Prose. David Erdman, ed. New York: Doubleday, 1988.
Ackroyd, Peter. *Blake*. New York: Knopf, 1996.
Erdman, David. *Blake: Prophet Against Empire*. Princeton: Princeton
    University Press, 1977.

The Tyger

Tyger! Tyger! burning bright
In the forests of the night,
What immortal hand or eye,
Could frame thy fearful symmetry?

In what distant deeps or skies
Burnt the fire of thine eyes?
On what wings dare he aspire?
What the hand dare seize the fire?

And what shoulder, & what art,
Could twist the sinews of thy heart?
And when thy heart began to beat,
What dread hand? & what dread feet?

What the hammer? what the chain,
In what furnace was thy brain?
What the anvil? what dread grasp,
Dare its deadly terrors clasp?

When the stars threw down their spears
And water'd heaven with their tears:
Did he smile his work to see?
Did he who made the Lamb make thee?

Tyger! Tyger! burning bright
In the forests of the night,
What immortal hand or eye,
Dare frame thy fearful symmetry?

COMPOSED 1793; PUBLISHED 1794. William Blake wrote "The Tyger" in 1793 and included it in a set of poems called *Songs of Experience,* published in 1794. There were also poems called *Songs of Innocence,* and some songs from the two sets make up contrasting pairs. Against the tiger of experience Blake put the lamb of innocence.

The poem is presented as the inner or outer speech of some person who is overwhelmed by the frightening but beautiful things of the world, like tigers and fire. The speaker, seemingly forced to talk to the world of experience, can do nothing but ask question after question. What does creation tell us about its creator? Many creatures in the world are strikingly beautiful but also annoying, unfriendly, dangerous, and even deadly—so much so that anyone can speculate about the producer of such mysterious products. "The Lamb" asks such questions: "Little Lamb, who made thee?" But in that poem Blake provides an answer: "He is called by thy name, / For he calls himself a Lamb." But, if God made humankind in his own image and the lamb after his own meek and mild nature, what do we do with a tiger? An adult male of certain subspecies can be twelve feet long from nose to tip of tail and weigh 650 pounds. It has long, sharp claws, massive teeth, and night vision five times better than ours. The tiger, an absolute carnivore, needs about fifteen pounds of meat per day.

Blake, a graphic artist as well as poet and printer, engraved a side-view picture of the Tyger to accompany the poem. The oldest surviving artworks in the world—cave paintings in southwestern Europe and rock drawings in Australia—almost always have to do with wild animals. (Blake's engraving of the Tyger in fact bears a striking resemblance to some of the figures on the so-called Lion Panel in Chauvet Cave, France.) Such beasts have been hunters' quarry and have also served humankind as sources of food, clothing, medicine, shelter, labor, transport, and recreation. They have also been turned into symbols in heraldry and allegory. Anybody with a couple of coins or bills will probably be carrying representations of eagles and other such creatures. Animals are still useful as entertainment (such as the Pink Panther and Roadrunner cartoons) and moral teaching (such as the Berenstain Bears). It may be that A. A. Milne's "Tigger" is a variation of "tiger" in the direction of comedy, much as Blake's "Tyger" is a variation in the direction of serious drama.

Other poems involving significant animals are "The Lamb" (the companion piece to this poem), "Jabberwocky," "The Darkling Thrush," "I Heard a Fly Buzz," "Leda and the Swan," "The Eagle," "The Windhover," "A Narrow Fellow in the Grass," "Ode to a Nightingale," and "To a Skylark."

FORM: Long measure rhyming *aabb.*

✣ London

I wander thro' each charter'd street,
Near where the charter'd Thames does flow.
And mark in every face I meet
Marks of weakness, marks of woe.

In every cry of every Man,
In every Infants cry of fear,
In every voice: in every ban,
The mind-forg'd manacles I hear,

How the Chimney-sweepers cry
Every blackning Church appalls,
And the hapless Soldiers sigh
Runs in blood down Palace walls,

But most thro' midnight streets I hear
How the youthful Harlots curse
Blasts the new-born Infants tear
And blights with plagues the Marriage hearse.

COMPOSED 1793; PUBLISHED 1794. Like "The Tyger," this poem first appeared in Blake's *Songs of Experience*. Unlike "The Tyger," which contains no "I" and no statements, "London" is spoken by an "I" and is nothing but vivid present-tense statements uttered by a speaker in direct passionate response to a common experience: walking in a city and looking at faces.

Blake's poem fits into a world to which anybody can relate, and he draws powerful emotions from everybody's ordinary fears and desires. At the same time, Blake wields a strikingly original style, which looks like some of the combinations of physical details seen in surrealist art: a sigh turns into blood running down a wall. Blake does not just condemn Prostitution or Disease or Oppression in the abstract: he presents a young whore whose life is reduced to a curse. He does not discuss his concern over Child Labor: he lets us hear the Chimney Sweeper's cry. In the first half of the poem, such abstractions as weakness, woe, and fear are mentioned, but the second half shoves before us nothing but actualities put together in extraordinary images of pity and terror.

For another picture of London two hundred years ago, see Wordsworth's "Composed upon Westminster Bridge, September 3, 1802."

FORM: Long measure (tetrameter quatrain rhyming *abab*).

And Did Those Feet in Ancient Time

And did those feet in ancient time
Walk upon England's mountains green?
And was the holy Lamb of God
On England's pleasant pastures seen?

And did the Countenance Divine
Shine forth upon our clouded hills?
And was Jerusalem builded here,
Among these dark Satanic Mills?

Bring me my Bow of burning gold:
Bring me my Arrows of desire:
Bring me my Spear: O clouds unfold!
Bring me my Chariot of fire!

I will not cease from Mental Fight,
Nor shall my Sword sleep in my hand,
Till we have built Jerusalem
In England's green & pleasant Land.

COMPOSED 1802–4; PUBLISHED 1804. This hymn introduces Blake's long prophetic poem *Milton*. For all his mysticism, Blake was a thoroughly practical man with a fine awareness of his physical and political identity. He was a very English Englishman, and in that role wrote one of the best-known English hymns (also called "Jerusalem"). Few hymns mention places outside the Holy Land, but this one calls England by name. It makes sense for a patriotic movie about English athletes to be called *Chariots of Fire*.

A tradition of struggle in politics and religion extends from John Milton and John Bunyan in the seventeenth century, through Blake and Wordsworth in the eighteenth and nineteenth, down to more recent times in writers as diverse as William Butler Yeats and Joyce Cary, to whom Blake was a model and an inspiration.

The hymn adapts visionary scriptural language to the actual landscape of modern England. Blake's visual artistry was not limited to engravings: most of his poems hammer their meaning home with physical images. Instead of vaguely promising to keep working in general terms, Blake takes up the language of a warrior: "I will not cease from Mental Fight, / Nor shall my Sword sleep in my hand."

FORM: Long measure (tetrameter quatrain) rhyming *abcb* or *abab*.

Little Lamb, who made thee?
　　Dost thou know who made thee?
Gave thee life and bid thee feed
By the stream and o'er the mead;
Gave thee clothing of delight,
Softest clothing, woolly, bright;
Gave thee such a tender voice,
Making all the vales rejoice?
　　Little Lamb, who made thee?
　　Dost thou know who made thee?

　　Little Lamb, I'll tell thee,
　　Little Lamb, I'll tell thee:
He is called by thy name,
For he calls himself a Lamb,
He is meek and he is mild;
He became a little child.
I a child, and thou a lamb,
We are called by his name.
　　Little Lamb, God bless thee!
　　Little Lamb, God bless thee!

COMPOSED AROUND 1788; PUBLISHED 1789. Blake included this poem among his *Songs of Innocence*. The corresponding poem in *Songs of Experience* is "The Tyger." And the contrast between the two poems is as vivid as the contrast between a real lamb and a real tiger as well as the manifold contrasts between innocence and experience. "The Tyger" is nothing but questions that end up at the same place where they began, and the rhythms are percussively insistent. Every line ends with a stressed rhyming syllable. "The Lamb" begins with questions but ends with answers. The inner lines of the stanzas have rhyme, but the outer couplets feature simple repetition ("made thee" four times, "tell thee" and "bless thee" twice each)—a much less emphatic effect. The speaker of "The Lamb" is identified as a child and seems to speak as a child.

FORM: Trimeter and tetrameter couplets.

To see a World in a Grain of Sand
And a Heaven in a Wild Flower,
Hold Infinity in the palm of your hand
And Eternity in an hour.

A Robin Redbreast in a Cage
Puts all Heaven in a Rage.
A dove house fill'd with doves and Pigeons
Shudders Hell thro' all its regions.
A dog starv'd at his Master's Gate
Predicts the ruin of the State.
A Horse misus'd upon the Road
Calls to Heaven for Human blood.
Each outcry of the hunted Hare
A fibre from the Brain does tear.
A Skylark wounded in the wing,
A Cherubim does cease to sing.
The Game Cock clip'd and arm'd for fight
Does the Rising Sun affright.
Every Wolf's and Lion's howl
Raises from Hell a Human Soul.
The wild deer, wand'ring here and there,
Keeps the Human Soul from Care.
The Lamb Misus'd breeds Public strife
And yet forgives the Butcher's Knife.
The Bat that flits at close of Eve
Has left the Brain that won't Believe.
The Owl that calls upon the Night
Speaks the Unbeliever's fright.
He who shall hurt the little Wren
Shall never be belov'd by Men.
He who the Ox to wrath has mov'd
Shall never be by Woman lov'd.
The wanton Boy that kills the Fly
Shall feel the Spider's enmity.

He who torments the Chafer's sprite
Weaves a Bower in endless Night.
The Catterpiller on the Leaf
Repeats to thee thy Mother's grief.
Kill not the Moth nor Butterfly,
For the Last Judgement draweth nigh.
He who shall train the Horse to War
Shall never pass the Polar Bar.
The Beggar's Dog and Widow's Cat,
Feed them and thou wilt grow fat.
The Gnat that sings his Summer's song
Poison gets from Slander's tongue.
The poison of the Snake and Newt
Is the sweat of Envy's Foot.
The Poison of the Honey Bee
Is the Artist's Jealousy.
The Prince's Robes and the Beggar's Rags
Are Toadstools on the Miser's Bags.
A truth that's told with bad intent
Beats all the Lies you can invent.
It is right it should be so;
Man was made for Joy and Woe;
And when this we rightly know
Thro' the World we safely go.
Joy and Woe are woven fine,
A Clothing for the Soul divine;
Under every grief and pine
Runs a joy with silken twine.
The Babe is more than swaddling Bands;
Throughout all these Human Lands
Tools were made, and Born were hands,
Every Farmer Understands.
Every Tear from Every Eye
Becomes a Babe in Eternity;
This is caught by Females bright
And return'd to its own delight.
The Bleat, the Bark, Bellow and Roar
Are Waves that Beat on Heaven's Shore.

The Babe that weeps the Rod beneath
Writes Revenge in realms of death.
The Beggar's Rags, fluttering in Air,
Does to Rags the Heavens tear.
The Soldier, arm'd with Sword and Gun,
Palsied strikes the Summer's Sun.
The poor Man's Farthing is worth more
Than all the Gold on Afric's Shore.
One Mite wrung from the Labrer's hands
Shall buy and sell the Miser's Lands:
Or, if protected from on high,
Does that whole Nation sell and buy.
He who mocks the Infant's Faith
Shall be mock'd in Age and Death.
He who shall teach the Child to Doubt
The rotting Grave shall ne'er get out.
He who respects the Infant's faith
Triumphs over Hell and Death.
The Child's Toys and the Old Man's Reasons
Are the Fruits of the Two seasons.
The Questioner, who sits so sly,
Shall never know how to Reply.
He who replies to words of Doubt
Doth put the Light of Knowledge out.
The Strongest Poison ever known
Came from Caesar's Laurel Crown.
Nought can deform the Human Race
Like to the Armour's iron brace.
When Gold and Gems adorn the Plow
To peaceful Arts shall Envy Bow.
A Riddle or the Cricket's Cry
Is to Doubt a fit Reply.
The Emmet's Inch and Eagle's Mile
Make Lame Philosophy to smile.
He who Doubts from what he sees
Will ne'er Believe, do what you Please.
If the Sun and Moon should doubt,
They'd immediately Go out.

To be in a Passion you Good may do,
But no Good if a Passion is in you.
The Whore and Gambler, by the State
Licenc'd, build that Nation's Fate.
The Harlot's cry from Street to Street
Shall weave Old England's winding Sheet.
The Winner's Shout, the Loser's Curse,
Dance before dead England's Hearse.
Every Night and every Morn
Some to Misery are Born.
Every Morn and every Night
Some are Born to sweet delight.
Some are Born to sweet delight,
Some are Born to Endless Night.
We are led to Believe a Lie
When we see not Thro' the Eye
Which was Born in a Night to perish in a Night
When the Soul Slept in Beams of Light.
God Appears and God is Light
To those poor Souls who dwell in Night,
But does a Human Form Display
To those who Dwell in Realms of day.

COMPOSED 1803; PUBLISHED 1863. Although these lines come from a sin-
gle part of a notebook kept in 1803, it is not clear whether they are a single work.
The title "Auguries of Innocence" may belong to the first four lines or to the
whole set of aphorisms or adages (short statements of some general truth). Blake
never published this work in his lifetime. It finally appeared in 1863, almost forty
years after the poet's death.

Readers familiar with Blake's much more compact "London" will recognize
many images and concepts, such as the soldier, the infant, and the "Harlot's cry
from Street to Street." These lines may be read as a general quarry from which
the more vivid and more dramatic "London" was taken.

FORM: Tetrameter lines rhyming in various patterns, mostly end-stopped self-
contained couplets but also longer groups and quatrains rhyming *abab*. Many
lines headless, as is the case also with Blake's "The Tyger" and "London."

Robert Burns

(1759–1796)

IT SEEMS VIRTUALLY IMPOSSIBLE to think of Robert Burns apart from Scotland. He is honored as the Scottish national poet, and for many readers, especially in America, knowledge of the language and landscape of Scotland is conveniently limited to the poetry of Burns.

At a time when poetry and learning were largely the preserve of the privileged classes, Burns overcame the odds. His father was a cottar, much like a tenant farmer, and much of Burns's life was given over to agricultural labor. He had little schooling other than that provided by his father. In the 1780s, while working as a farmer himself, he began writing poems that were first gathered in a volume in 1786. The book was a hit, and its second edition brought Burns enough money to permit him to marry and settle down. It has to be said that marriage did not make him faithful and settling down did not make him give up drinking.

His countryman James Johnson published a series called the *Scots Musical Museum*, to which Burns contributed scores of songs, some of them original, some of them reworkings of folk material. Burns's "Auld Lang Syne" remains the favored anthem of New Year's Eve, even though few know what the words mean. His "Scots Wha Hae" celebrates the same hero as the one portrayed by Mel Gibson in the movie *Braveheart* (1995), and it is a distinction for Burns that his "Comin' thro' the Rye" could be called the source of the title of J. D. Salinger's *The Catcher in the Rye*.

Further Reading

The Poems and Songs. James Kinsley, ed. Oxford: Clarendon, 1968.
Daiches, David. *Robert Burns: The Poet*. Edinburgh: Saltire Society, 1994.
McIntyre, Ian. *Dirt and Deity: A Life of Robert Burns*. London: HarperCollins, 1995.

A Red, Red Rose

O my Luve's like a red, red rose,
    That's newly sprung in June.
O, my Luve's like a melodie,
    That's sweetly played in tune!

As fair art thou, my bonnie lass,
    So deep in luve am I;
And I will luve thee still, my dear,
    Till a' the seas gang dry.

Till a' the seas gang dry, my dear,
    And the rocks melt wi' the sun;
And I will luve thee still, my dear,
    While the sands o' life shall run.

And fare thee well, my only Luve!
    And fare thee well a while!
And I will come again, my Luve,
    Though it were ten thousand mile.

Composed around 1790; published 1796. Burns liked to write new words for old tunes and to dress up some old verses for old tunes. His research into popular songs, especially in Scotland, led him to agree with a critic who claimed that the only fit themes for songwriting are love and wine. And Burns admitted of himself, "As I have been all along, a miserable dupe to love, and have been led into a thousand weakness & follies because of it, for that reason I put more confidence in my critical skill in distinguishing foppery & conceit, from real passion & nature."

In the manner of folk songs, this poem is a series of statements about how and how much the poet loves his lass. Among many other such poems, the most familiar to many readers is "How Do I Love Thee? Let Me Count the Ways." Burns's poems almost reach the extreme of bragging. The first stanza is *about* the lass, the others are addressed *to* her.

Form: Ballad measure: alternating tetrameter and trimeter lines rhyming *abcb;* in the two last stanzas, lines 1 and 3 end with the same word.

WILLIAM WORDSWORTH
(1770–1850)

AFTER BEING RAISED in Cumberland (in the Lake District of northwest England) and educated at Cambridge, Wordsworth spent some time in France at the height of its Revolution. There, also, he and Annette Vallon became the parents of a daughter, Caroline, but for complex reasons they did not marry. A succession of legacies, settlements, and sinecures permitted Wordsworth and his sister Dorothy to live simply without needing to work. They occupied dwellings in Dorset, then in Somerset, near Coleridge, at Grasmere in the Lake Country, and finally—in 1813, after he had married Mary Hutchinson—at Rydal Mount.

An on-again-off-again friendship with Coleridge was clearly the most important association of Wordsworth's literary life. The two collaborated on the volume called *Lyrical Ballads, with a Few Other Poems*, containing Coleridge's "The Rime of the Ancient Mariner" and a number of Wordsworth's poems, including the meditative masterpiece, "Tintern Abbey."

Wordsworth's presence remains colossal, as both inspiration and irritation. After a radically revolutionary youth, he seemed to turn increasingly toward conservatism and solemnity. Byron repeatedly ribbed Wordsworth; there are notable caricatures and burlesques of Wordsworth in Byron's *English Bards and Scotch Reviewers* and in *Don Juan*. In 1816, Shelley addressed a sonnet of mild reprimand "To Wordsworth," and in 1845, after the elderly Wordsworth had accepted a government pension of £300 and the office of Poet Laureate, Robert Browning hotheadedly wrote "The Lost Leader":

> Just for a handful of silver he left us,
>> Just for a riband to stick in his coat . . . .
> We that had loved him so, followed him, honored him,
>> Lived in his mild and magnificent eye,
> Learned his great language, caught his clear accents,
>> Made him our pattern to live and to die!
> Shakespeare was of us, Milton was for us,

Burns, Shelley, were with us,—they watch from their graves!
He alone breaks from the van and the freemen,
    —He alone sinks to the rear and the slaves!

In time Browning was sorry for his intemperate attack. The next generation of literary revolutionaries, including T. S. Eliot, Ezra Pound, and Aldous Huxley, again attacked Wordsworth. Even so, now it is quite clear that, in his long and eventful life, Wordsworth had more to do with shaping the nature of English poetry than any other poet of the past two centuries.

Further Reading

The Poems. John O. Hayden, ed. New Haven: Yale University Press, 1981.
Abrams, M. H. *Wordsworth: A Collection of Critical Essays*. Englewood Cliffs, NJ: Prentice-Hall, 1972.
Gill, Stephen. *William Wordsworth: A Life*. Oxford: Clarendon, 1989.

She dwelt among the untrodden ways
   Beside the springs of Dove,
A Maid whom there were none to praise
   And very few to love:

A violet by a mossy stone
   Half hidden from the eye!
Fair as a star, when only one
   Is shining in the sky.

She lived unknown, and few could know
   When Lucy ceased to be;
But she is in her grave, and oh,
   The difference to me!

COMPOSED 1799; PUBLISHED 1800. This poem, along with "A Slumber Did My Spirit Seal" and four others, is part of a group of short lyrics known as the "Lucy Poems." The identity of the woman has never been established; indeed, the poet could have made the whole thing up.

The poem tells the simplest of stories. Someone lived unknown and nearly alone in a remote place. In two quick metaphors the poem sets up her situation, isolated but lovely, like a flower or a star; and then nothing.

Coming after several ages of heroics, small quiet poems like this one—so pure and clear—seem like drinks of cold water. In another poem, "Lines Written a Few Miles Above Tintern Abbey," Wordsworth calls a good man's "little, nameless, unremembered acts / Of kindness and of love" the "best portion" of his life. Here is a person who is herself almost nameless and all but unremembered.

FORM: Three ballad measure stanzas rhyming *abab*.

The world is too much with us; late and soon,
Getting and spending, we lay waste our powers:
Little we see in Nature that is ours;
We have given our hearts away, a sordid boon!
This Sea that bares her bosom to the moon;
The winds that will be howling at all hours,
And are up-gathered now like sleeping flowers;
For this, for everything, we are out of tune;
It moves us not.—Great God! I'd rather be
A Pagan suckled in a creed outworn;
So might I, standing on this pleasant lea,
Have glimpses that would make me less forlorn;
Have sight of Proteus rising from the sea;
Or hear old Triton blow his wreathèd horn.

COMPOSED 1802–4; PUBLISHED 1807. Wordsworth was in his thirties before he began writing sonnets with much emotion. The particular inspiration came not from Petrarch or Shakespeare but from Milton, who wrote sonnets with such originality that the form, practically exhausted, went into hibernation after his death in 1674. Wordsworth, born almost a century after Milton's death, woke the sonnet up from a sleep of 130 years. Like Milton, Wordsworth put personal feelings as well as political reflections into the sonnet.

"The World Is Too Much with Us" is a sort of writing that can be called a complaint. After a list of woes, the poet may offer some resolution. Here the poet addresses humankind in a generalized complaint about the ways in which culture ("the world") usurps the glory of nature. Worn out by work and care, we cannot see much of the world beyond our jobs. Distracted by this sentiment, the pious poet would almost be willing to give up his creed and adopt an older system of belief, in which nature was animated by so much energy that people perceived gods and other superhuman presences in all parts of nature.

FORM: Italian sonnet rhyming *abbaabbacdcdcd*.

The Solitary Reaper

Behold her, single in the field,
Yon solitary Highland Lass!
Reaping and singing by herself;
Stop here, or gently pass!
Alone she cuts and binds the grain,
And sings a melancholy strain;
O listen! for the Vale profound
Is overflowing with the sound.

No Nightingale did ever chaunt
More welcome notes to weary bands
Of travelers in some shady haunt,
Among Arabian sands:
A voice so thrilling ne'er was heard
In spring-time from the Cuckoo-bird,
Breaking the silence of the seas
Among the farthest Hebrides.

Will no one tell me what she sings?—
Perhaps the plaintive numbers flow
For old, unhappy, far-off things,
And battles long ago:
Or is it some more humble lay,
Familiar matter of today?
Some natural sorrow, loss, or pain,
That has been, and may be again?

Whate'er the theme, the Maiden sang
As if her song could have no ending;
I saw her singing at her work,
And o'er the sickle bending:—
I listened, motionless and still;
And, as I mounted up the hill,
The music in my heart I bore,
Long after it was heard no more.

COMPOSED 1805; PUBLISHED 1807. Reading Thomas Wilkinson's *Tour of Scotland* gave Wordsworth the idea for this poem. Like Hardy's "The Darkling Thrush" and Keats's "Ode to a Nightingale," this is a poem about trying to understand what we hear. Interpretation of the reaper's song is hard because she is singing in the Erse language.

Bringing the reader right into the scene, the first stanza is in the present tense: "Behold her . . . O listen!" The second stanza, shifting to a generalized past, gives the present song a context. The third stanza comes back to the present and even touches the future ("Will no one tell me what she sings?"); and finally, the fourth stanza settles into a narrative past and testifies to the strength of the music, whatever its meaning.

FORM: Eight-line stanza rhyming either *abcbddee* or *ababccdd*, fourth line trimeter, all others tetrameter.

❧ Composed upon Westminster Bridge, September 3, 1802

Earth has not anything to show more fair:
Dull would he be of soul who could pass by
A sight so touching in its majesty:
This City now doth, like a garment, wear
The beauty of the morning; silent, bare,
Ships, towers, domes, theaters, and temples lie
Open unto the fields, and to the sky;
All bright and glittering in the smokeless air.
Never did sun more beautifully steep
In his first splendor, valley, rock, or hill;
Ne'er saw I, never felt, a calm so deep!
The river glideth at his own sweet will:
Dear God! the very houses seem asleep;
And all that mighty heart is lying still!

COMPOSED 1802; PUBLISHED 1807. Wordsworth's "The World Is Too Much with Us" begins, "The world"; this other Wordsworth sonnet begins, "Earth." But the poems are almost opposite in their ideas. Standing on Westminster Bridge, the poet sees a world of culture that can be as touching as a world of nature, so that the two worlds come together. In "The World Is Too Much with Us," however, the world of culture makes us unable to enjoy the world of nature, because we are too busy earning a living to live.

In fact, Wordsworth had the experience in July and not in September, so that we are dealing with a summer morning scene, when a city can be at its best. Westminster Bridge is upriver from Tower Bridge and London Bridge, but, like them, it touches the section of London known as the City: the oldest part of London, known for its many fine churches and also for its financial institutions. Until recently the City also housed the great and boisterous fish-market known as Billingsgate.

FORM: Italian sonnet rhyming *abbaabbacdcdcd*.

✺ *A Slumber Did My Spirit Seal*

A slumber did my spirit seal;
    I had no human fears:
She seemed a thing that could not feel
    The touch of earthly years.

No motion has she now, no force;
    She neither hears nor sees;
Rolled round in earth's diurnal course,
    With rocks, and stones, and trees.

COMPOSED 1799; PUBLISHED 1800. This poem, along with "She Dwelt Among the Untrodden Ways" and four others, make up a group of short lyrics known as the "Lucy Poems." The identity of the woman has never been established; indeed, the poet could have made the whole thing up.

FORM: Two ballad measure stanzas rhyming *abab*.

SAMUEL TAYLOR COLERIDGE
(1772–1834)

COLERIDGE BELONGS in the company of the great collaborators, the great poet-critics, and—paradoxically—the great popular poets. The paradox is that the most philosophical of philosophical critics, fit for the company of Plato and Bacon, should also be the least philosophical of poets, fit for the company of the anonymous authors of "Sir Patrick Spens" and "Edward, Edward."

The son of a vicar, Coleridge received a sporadic but stimulating education and led a peculiarly vexed life, which included a dependency on opium. He was in and out of school, and interrupted his stay at Cambridge to spend a short time in the military. That a person so peculiar could believe for a minute that he ought to join the cavalry is one indication of just how peculiar he was. His ambitions outran his performance, and he started a dozen projects for every one that he even came close to finishing. He was married to a woman whom he scarcely loved, and he tended to fall in love with women he could not marry.

He was, however, most fortunate in his associations; he was close to Charles Lamb, William Wordsworth, and Robert Southey. He and Southey worked out an elaborate scheme for an ideal community based on a concept called Pantisocracy. They planned a model life to be pursued on the banks of the Susquehanna River in Pennsylvania (they were probably influenced more by the beautiful name of the river than by any workable ideas). Coleridge was supported for several years by the philanthropy of Josiah and Thomas Wedgwood, of the great Staffordshire family that is still famous for fine china.

Coleridge's most productive association was with Wordsworth, and a tourist can still visit many places that were the sites, two hundred years ago, of their dwellings. In Somerset, in the southwest of England next to the Dorset of Thomas Hardy, a "Coleridge Cottage" still exists in the village of Nether Stowey. Not far away is Alfoxden Park, a house once occupied by Wordsworth when he and Coleridge were collaborating on some of their most important works. The house is now a hotel.

Coleridge remains a most influential presence. His personality was so vividly distinguished that he still seems a living person, and many of his poems are the most effective and haunting in the language. His greatest sustained prose work, *Biographia Literaria*, which combines autobiography with criticism, remains a masterpiece of wisdom and insight into the subtlest of human arts. Coleridge's genius recognized that poetry is not one monotonously consistent thing but a complex of contradictory things with a power revealed "in the balance or reconciliation of opposite or discordant qualities: of sameness, with difference; of the general, with the concrete; the idea, with the image; the individual, with the representative; the sense of novelty and freshness, with old and familiar objects; a more than usual state of emotion, with more than usual order; judgment ever awake and steady self-possession, with enthusiasm and feeling profound or vehement."

Readers baffled by a poem that seems both mechanically measured and rapturously emotional can relax: that's the way it's supposed to be; and we know that because Coleridge told us, in clear and forcible language.

Further Reading

The Collected Works. Coburn and Bart Winer, eds. Princeton: Princeton University Press, 1969–90.

Crawford, Walter B. *Reading Coleridge*. Ithaca: Cornell University Press, 1979.

Doughty, Oswald. *Perturbed Spirit*. East Brunswick, NJ: Associated University Presses, 1981.

Lowes, John Livingston. *The Road to Xanadu*. Boston: Houghton, 1927.

⚘ *Kubla Khan*

Or, a Vision in a Dream. A Fragment.

In Xanadu did Kubla Khan
A stately pleasure-dome decree:
Where Alph, the sacred river, ran
Through caverns measureless to man
    Down to a sunless sea.
So twice five miles of fertile ground
With walls and towers were girdled round;
And there were gardens bright with sinuous rills,
Where blossomed many an incense-bearing tree;
And here were forests ancient as the hills,
Enfolding sunny spots of greenery.

But oh! that deep romantic chasm which slanted
Down the green hill athwart a cedarn cover!
A savage place! as holy and enchanted
As e'er beneath a waning moon was haunted
By woman wailing for her demon-lover!
And from this chasm, with ceaseless turmoil seething,
As if this earth in fast thick pants were breathing,
A mighty fountain momently was forced:
Amid whose swift half-intermitted burst
Huge fragments vaulted like rebounding hail,
Or chaffy grain beneath the thresher's flail:
And 'mid these dancing rocks at once and ever
It flung up momently the sacred river.
Five miles meandering with a mazy motion
Through wood and dale the sacred river ran,
Then reached the caverns measureless to man,
And sank in tumult to a lifeless ocean:
And 'mid this tumult Kubla heard from far
Ancestral voices prophesying war!

The shadow of the dome of pleasure
Floated midway on the waves;
Where was heard the mingled measure
From the fountain and the caves.
It was a miracle of rare device,
A sunny pleasure-dome with caves of ice!

A damsel with a dulcimer
In a vision once I saw:
It was an Abyssinian maid,
And on her dulcimer she played,
Singing of Mount Abora.
Could I revive within me
Her symphony and song,
To such a deep delight 'twould win me,
That with music loud and long,
I would build that dome in air,
That sunny dome! those caves of ice!
And all who heard should see them there,
And all should cry, Beware! Beware!
His flashing eyes, his floating hair!
Weave a circle round him thrice,
And close your eyes with holy dread,
For he on honey-dew hath fed,
And drunk the milk of Paradise.

COMPOSED ABOUT 1798; PUBLISHED 1816. The full title is "Kubla Khan; or, A Vision in a Dream: A Fragment." Coleridge offered an account of the strange genesis of the poem. In the summer of 1797, he suffered "a slight indisposition" for which opium was prescribed. The opium made him fall into a sleep or a reverie just as he was reading a sentence about Kubla Khan in Samuel Purchas's book called *Purchas His Pilgrimage* (1613). The Chinese emperor, whose name is now usually spelled "Kublai Khan," built in what is now Xamdu a stately palace in a walled enclosure with a "sumptuous house of pleasure" in the middle. Coleridge reported that for about three hours he was in a strange condition during which he effortlessly composed hundreds of lines of poetry. When he woke, he began to write down the poetry, of which he had a "distinct recollection." He managed to write down the fifty-odd lines that we now have, but, with much remaining to be written, he was interrupted by "a person on business" who detained him for more than an hour. When Coleridge was able to resume his work, he found that most of what he had distinctly recollected earlier "had passed away like the images on the surface of a stream into which a stone has been cast."

The poem resembles a dream, maybe even a dream within a dream. It is sensual, indefinite, both exotic and immediate. First the dreamer dreams about a paradise (which literally means "walled enclosure"), seen at first from a distance. Then the sacred river is traced to a turbulent source, and the first human presence is introduced: "Ancestral voices prophesying war." Here the strange combinations come to the fore: sun and ice, war and pleasure, holiness and demonic wailing. Then a sort of resolution is reached by a vision inside the dream: a woman singing to her own accompaniment and setting an example of the power of art.

"Kubla Khan" resembles Coleridge's "The Rime of the Ancient Mariner" in its reliance on enchantment and the supernatural. Keats's "La Belle Dame sans Merci" shares such a combination of dread and sensuality, and Wordsworth's "The Solitary Reaper" includes a woman making music with powerful influence on a hearer. Milton's "Lycidas" also mentions the sacred river Alpheus, the likely source of Coleridge's "Alph."

FORM: Irregular.

George Gordon Byron, 6th Baron Byron

(1788–1824)

EVEN AMONG THE STELLAR COMPANY of these great poets, Lord Byron stands out as uniquely distinguished—maybe more for his personality and life than for his poetry as such, although he is widely regarded as a very great poet indeed, especially as a wit and satirist. Byron was not only a genius, he was also a millionaire, a hero, a nobleman, a sinner, and a beauty. The world is still learning how to catch up with him.

He was born into a tormented and tempestuous family; his father, who died when Byron was three, was nicknamed "Mad Jack." Byron succeeded to the family title when he was ten. As a hereditary baron, he is the highest-ranking poet in this collection, edging out Tennyson, who was born a commoner and created a baron. Byron's schooling was at Harrow and Cambridge. He began publishing poetry while still in his teens, and by 1812 was among the most famous poets in England. He married most unhappily in 1815, and in the next year—hounded by accusations of insanity and incest—he exiled himself, never to come home. He spent some time in Switzerland but devoted most of his remaining life to working in Italy, often in the company of Shelley and his wife Mary. During one summer, Byron and the Shelleys passed the time by writing and telling ghost stories and other such entertainments, and it was in this setting that Mary Shelley produced her novel *Frankenstein*. In James Whale's classic *Bride of Frankenstein* (1935), Byron and the Shelleys are shown at the beginning in a frame story, with Mary Shelley portrayed by Elsa Lanchester, who also appears as the Bride. A much less successful film, *The Haunted Summer* (1988), concerns the same general situation, but the chief conclusion one can draw is that Laura Dern is no Elsa Lanchester.

Byron exploited the same fashion for things Scottish that first made Robert Burns famous a generation earlier. In addition to a number of excellent short lyrics, Byron is remembered today for his two most ambitious poems, *Childe Harold's Pilgrimage* and *Don Juan*. There have been better poets, but none has surpassed Byron in personal influence: the "Byronic hero" is still with us—dark, moody, aloof, misanthropic, courageous, brilliant, tortured. He died, aged thirty-six, while in Greece to help the cause of liberty. Although he died of fever and not of wounds—and, indeed, never saw combat—he was there, and patriotic Greeks still remember him enough to name their sons "Byron."

Further Reading

The Complete Poetical Works. Jerome McGann, ed. Oxford: Clarendon, 1980–continuing.

Grosskurth, Phyllis. *Byron: The Flawed Angel*. Boston: Houghton Mifflin, 1997.

Marchand, Phyllis. *Byron: A Portrait*. New York: Knopf, 1970.

✍ *So, We'll Go No More a-Roving*

So, we'll go no more a-roving
   So late into the night,
Though the heart be still as loving,
   And the moon be still as bright.

For the sword outwears its sheath,
   And the soul wears out the breast,
And the heart must pause to breathe,
   And love itself have rest.

Though the night was made for loving,
   And the day returns too soon,
Yet we'll go no more a-roving
   By the light of the moon.

COMPOSED 1817; PUBLISHED 1830. Byron was not yet thirty when he wrote this poem of farewell to his earlier life of staying up till all hours getting into various kinds of mischief. The day comes when the excesses of youth just cannot be kept up any more. In this poem, Byron has added some new material to an old Scottish song.

FORM: Trimeter quatrains rhyming *abab*.

She Walks in Beauty

I

She walks in Beauty, like the night
    Of cloudless climes and starry skies;
And all that's best of dark and bright
    Meet in her aspect and her eyes:
Thus mellowed to that tender light
    Which Heaven to gaudy day denies.

II

One shade the more, one ray the less,
    Had half impaired the nameless grace
Which waves in every raven tress,
    Or softly lightens o'er her face;
Where thoughts serenely sweet express,
    How pure, how dear their dwelling-place.

III

And on that cheek, and o'er that brow,
    So soft, so calm, yet eloquent,
The smiles that win, the tints that glow,
    But tell of days in goodness spent,
A mind at peace with all below,
    A heart whose love is innocent!

COMPOSED 1814; PUBLISHED 1815. Byron wrote this lyric for a volume called *Hebrew Melodies*, with traditional music adapted by Isaac Nathan. Most things about Byron are fabulously romantic, including the story that he met a lovely cousin by marriage at a ball and wrote "She Walks in Beauty" the next morning. She was Lady Wilmot Horton.

FORM: Three six-line tetrameter stanzas rhyming *ababab*.

PERCY BYSSHE SHELLEY
(1792–1822)

SHELLEY WAS BORN into a substantial Sussex family and educated at Eton and Oxford. During his first year at Oxford, he was expelled on account of a pamphlet in favor of atheism. His life was complex and turbulent, with an early marriage to the sixteen-year-old Harriet Westbrook, whom he subsequently abandoned to take up with Mary, the daughter of the radical thinker William Godwin and his first wife, Mary Wollstonecraft. When Harriet committed suicide in 1816, Shelley and Mary were married (in 1818 she published *Frankenstein, or the Modern Prometheus*). Shelley fathered five children: two by Harriet, three by Mary.

Shelley resembles Blake in his originality and his dedication to radical causes; he resembles Coleridge in his high-minded intellect and critical faculty; he resembles his close friend Byron in his love for liberty and his affection for the south of Europe, especially Italy; and he resembles Keats (on whose death he wrote the noble pastoral elegy "Adonais") in the range and depth of his lyrics. Shelley was a resourceful translator as well as a great lyric and dramatic poet. He died by drowning when his yacht *Ariel* foundered in a storm off the Italian coast near Leghorn. His body, which washed ashore after a week, was cremated in the presence of Leigh Hunt and Byron.

Later during the nineteenth century, Shelley attracted some enthusiastic supporters, including Robert Browning and Thomas Hardy. Others, including Matthew Arnold, were less enthusiastic. Arnold wrote, "It always seems to me that the right sphere for Shelley's genius was the sphere of music, not of poetry; the medium of sounds he can master, but to master the more difficult medium of words he has neither intellectual force enough nor sanity enough." Later, Arnold summed up Shelley as a "beautiful and ineffectual angel, beating in the void his luminous wings in vain." Later critics, such as T. S. Eliot and D. H. Lawrence, were even more skeptical, but, after about 1970, Shelley's stock has been rising again, especially with more tolerant critics, such as Harold Bloom. It is not likely, however, that Shelley will ever live down the fact that most people know him chiefly as the husband of the author of *Frankenstein*.

Further Reading

Poetry and Prose. Donald Reiman and Sharon Powers, eds. New York: Norton, 1977.

Bloom, Harold, ed. *Percy Bysshe Shelley*. New York: Chelsea House, 1985.

Holmes, Richard. *Shelley: The Pursuit*. New York: Dutton, 1975.

Ode to the West Wind

I

O wild West Wind, thou breath of Autumn's being,
Thou, from whose unseen presence the leaves dead
Are driven, like ghosts from an enchanter fleeing,

Yellow, and black, and pale, and hectic red,
Pestilence-stricken multitudes: O Thou,
Who chariotest to their dark wintry bed

The winged seeds, where they lie cold and low,
Each like a corpse within its grave, until
Thine azure sister of the Spring shall blow

Her clarion o'er the dreaming earth, and fill
(Driving sweet buds like flocks to feed in air)
With living hues and odors plain and hill:

Wild Spirit, which art moving everywhere;
Destroyer and Preserver; hear, O hear!

II

Thou on whose stream, mid the steep sky's commotion,
Loose clouds like earth's decaying leaves are shed,
Shook from the tangled boughs of Heaven and Ocean,

Angels of rain and lightning: there are spread
On the blue surface of thine aëry surge,
Like the bright hair uplifted from the head

Of some fierce Maenad, even from the dim verge
Of the horizon to the zenith's height,
The locks of the approaching storm. Thou dirge

Of the dying year, to which this closing night
Will be the dome of a vast sepulcher,
Vaulted with all thy congregated might

Of vapors, from whose solid atmosphere
Black rain, and fire, and hail will burst: O hear!

III

Thou who didst waken from his summer dreams
The blue Mediterranean, where he lay,
Lulled by the coil of his crystalline streams,

Beside a pumice isle in Baiae's bay,
And saw in sleep old palaces and towers
Quivering within the wave's intenser day,

All overgrown with azure moss and flowers
So sweet, the sense faints picturing them! Thou
For whose path the Atlantic's level powers

Cleave themselves into chasms, while far below
The sea-blooms and the oozy woods which wear
The sapless foliage of the ocean, know

Thy voice, and suddenly grow gray with fear,
And tremble and despoil themselves: O hear!

IV

If I were a dead leaf thou mightest bear;
If I were a swift cloud to fly with thee;
A wave to pant beneath thy power, and share

The impulse of thy strength, only less free
Than thou, O uncontrollable! If even
I were as in my boyhood, and could be

The comrade of thy wanderings over Heaven,
As then, when to outstrip thy skiey speed
Scarce seemed a vision; I would ne'er have striven

As thus with thee in prayer in my sore need.
Oh, lift me as a wave, a leaf, a cloud!
I fall upon the thorns of life! I bleed!

A heavy weight of hours has chained and bowed
One too like thee: tameless, and swift, and proud.

V

Make me thy lyre, even as the forest is:
What if my leaves are falling like its own!
The tumult of thy mighty harmonies

Will take from both a deep, autumnal tone,
Sweet though in sadness. Be thou, Spirit fierce,
My spirit! Be thou me, impetuous one!

Drive my dead thoughts over the universe
Like withered leaves to quicken a new birth!
And, by the incantation of this verse,

Scatter, as from an unextinguished hearth
Ashes and sparks, my words among mankind!
Be through my lips to unawakened earth

The trumpet of a prophecy! O Wind,
If Winter comes, can Spring be far behind?

COMPOSED ABOUT 1819; PUBLISHED 1820. Shelley wrote this ode in Italy, one autumn two or three years before his death. The word "ode" means "song," and odes offer some musical charm while handling a serious subject with dignity. This ode soars on a few elementary parts of life: the seasons, the elements, the points of the compass, primary colors. The poem passionately unites all its elements and connects the death of leaves in autumn to the birth of new plants from seeds in the spring to come.

In another union, the poet becomes the world over which the wind blows, and then he himself becomes the wind. It may be hard to take the melodramatic exaggeration of "I fall upon the thorns of life! I bleed!" but most readers see some truth in what the poem is singing about: when we encounter the world, we encounter ourselves also. Having made himself and ourselves into waves, leaves, clouds, and lyres, Shelley has no trouble in claiming for himself the role of prophet. Some poems in this collection are about art (see "Musée des Beaux Arts"); some are about poetry ("Shall I Compare Thee to a Summer's Day?"); Shelley's ode, among all the other matters that it is about, is a poem about itself.

FORM: Terza rima sonnet (*aba bcb cdc ded ee*) used as stanza.

❧ *Ozymandias*

I met a traveler from an antique land
Who said: Two vast and trunkless legs of stone
Stand in the desert. Near them, on the sand,
Half sunk, a shattered visage lies, whose frown,
And wrinkled lip, and sneer of cold command,
Tell that its sculptor well those passions read
Which yet survive, stamped on these lifeless things,
The hand that mocked them and the heart that fed;
And on the pedestal these words appear:
"My name is Ozymandias, king of kings:
Look on my works, ye Mighty, and despair!"
Nothing beside remains. Round the decay
Of that colossal wreck, boundless and bare
The lone and level sands stretch far away.

COMPOSED 1817; PUBLISHED 1818. Shelley wrote this poem at a time
when Egyptian antiquities were on show in London. Quite a few monuments
and inscriptions in praise of Ozymandias (one of the many names of Ramses II)
have survived, and there is a fallen statue of him in a mortuary temple in Thebes.
Ramses Square in Cairo today holds a thirty-one-foot-high, ninety-ton rose
granite statue of Ramses II.

Shelley provides an outer story (or "frame") about hearing a traveler tell a
story. That story is the rest of the poem. Inside the inner story is yet another
story: the two lines from the pedestal. This kind of complication is common in
poems. "Leda and the Swan" and "Musée des Beaux Arts" are poems about
paintings of myths. "Ozymandias" is a poem about a story about an inscription
on a ruined statue. Ozymandias boasted, and now almost nothing remains of
him. The ancients seemed to enjoy these lessons in humility, and we are no different.

FORM: Irregular sonnet, rhyming *ababacdcefegeg*.

To a Skylark

Hail to thee, blithe spirit!
   Bird thou never wert,
That from heaven, or near it,
   Pourest thy full heart
In profuse strains of unpremeditated art.

Higher still and higher,
   From the earth thou springest
Like a cloud of fire;
   The blue deep thou wingest,
And singing still dost soar, and soaring ever singest.

In the golden lightning
   Of the sunken sun,
O'er which clouds are bright'ning,
   Thou dost float and run,
Like an unbodied joy whose race is just begun.

The pale purple even
   Melts around thy flight;
Like a star of heaven
   In the broad daylight
Thou art unseen, but yet I hear thy shrill delight.

Keen as are the arrows
   Of that silver sphere,
Whose intense lamp narrows
   In the white dawn clear,
Until we hardly see, we feel that it is there.

All the earth and air
   With thy voice is loud,
As, when night is bare,
   From one lonely cloud
The moon rains out her beams, and heaven is overflowed.

What thou art we know not;
  What is most like thee?
From rainbow clouds there flow not
  Drops so bright to see,
As from thy presence showers a rain of melody.

Like a poet hidden
  In the light of thought,
Singing hymns unbidden,
  Till the world is wrought
To sympathy with hopes and fears it heeded not:

Like a high-born maiden
  In a palace tower,
Soothing her love-laden
  Soul in secret hour
With music sweet as love, which overflows her bower:

Like a glow-worm golden
  In a dell of dew,
Scattering unbeholden
  Its aerial hue
Among the flowers and grass, which screen it from the view:

Like a rose embowered
  In its own green leaves,
By warm winds deflowered,
  Till the scent it gives
Makes faint with too much sweet those heavy-winged thieves:

Sound of vernal showers
  On the twinkling grass,
Rain-awakened flowers,
  All that ever was,
Joyous, and clear, and fresh, thy music doth surpass.

Teach us, sprite or bird,
  What sweet thoughts are thine:

I have never heard
    Praise of love or wine
That panted forth a flood of rapture so divine.

Chorus hymeneal,
    Or triumphal chaunt,
Matched with thine would be all
    But an empty vaunt—
A thing wherein we feel there is some hidden want.

What objects are the fountains
    Of thy happy strain?
What fields, or waves, or mountains?
    What shapes of sky or plain?
What love of thine own kind? what ignorance of pain?

With thy clear keen joyance,
    Languor cannot be:
Shadow of annoyance
    Never came near thee:
Thou lovest, but never knew love's sad satiety.

Waking as asleep,
    Thou of death must deem
Things more true and deep
    Than we mortals dream,
Or how could thy notes flow in such a crystal stream?

We look before and after,
    And pine for what is not:
Our sincerest laughter
    With some pain is fraught;
Our sweetest songs are those that tell of saddest thought.

Yet if we could scorn
    Hate, and pride, and fear;
If we were things born
    Not to shed a tear,
I know not how thy joy we ever should come near.

Better than all measures
    Of delightful sound,
Better than all treasures
    That in books are found,
Thy skill to poet were, thou scorner of the ground!

Teach me half the gladness
    That thy brain must know,
Such harmonious madness
    From my lips would flow,
The world should listen then, as I am listening now.

COMPOSED AND PUBLISHED 1820. Shelley wrote this poem toward the end of his life while living near Leghorn (Livorno), Italy. The behavior of the common European *Alauda arvensis* is described in colorful terms by a guidebook: "Noisy in flight, with pleasing but variable 'chrriup,' 'trruwee' or similar. Song unmistakable, a continuous stream of trilling and babbling series, often with interwoven mimicry, given mostly in fluttering stationary flight high up in air. Sings from first light and during all daylight hours" (Lars Jonsson, *Birds of Europe* [Princeton University Press, 1993]). The collective name of larks in flight is *exaltation*. The high flight, the song, and the appearance in early morning have given the skylark a place in poems by Shakespeare, Hopkins, Wordsworth (who wrote two poems called "To a Skylark"), Ted Hughes, and many others.

Shelley's poem cannot be summarized easily. The bird hardly exists, since the poem begins by hailing a spirit: "Bird thou never wert." By its flight and song the bird passes completely beyond the ordinary world and can be understood only by means of a series of comparisons. Just as Keats in "Ode to a Nightingale" is reminded of the "viewless wings of Poesy," Shelley here likens the bird to a "Poet hidden / In the light of thought." There is more than a pun between "bird" and "bard."

Sixty-five years after Shelley's death, Thomas Hardy passed by Leghorn on a trip through Italy and wrote "Shelley's Skylark":

Somewhere afield here something lies
In Earth's oblivious eyeless trust
That moved a poet to prophecies . . .

In nautical slang, "skylarking" is goofing off. At age eighty, Robert Frost wrote a long poem called "Kitty Hawk" about the Wright brothers' first flight (1903). The poem, which alludes to Shelley, is labeled "a skylark . . . in three-beat phrases."

FORM: Five-line stanza rhyming *ababb* (in seventeen of the twenty-one stanzas, the *a* rhyme is feminine). The first four lines of each stanza are trimeter, the fifth is hexameter. Many lines are headless.

JOHN KEATS
(1795–1821)

IT IS PROBABLE that John Keats produced more great poetry at an earlier age than any other poet in this collection. Readers sometimes play a game that asks, "What would Shakespeare's (or Milton's, or whosever) reputation be if he or she had died, like Keats, at twenty-five?" In almost every case, the answer is "Nothing."

Keats's father, who kept a livery stable, died in a mishap in 1804; his mother died of consumption a few years later, when Keats was fourteen. As a teenager Keats was apprenticed to a surgeon and was qualified as a "dresser" and subsequently as a surgeon, in accordance with the medical regulations of the day. Keats's first poems were written under the influence of Edmund Spenser, and all of Keats's work shows something of a Spenserian blend of sensuousness and intellectual depth. Keats renders the sights and sounds that we are accustomed to in poetry, but, more than any other, he also attends to the tastes, odors, and tactile qualities. "The Eve of St. Agnes," for example, is a Spenserian romance in design, but many of the details are devoted to registering the exact feeling of bitter cold or exquisite sweetness.

Keats's brief career as a poet was aided immeasurably by his friendship with the poet and editor Leigh Hunt, who published Keats's early poetry in the *Examiner*. Thanks again to Hunt, Keats met Wordsworth and Shelley and began to participate in the activities of literary people in London. When his poetry was viciously attacked in conservative magazines, Keats retreated somewhat into himself, at the same time having to take care of his younger siblings (two brothers and one sister) who depended on their eldest brother for friendship and support. His brother Tom, gravely ill with consumption, especially needed care; Tom died in December 1818, becoming part of the world "Where youth grows pale, and spectre-thin, and dies," in a passage of "Ode to a Nightingale" that surely refers to the dying younger brother.

Toward the end of his life Keats lived in Hampstead, where he shared a house with his friend Charles Brown. The family of Keats's fiancée Fanny Brawne lived next door. By 1819 Keats was ill with tuberculosis, which he may have contracted from Tom. Later, in search of a more wholesome climate, he went to Italy, but he died in Rome in early 1821. He had asked that his epitaph read, "Here lies one whose name was writ in water."

Keats was never a formal critic of the sort who writes essays, reviews, and dissertations, but in his marvelous letters, he displays one of the finest critical intelligences in English literature. He was, moreover, one of the most brilliant readers that the poetry of Spenser, Shakespeare, and Milton has ever had.

Further Reading

Poetical Works. H. W. Garrod, ed. Oxford: Oxford University Press, 1958.

Bate, Walter Jackson. *John Keats*. Cambridge: Harvard University Press, 1963.

Ende, Stuart A. *Keats and the Sublime*. New Haven: Yale University Press, 1976.

To Autumn

I

Season of mists and mellow fruitfulness,
    Close bosom-friend of the maturing sun;
Conspiring with him how to load and bless
    With fruit the vines that round the thatch-eves run;
To bend with apples the mossed cottage-trees,
    And fill all fruit with ripeness to the core;
        To swell the gourd, and plump the hazel shells
    With a sweet kernel; to set budding more,
And still more, later flowers for the bees,
Until they think warm days will never cease,
        For summer has o'er-brimmed their clammy cells.

II

Who hath not seen thee oft amid thy store?
    Sometimes whoever seeks abroad may find
Thee sitting careless on a granary floor,
    Thy hair soft-lifted by the winnowing wind;
Or on a half-reaped furrow sound asleep,
    Drowsed with the fume of poppies, while thy hook
        Spares the next swath and all its twinèd flowers:
    And sometimes like a gleaner thou dost keep
Steady thy laden head across a brook;
Or by a cider-press, with patient look,
        Thou watchest the last oozings hours by hours.

III

Where are the songs of Spring? Ay, where are they?
    Think not of them, thou hast thy music too,—
While barrèd clouds bloom the soft-dying day,
    And touch the stubble-plains with rosy hue;
Then in a wailful choir the small gnats mourn

Among the river swallows, borne aloft
   Or sinking as the light wind lives or dies;
And full-grown lambs loud bleat from hilly bourn;
Hedge-crickets sing; and now with treble soft
The red-breast whistles from a garden-croft;
   And gathering swallows twitter in the skies.

COMPOSED 1819, PUBLISHED 1820. "To Autumn" has been anthologized more often than any other poem in English. Keats wrote it at the very beginning of the next-to-last autumn he would see: September 19, 1819 (he died in February 1821, aged twenty-five). Born in October, he could consider autumn his own season. At the time, he was staying in Winchester, county seat of Hampshire in south-central England, still today an agricultural region known for cider.

The poem is set in the autumn of the year and also in what could be called the autumn of the day: evening ("soft-dying day"). A speaker talks *about* autumn by talking *to* autumn. He addresses the season as though it were human (personifying it). In praising autumn, the poem offers consolation, too, since so many songs insist on praising spring and summer for their beauties while dismissing autumn and winter as unfriendly. The poem offers a catalogue of sensual details having to do with the harvest season when crops are gathered, honey is collected, and by-products like flour and cider are turned out.

This poem and Shakespeare's "That Time of Year Thou Mayst in Me Behold" both suggest autumn evenings. See also Shelley's "Ode to the West Wind," Hopkins's "Spring and Fall," and Wordsworth's "The Solitary Reaper."

FORM: Eleven-line pentameter stanzas rhyming *ababcdedcce*.

La Belle Dame sans Merci

O what can ail thee, Knight at arms,
    Alone and palely loitering?
The sedge has withered from the Lake
    And no birds sing!

O what can ail thee, Knight at arms,
    So haggard, and so woe begone?
The Squirrel's granary is full
    And the harvest's done.

I see a lily on thy brow
    With anguish moist and fever dew,
And on thy cheeks a fading rose
    Fast withereth too—

I met a Lady in the Meads,
    Full beautiful, a faery's child
Her hair was long, her foot was light
    And her eyes were wild—

I made a Garland for her head,
    And bracelets too, and fragrant Zone;
She look'd at me as she did love
    And made sweet moan—

I set her on my pacing steed
    And nothing else saw all day long
For sidelong would she bend and sing
    A faery's song—

She found me roots of relish sweet
    And honey wild and manna dew
And sure in language strange she said
    I love thee true—

She took me to her elfin grot
    And there she wept, and sigh'd full sore,
And there I shut her wild wild eyes
    With kisses four.

And there she lulled me asleep
    And there I dream'd—Ah Woe betide!
The latest dream I ever dreamt
    On the cold hill side.

I saw pale Kings, and Princes too
    Pale warriors, death pale were they all;
They cried, La belle dame sans merci
    Hath thee in thrall.

I saw their starv'd lips in the gloam
    With horrid warning gaped wide,
And I awoke, and found me here
    On the cold hill's side.

And this is why I sojourn here
    Alone and palely loitering;
Though the sedge is withered from the Lake
    And no birds sing—

COMPOSED 1819–1820; PUBLISHED 1820. Keats wrote one version of this ballad in 1819 and another, revised slightly in keeping with suggestions from his mentor Leigh Hunt, in 1820. The version given here is the earlier.

The old ballad form had been revived in the late eighteenth century by Robert Burns and Sir Walter Scott, and their lead was quickly followed by Wordsworth, Coleridge, and Byron. They were all poets of learning and sophistication, but they found excitement in an antique style that emphasized vivid drama, conflict, violence, and the mysterious power of the supernatural. The settings are remote from cities and civilization, the action is elementary, and the presentation can be as primitive as a puppet show.

"La Belle Dame sans Merci" begins at the story's end, with a speaker asking questions of someone who is either a "Knight at arms" or a "wretched wight."

The speaker's questions set the scene at the end of autumn and sketch the other's haggard appearance in a waste landscape that has been abandoned by plant and animal life. The Knight's tale begins with the fourth stanza, "I met a Lady" and continues to the end of the poem. After a time of dalliance, he fell into a sleep and dreamed that many pale men of his noble class warned him that he had been enchanted by a mysterious woman, lovely but without love's mercy. She is a *femme fatale* or "deadly woman" of a type familiar throughout history, from Judith, Delilah, Helen, Cleopatra, and Salome in antiquity to troublemakers played by Lana Turner, Glenn Close, Sharon Stone, and Madonna in movies. Vladimir Nabokov's Lolita may be a teenage variation of the theme, also exhibited in Thomas Pynchon's *V.* and studied in Robert Graves's *The White Goddess.*

The folk ballads in this collection are "Sir Patrick Spens" and "Edward, Edward." Poems of dangerous or deadly beauty include "The Tyger," "The Windhover," "They Flee from Me That Sometime Did Me Seek," "Leda and the Swan," "Why So Pale and Wan, Fond Lover?," and "A Narrow Fellow in the Grass."

FORM: Quatrain rhyming *abcb*, the lines being tetrameter, tetrameter, tetrameter, dimeter.

Much have I traveled in the realms of gold,
　　And many goodly states and kingdoms seen;
　　Round many western islands have I been
Which bards in fealty to Apollo hold.
Oft of one wide expanse had I been told
　　That deep-browed Homer ruled as his demesne,
　　Yet did I never breathe its pure serene
Till I heard Chapman speak out loud and bold.
Then felt I like some watcher of the skies
　　When a new planet swims into his ken;
Or like stout Cortez when with eagle eyes
　　He stared at the Pacific—and all his men
Looked at each other with a wild surmise—
　　Silent, upon a peak in Darien.

COMPOSED 1816; PUBLISHED 1817. It may be hard to believe, but Keats
was such a great poet that he could make a memorable sonnet out of something
as unexciting as—hold on to your hat—an Educational Experience. Not able to
read Greek, he had been cut off from many fulfilling experiences. A good trans-
lation can be a second-best solution, however, and Keats thought he had found
a very good second-best in the translations of Homer's *Iliad* and *Odyssey* by
Shakespeare's contemporary George Chapman (about 1559–1634). Some schol-
ars identify Chapman as the "rival poet" mentioned in some of Shakespeare's
sonnets.

Keats would have been inclined to pass over the too-classical Homeric trans-
lations of Alexander Pope in the eighteenth century; Keats preferred the more
vigorous and, one could say, more heroically Homeric writers of the late six-
teenth and early seventeenth centuries. One of Keats's first models was Edmund
Spenser, a poet of romantic epic and a contemporary of Chapman and
Shakespeare.

Keats chose two excellent metaphors to register his excitement at getting a
glimpse of Homer. He felt like an astronomer who has discovered a new planet
or an explorer who has discovered a sea. No new planet has been found since

1930, but the thrill is easy to imagine. Keats erred in giving Cortez credit for what Balboa did, but it was a stroke of genius to connect Renaissance explorers and more recent scientists. And there is something Homeric about the travels of people like Cortez and Balboa, and something heroic about the labors of people like William Herschel, who discovered Uranus in 1781. That we call planets by such names as Uranus, Neptune, and Pluto suggests that we are not after all so very far from the mythic world of classical antiquity.

Other poems linked to Homer and other writers of ancient Greece and Rome are "Dover Beach," "Miniver Cheevy," "Leda and the Swan," and "Ulysses."

FORM: Italian sonnet rhyming *abbaabbacdcdcd*.

Ode to a Nightingale

I

My heart aches, and a drowsy numbness pains
    My sense, as though of hemlock I had drunk,
Or emptied some dull opiate to the drains
    One minute past, and Lethe-wards had sunk:
'Tis not through envy of thy happy lot,
    But being too happy in thine happiness,—
        That thou, light-wingèd Dryad of the trees,
            In some melodious plot
    Of beechen green, and shadows numberless,
        Singest of summer in full-throated ease.

II

O, for a draught of vintage! that hath been
    Cool'd a long age in the deep-delvèd earth,
Tasting of Flora and the country green,
    Dance, and Provençal song, and sunburnt mirth!
O for a beaker full of the warm South,
    Full of the true, the blushful Hippocrene,
        With beaded bubbles winking at the brim,
            And purple-stainèd mouth;
    That I might drink, and leave the world unseen,
        And with thee fade away into the forest dim:

III

Fade far away, dissolve, and quite forget
    What thou among the leaves hast never known,
The weariness, the fever, and the fret
    Here, where men sit and hear each other groan;
Where palsy shakes a few, sad, last gray hairs,
    Where youth grows pale, and specter-thin, and dies;
        Where but to think is to be full of sorrow
            And leaden-eyed despairs,

Where Beauty cannot keep her lustrous eyes,
    Or new Love pine at them beyond to-morrow.

IV

Away! away! for I will fly to thee,
    Not charioted by Bacchus and his pards,
But on the viewless wings of Poesy,
    Though the dull brain perplexes and retards:
Already with thee! tender is the night,
    And haply the Queen-Moon is on her throne,
        Cluster'd around by all her starry Fays;
            But here there is no light,
    Save what from heaven is with the breezes blown
        Through verdurous glooms and winding mossy ways.

V

I cannot see what flowers are at my feet,
    Nor what soft incense hangs upon the boughs,
But, in embalmèd darkness, guess each sweet
    Wherewith the seasonable month endows
The grass, the thicket, and the fruit-tree wild;
    White hawthorn, and the pastoral eglantine;
        Fast fading violets cover'd up in leaves;
            And mid-May's eldest child,
    The coming musk-rose, full of dewy wine,
        The murmurous haunt of flies on summer eves.

VI

Darkling I listen; and for many a time
    I have been half in love with easeful Death,
Call'd him soft names in many a musèd rhyme,
    To take into the air my quiet breath;
Now more than ever seems it rich to die,
    To cease upon the midnight with no pain,
        While thou art pouring forth thy soul abroad
            In such an ecstasy!

Still wouldst thou sing, and I have ears in vain—
    To thy high requiem become a sod.

VII

Thou wast not born for death, immortal Bird!
    No hungry generations tread thee down;
The voice I hear this passing night was heard
    In ancient days by emperor and clown:
Perhaps the self-same song that found a path
    Through the sad heart of Ruth, when, sick for home,
      She stood in tears amid the alien corn;
        The same that oft-times hath
    Charm'd magic casements, opening on the foam
      Of perilous seas, in faery lands forlorn.

VIII

Forlorn! the very word is like a bell
    To toll me back from thee to my sole self!
Adieu! the fancy cannot cheat so well
    As she is fam'd to do, deceiving elf.
Adieu! adieu! thy plaintive anthem fades
    Past the near meadows, over the still stream,
      Up the hill-side; and now 'tis buried deep
        In the next valley-glades:
    Was it a vision, or a waking dream?
      Fled is that music:—Do I wake or sleep?

COMPOSED 1819; PUBLISHED 1820. Keats wrote this poem very quickly one spring morning in 1819 in the garden of a house in Hampstead. Charles Brown, with whom Keats was living, said that a nightingale had been nesting in a plum tree and that "Keats felt a tranquil and continual joy in her song."

    Luscinia megarhynchos here—like *Turdus viscivorus* in Hardy's "The Darkling Thrush," *Falco tinnunculus* in Hopkins's "The Windhover," and *Alauda arvensis* in Shelley's "To a Skylark"—is not a bird with which Americans are familiar, unless they travel in Europe. On the other hand, even Americans who never leave home except to travel in the "realms of gold" provided by poetry know these European birds better than they know some of their New World cousins which have never been memorably celebrated. Keats's nightingale, with its habit of singing beautifully at night, has become *the* bird of poetry, the most significant creature that concentrates the meaning of the world into a song. In many of the celebrated bird poems in this collection, the bird is an intermediary between the human and the animal, between ourselves and nature, and even between ourselves and the divine. A bird's flight, as in "The Windhover," can be a formula for the meaning of all motion and all life; a bird's song can be, as in this poem, a formula for the meaning of everything we hear.

As a story, the poem hardly covers more than a few minutes. In a somber mood, a person hears a bird singing beautifully at night and almost loses himself in the song. He almost wishes to join the bird and to escape the world of affairs and diseases where "youth" (like Keats's younger brother Tom) "grows pale, and spectre-thin, and dies." The meditation deepens as the speaker realizes that his wish to escape is not a wish to die, but rather to live more, with experience made richer by music and poetry. After some back and forth, the poem ends on a note of compromise between sleeping and waking. The complex movements between life and death receive a tenderly humorous treatment in Larry McMurtry's novel *The Last Picture Show*; in the movie version, John Hillerman played the high school teacher who presents "Ode to a Nightingale" to an appreciative but bewildered class.

Keats's "Ode to a Nightingale" does such a good job in presenting what all poems try to present that it has become what might be called The Poem of Poems. It lives on in many other works, including T. S. Eliot's "Sweeney Among the Nightingales" and *The Waste Land* as well as two poems by Thomas Hardy. "The Selfsame Song" begins "A bird sings the selfsame song" and ends "But it's not the selfsame bird. — / No: perished to dust is he." At age eighty, Hardy wrote "At a House in Hampstead," which begins

> O poet, come you haunting here
> Where streets have stolen up all around,
> And never a nightingale pours one
> Full-throated sound?

Keats's poem is even tough enough to withstand some amiable kidding. It is the leadoff number in a feature called "Famous First Drafts" in *The Brand New Monty Python Bok* (yes: *Bok*). There, Keats is imagined to have started on an "Ode to a Gynaecologist," decided instead to write an "Ode to a Nightwatchman," then changed "Nightwatchman" to "Nightingale."

FORM: Pentameter stanza rhyming *ababcdecde* (eighth line is trimeter).

ELIZABETH BARRETT BROWNING
(1806–1861)

THE BROWNINGS ARE the only married couple in this collection. One can speculate about what that fact means for poetry and for matrimony, but it tells much about the great distinction of both Brownings as poets. She was some years older than Robert, and, when they first met, she was the more famous poet. Her first book, *Essay on Mind, with Other Poems*, was published in 1826, when she was barely twenty and he was still in his teens. She died twenty-eight years before he did, and he spent the last quarter of his life as a lonely widower.

Their story still reads like a soap opera with many melodramatic features, including bodily illness, paternal opposition, romantic art, and a secret wedding. Elizabeth developed a lingering affliction in 1838 and was an invalid for several years thereafter. Robert wrote to her in 1845, praising her work, and they soon met and began corresponding. In September of 1846 they were wed in secrecy and fled to Italy, where they lived for most of the rest of her life.

With only one poem in this collection, she stands some risk of being dismissed as a romantic sonneteer with little scope or depth. But the full range of her publications tells a very different story. *The Seraphim and Other Poems* (1838) and *Poems* (1844) show a great variety of subjects and styles. It may be that *Sonnets from the Portuguese* (first published in 1850) are like other wildly popular but also wildly untypical works, such as Walt Whitman's "Oh Captain, My Captain" and T. S. Eliot's *Old Possum's Book of Practical Cats*: if you knew nothing else about the writer, you would in effect know nothing. If you stopped with "How Do I Love Thee? Let Me Count the Ways," you would be missing *Aurora Leigh* (1857), Elizabeth Barrett Browning's 11,000-line "novel in verse" about a woman writer—one of the boldest and most audacious experiments in English literature.

When she died in 1861, Edward FitzGerald, famous as the translator of *The Rubáiyát of Omar Khayyám*, wrote in a letter, "Mrs. Browning's death is rather a relief to me. I must say: no more Aurora Leighs." Robert Browning came across these unkind words many years later, after FitzGerald's death in 1883, and wrote "To Edward FitzGerald":

I chanced upon a new book yesterday;
I opened it, and, where my finger lay
    'Twixt page and uncut page, these words I read—
Some six or seven at most—and learned thereby
That you, FitzGerald, whom by ear and eye
    She never knew, "thanked God my wife was dead."
Aye, dead! And were yourself alive, good Fitz,
How to return you thanks would task my wits.
    Kicking you seems the common lot of curs—
While more appropriate greeting lends you grace;
Surely to spit there glorifies your face—
    Spitting from lips once sanctified by hers.

Further Reading

The Complete Works. New York: AMS Press, 1973.

Besier, Rudolph. *The Barretts of Wimpole Street*. Boston: Little, Brown, 1930.

Cooper, Helen. *Elizabeth Barrett Browning: Woman and Artist*. Chapel Hill:
    University of North Carolina Press, 1988.

Mermin, Dorothy. *Elizabeth Barrett Browning: The Origins of a New Poetry*.
    Chicago: University of Chicago Press, 1989.

How do I love thee? Let me count the ways.
I love thee to the depth and breadth and height
My soul can reach, when feeling out of sight
For the ends of Being and ideal Grace.
I love thee to the level of every day's
Most quiet need; by sun and candle-light.
I love thee freely, as men strive for Right;
I love thee purely, as they turn from Praise.
I love thee with the passion put to use
In my old griefs, and with my childhood's faith.
I love thee with a love I seemed to lose
With my lost saints,—I love thee with the breath,
Smiles, tears, of all my life!—and, if God choose,
I shall but love thee better after death.

COMPOSED AROUND 1845; PUBLISHED 1850. *Sonnets from the Portuguese* appeared in 1850. An earlier title was *Sonnets Translated from the Bosnian*. The sonnets are not translated from the Portuguese or the Bosnian, but the suggestion of indirection may keep the poems from seeming too personal.

The sequence contains forty-four sonnets; this one comes next to last. Some of the poems talk about the beloved in the third person, but many talk to the beloved in the poetic second person of *thou* and *thee*.

FORM: Italian sonnet rhyming *abbaabbacdcdcd*.

Edgar Allan Poe

(1809–1849)

POE'S LIFE WAS SHORT; he was evidently an undiagnosed diabetic, on whom alcohol had a terrible effect (although, as one student of his life has remarked, the sad thing is less a matter of Poe's drinking so much as of his eating so little). He was born in Boston but, having been orphaned at an early age, raised in Virginia. Between 1811 and 1815 he lived in Richmond, then he went with his adoptive family to England until 1820. He spent a short time at the University of Virginia, then left to join the Army, eventually going to the U.S. Military Academy at West Point for a year. From about the age of fourteen he had been writing poetry, and after his dismissal from West Point in 1831 lived hand-to-mouth in various literary and journalistic jobs all over the eastern seaboard: in New York, Baltimore, Richmond, and Philadelphia. In 1835 he received a license to marry his cousin, Virginia Clemm, who was thirteen at the time. They married in 1836 and seem to have lived together happily until her death from tuberculosis in 1845. Poe himself died in Baltimore in 1849 under mysterious circumstances. A century and a half after his death, a dispassionate diagnostician reviewing the facts in the case concluded that Poe probably died of rabies.

Poe spent most of his adult life as a literary editor and journalist. In a pitifully abbreviated career, he managed to make himself famous as a fabulous inventor—a true American Daedalus—so that it can be persuasively argued that Poe, just about single-handedly, invented the short story, science fiction, detective fiction, the symbolist poem, and the New Criticism.

For various reasons, some of which remain mysterious, Poe has enjoyed, all along, a higher reputation in France than in America or England. True, Poe's diction can be lurid and his verbal effects may seem vulgar, but it seems unfair to say—as both Walter Pater and T. S. Eliot suggested—that the full appreciation of Poe can come only to those whose knowledge of English is imperfect. Since Poe was a great inventor and explorer in one of the oldest American traditions, William Carlos Williams called him "a new DeSoto."

It is certain that Poe remains the American writer with the farthest-reaching influence: he understood our deepest fears and desires, and his shadow stretches over many literary provinces, from Jules Verne to Vladimir Nabokov to the films of Stanley Kubrick (the secret code letters in *Dr. Strangelove* are "P.O.E.," after all).

Further Reading

Complete Works. Thomas Olive Mabbott, ed. Cambridge: Harvard University Press, 1969–1978.

Miller, John Carl. *Building Poe Biography*. Baton Rouge: Louisiana State University Press, 1977.

Zayed, Georges. *The Genius of Edgar Allan Poe*. Cambridge, Mass.: Schwenkman, 1985.

✗ *To Helen*

Helen, thy beauty is to me
    Like those Nicéan barks of yore,
That gently, o'er a perfumed sea,
    The weary, way-worn wanderer bore
    To his own native shore.

On desperate seas long wont to roam,
    Thy hyacinth hair, thy classic face,
Thy Naiad airs have brought me home
    To the glory that was Greece,
And the grandeur that was Rome.

Lo! in yon brilliant window-niche
    How statue-like I see thee stand,
    The agate lamp within thy hand!
Ah, Psyche, from the regions which
    Are Holy-Land!

POSSIBLY BEGUN AS EARLY AS 1823; FIRST PUBLISHED 1831, REVISED THEREAFTER THROUGH 1845. Poe said that he began this poem, at age fourteen, in praise of a woman named Jane Stith Stanard, who was a good friend of the sort that gives comfort and shelter to a young person with problems. Poe memorialized her by elevating her affection to an extraordinary beauty powerful enough to deserve comparison with the joy of homecoming. Such beauty is not so much a physical attribute as an emotional effect. "Being with you is like coming home after a long absence," the poem suggests, although in extremely vivid images. Vivid, yes, but also vague. The poem bewitchingly mixes the definite with the indefinite, and, for at least 150 years, readers have been debating the meaning of "Nicéan" and much else in the poem. Its terrific power probably comes more from mystery and suggestion of the idealized woman than from any outright reference to a particular Helen or Holy Land. Her presence calls up other classical presences, including the refuge of classical antiquity, which is, in a way, a home to which we long to return.

FORM: Five-line stanzas with inconsistent meter and rhyme pattern, varying between two and four stresses per line. The stanzas rhyme *ababb cdcdc effef*. As part of the enchanting irregularity, no two stanzas have quite the same rhyme scheme; "face" and "Greece" rhyme too little (the vowels do not match), "roam" and "Rome" rhyme too much (they sound just alike from beginning to end).

✒ *Annabel Lee*

It was many and many a year ago,
    In a kingdom by the sea,
That a maiden there lived whom you may know
    By the name of Annabel Lee;
And this maiden she lived with no other thought
    Than to love and be loved by me.

She was a child and *I* was a child,
    In this kingdom by the sea,
But we loved with a love that was more than love—
    I and my Annabel Lee—
With a love that the wingèd seraphs of Heaven
    Coveted her and me.

And this was the reason that, long ago,
    In this kingdom by the sea,
A wind blew out of a cloud by night
    Chilling my Annabel Lee;
So that her high-born kinsmen came
    And bore her away from me,
To shut her up in a sepulchre
    In this kingdom by the sea.

The angels, not half so happy in Heaven,
    Went envying her and me:—
Yes! that was the reason (as all men know,
    In this kingdom by the sea)
That the wind came out of the cloud chilling,
    And killing my Annabel Lee.

But our love it was stronger by far than the love
    Of those who were older than we—
    Of many far wiser than we—
And neither the angels in Heaven above
    Nor the demons down under the sea

Can ever dissever my soul from the soul
    Of the beautiful Annabel Lee:—

For the moon never beams without bringing me dreams
    Of the beautiful Annabel Lee;
And the stars never rise but I feel the bright eyes
    Of the beautiful Annabel Lee:
And so all the night-tide, I lie down by the side
Of my darling, my darling, my life and my bride
    In the sepulchre there by the sea—
    In her tomb by the side of the sea.

COMPOSED 1849; PUBLISHED 1850. Poe wrote several versions of this poem between May and September 1849. The latest is given here. The earlier versions are generally considered inferior, with the exception of the last line. In the earliest text, the poem ends "by the sounding sea"—a touching echo of "sounding seas" in Milton's "Lycidas." Since Poe died in October 1849, "Annabel Lee" is usually considered his last poem.

Scholars have traced some incidental elements of the poem to the work of others. Poe knew of a novel called *The Ladye Annabel* and a poem called "Young Rosalie Lee," and he was probably familiar with Sir Walter Scott's *Marmion*, which contains the line "There was racing and chasing on Cannobie Lea." The force of Poe's genius, even so, unified all the elements into a wholly original and enduring poem. "Annabel Lee" is the single most important ancestor of Vladimir Nabokov's *Lolita*.

Although the story of young love and early death in a kingdom by the sea is obviously not autobiographical, many have related the mood of the poem to Poe's grief over the early death of his wife Virginia, whom he had married when she was thirteen.

One cannot say for sure whether the speaker is alive or dead. Characteristically, Poe's art furnishes many things that we want, even if they contradict one another. On the one hand, the poem presents definite outlines and solid rhythms (here a combination of iambs and anapests, also found in Tennyson's "Break, Break, Break.") On the other hand, there are indefinite references and grammatical inconsistencies ("And this maiden she lived"). Poe called the poem a ballad, and it may recall such "art ballads" (as opposed to "folk ballads") as Burns's "A Red, Red Rose" and Byron's "So, We'll Go No More a-Roving."

With its setting in the long ago and far away, and with angels and demons and aristocrats, the poem seems to belong to the world of folklore and fairy tale. With its obsessive repetition of key words and sounds—"sea," "Lee," "me," along with a "we" or two—the poem is as haunting as a recurrent dream.

FORM: Irregular strophes of iambs and anapests, mixing tetrameters and trimeters in an elaboration of the ballad measure, with twenty of the forty-one lines ending with an "-ee" rhyme; also internal rhymes in many lines.

ALFRED, LORD TENNYSON
(1809–1892)

BY THE CENTENNIAL of Tennyson's death, a pretty good case could have been made to the effect that it has been a full hundred years since the Poet Laureate and the greatest living English poet were arguably the same person. Disputes, as always, may develop about any of the terms of that case, but it remains true that Tennyson was one of the greatest poets who have held the Laureateship.

Tennyson was born in Lincolnshire and educated at Cambridge, where he was one of a bright constellation of promising students. Another member of the group was the brilliant Arthur Henry Hallam, a dear friend whose early death in 1833 stimulated Tennyson to write the noble and eloquent elegy *In Memoriam* (published in 1850). Much else that Tennyson wrote in the during the ten years after 1833 was colored by memories of Hallam, including "Ulysses" and "Break, Break, Break."

The publication of *In Memoriam* happened to coincide with the death of Wordsworth, who had been the Poet Laureate since 1843. Tennyson was young for the position, but he carried out the office of the Laureate with matchless skill. Some have thought, in fact, that he was too much of a Laureate and not enough of a poet, churning out jingoistic pieces like "The Charge of the Light Brigade" (the inspiration of two very different movies in 1936 and 1968). But such poems, even if guilty as charged, are in the minority of his large output.

With a certain measure of popular success and the celebrity of the Laureateship, Tennyson finally achieved some repose. He was at last able to marry Emily Sellwood, after delays over twenty years, and he lived comfortably in large houses: "Farringford" near Freshwater Bay on the Isle of Wight (1853–68) and "Aldworth" near Haslemere in Surrey (1868–92, with some summers back on the Isle of Wight).

Tennyson excelled in the short musical lyric, the dramatic monologue, the long narrative, and certain boldly mixed forms for which we still lack accurate names, such as *The Princess* and *Maud*.

Further Reading

The Poems. Christopher Ricks, ed. London: Longmans, 1987.

Ebbatson, Roger. *Tennyson: Penguin Critical Studies*. New York: Viking Penguin, 1988.

Martin, Robert Bernard. *Tennyson, the Unquiet Heart: A Biography*. Oxford: Clarendon, 1980.

Break, Break, Break

Break, break, break,
   On thy cold gray stones, O Sea!
And I would that my tongue could utter
   The thoughts that arise in me.

O, well for the fisherman's boy,
   That he shouts with his sister at play!
O, well for the sailor lad,
   That he sings in his boat on the bay!

And the stately ships go on
   To their haven under the hill;
But O for the touch of a vanished hand,
   And the sound of a voice that is still!

Break, break, break,
   At the foot of thy crags, O Sea!
But the tender grace of a day that is dead
   Will never come back to me.

COMPOSED AFTER 1833; PUBLISHED 1842. Tennyson wrote this poem from the same experience that gave him *In Memoriam*: that is, the death of his dear friend Arthur Henry Hallam in 1833.

England is an island, small enough that one is never far from the sea. Tennyson wrote this poem near Bristol. The poem, addressing the sea directly, takes the breaking waves as a measure of time passing, with reminders of what is permanent and what is temporary. (Similar seaside reflections animate Arnold's "Dover Beach" and Eliot's "The Love Song of J. Alfred Prufrock.") In another poem, Tennyson gives a brook this song: "For men may come and men may go, / But I go on forever."

FORM: Quatrains rhyming *abcb*: the first and second are all trimeter, the third and fourth have a tetrameter in the third line (a pattern equivalent to the Short Measure of the hymnals); some lines consist of monosyllabic feet ("Break, break, break"), others of anapests ("And the sound of a voice that is still"), others of a combination of iambs and anapests.

ᓚ *The Eagle*

FRAGMENT

He clasps the crag with crooked hands;
Close to the sun in lonely lands,
Ringed with the azure world, he stands.

The wrinkled sea beneath him crawls;
He watches from his mountain walls,
And like a thunderbolt he falls.

COMPOSED AROUND 1850; PUBLISHED 1851. This vivid fragment closely examines the physical details of a bird often given heraldic or symbolic significance. If you have a dollar bill or a quarter handy, you can see an effigy of an eagle much less genuine than Tennyson's exciting word-picture.

Other meaningful birds are in "The Darkling Thrush," "Leda and the Swan," "The Windhover," "Ode to a Nightingale," and "To a Skylark."

FORM: Two tetrameter triplets rhyming *aaa*.

Ulysses

It little profits that an idle king,
By this still hearth, among these barren crags,
Matched with an agèd wife, I mete and dole
Unequal laws unto a savage race
That hoard, and sleep, and feed, and know not me.
I cannot rest from travel; I will drink
Life to the lees. All times I have enjoyed
Greatly, have suffered greatly, both with those
That loved me, and alone; on shore, and when
Through scudding drifts the rainy Hyades
Vexed the dim sea. I am become a name;
For always roaming with a hungry heart
Much have I seen and known—cities of men
And manners, climates, councils, governments,
Myself not least, but honored of them all—
And drunk delight of battle with my peers,
Far on the ringing plains of windy Troy.
I am a part of all that I have met;
Yet all experience is an arch wherethrough
Gleams that untraveled world whose margin fades
Forever and forever when I move.
How dull it is to pause, to make an end,
To rust unburnished, not to shine in use!
As though to breathe were life! Life piled on life
Were all too little, and of one to me
Little remains; but every hour is saved
From that eternal silence, something more,
A bringer of new things; and vile it were
For some three suns to store and hoard myself,
And this gray spirit yearning in desire
To follow knowledge like a sinking star,
Beyond the utmost bound of human thought.
    This is my son, mine own Telemachus,
To whom I leave the scepter and the isle—
Well-loved of me, discerning to fulfill

This labor, by slow prudence to make mild
A rugged people, and through soft degrees
Subdue them to the useful and the good.
Most blameless is he, centered in the sphere
Of common duties, decent not to fail
In offices of tenderness, and pay
Meet adoration to my household gods,
When I am gone. He works his work, I mine.
　　There lies the port; the vessel puffs her sail;
There gloom the dark, broad seas. My mariners,
Souls that have toiled, and wrought, and thought with me—
That ever with a frolic welcome took
The thunder and the sunshine, and opposed
Free hearts, free foreheads—you and I are old;
Old age hath yet his honor and his toil.
Death closes all; but something ere the end,
Some work of noble note, may yet be done,
Not unbecoming men that strove with Gods.
The lights begin to twinkle from the rocks;
The long day wanes, the slow moon climbs; the deep
Moans round with many voices. Come, my friends,
'Tis not too late to seek a newer world.
Push off, and sitting well in order smite
The sounding furrows; for my purpose holds
To sail beyond the sunset, and the baths
Of all the western stars, until I die.
It may be that the gulfs will wash us down;
It may be we shall touch the Happy Isles,
And see the great Achilles, whom we knew.
Though much is taken, much abides; and though
We are not now that strength which in old days
Moved earth and heaven, that which we are, we are—
One equal temper of heroic hearts,
Made weak by time and fate, but strong in will
To strive, to seek, to find, and not to yield.

COMPOSED AROUND 1833; PUBLISHED 1842. According to his own testimony, Tennyson said that "Ulysses," written shortly after the death of Arthur Henry Hallam, "gave my feeling about the need of going forward and braving the struggle of life." Tennyson and Hallam had some things in common with John Milton and Edward King. All were poets who were undergraduates at Cambridge. King's early death prompted Milton, who was three years his senior, to write "Lycidas"; Hallam's early death prompted Tennyson, who was two years his senior, to write *In Memoriam* and several other poems, including "Break, Break, Break" and "Ulysses."

In elementary terms, "Ulysses" works as a poem of resolution and strength. It takes a legendary hero from classical antiquity and shows him toward the end of his life, still restless to travel, explore, ever seeking new knowledge and experience. In these respects he is like any number of versatile British heroes, such as Sir Walter Ralegh and Sir Francis Drake, who enlarged the realm of Queen Elizabeth I, and Sir Richard Francis Burton and Cecil Rhodes, restlessly exploring and forging new realms of Victoria's empire. A similar spirit animated the life of Commander Robert Falcon Scott (1868–1912), who led a small party to the South Pole in January 1912, only to find out that Roald Amundsen had beaten them there by one month. Scott and his party perished on their way back from the Pole. On the memorial cross erected near where they died is an inscription that ends with the last line of "Ulysses": "To strive, to seek, to find, and not to yield." (On television, a Swiss bank has advertised its reliability by presenting Sir John Gielgud, aged ninety-two, intoning the finale of "Ulysses.")

Such resolute language, however, points the way to other aspects of Ulysses that practically suggest a whole other poem lurking under the surface of inspirational rhetoric. "To strive, to seek, to find, and not to yield" sounds very much like the blank verse of another plucky and resourceful aristocratic explorer of alien worlds rallying his companions to join him with "courage never to submit or yield." That line comes from a speech early in Milton's *Paradise Lost* (I, 108) in which the fallen Satan, newly arrived in hell, addresses Beelzebub and tries to cheer him up. And that scene in hell recalls another infernal episode involving the same Ulysses with whom we started. To Dante, Ulysses, although a hero, was also a false counselor, an unfaithful husband, a negligent parent, a despoiler of religious shrines, and a cunning deceiver (the Wooden Horse was his idea, and he is usually identified as a trickster). His lust for experience and knowledge is nothing to be admired since, according to a non-Homeric legend preserved in Dante's *Inferno*, Ulysses and all his crew perished on the final voyage that presumably came after the speech represented in Tennyson's "Ulysses." Dante places Ulysses far down in hell, in the eighth pit of the eighth circle of the Abyss. The

Inferno has thirty-four cantos, and Ulysses tells his story in Canto XXVI, just ahead of the canto in which Guido da Montefeltro, another deceiver, speaks the words preserved in the epigraph of Eliot's "The Love Song of J. Alfred Prufrock."

It seems fitting that such a complex figure should have two names: Odysseus in Greek (source of "odyssey") and Ulysses in Latin. He is almost as complicated as a real person! The hero may seem more like a corporation (Odysseus, Inc.) than a single man. Tennyson here joins a large company of poets who have written about Odysseus-Ulysses, dating back to Homer, Euripides, Horace, Dante, Shakespeare, and Pope, to say nothing of the translation memorialized in Keats's "On First Looking into Chapman's Homer," which also invokes discoverers and explorers. This "Ulysses" looks back and also forward, since variations of the *Odyssey* have occupied a number of later writers, such as James Joyce (*Ulysses*, 1922) and Ezra Pound (*The Cantos*, 1904–1972). Both modern writers admired the original hero's resourcefulness and vivacity, regarding his inventiveness as a particularly significant talent for the modern world. Many regard Joyce's *Ulysses*—which is not about Ulysses himself but about a modern incarnation whose one-day journey around Dublin on June 16, 1904, is parallel to Ulysses' ten-year journey around the Mediterranean—as the greatest modern novel.

FORM: Blank verse.

Robert Browning
(1812–1889)

The most sensational episode in Robert Browning's life was his elopement with Elizabeth Barrett, a piece of history made perhaps all too familiar in the popular play *The Barretts of Wimpole Street*. Even so, they were in love, and they did escape to Italy, and a little bit of romantic adventure, even if exaggerated, won't do any harm. As an adolescent and young man, Browning experimented with a great variety of types of poetry, but his subsequent reputation owes most to his perfection of the dramatic monologue. Some of these poems are more properly classified as soliloquies or epistles, but the fundamental idea is the same: one person speaks or writes a single sustained expression under some pressure that causes a revelation of character. Since the informal regulations limit such poetry, Browning did not often invent characters from scratch. Instead, he took existing literary figures (such as Caliban from Shakespeare's *The Tempest*), real historical characters (such as Fra Lippo Lippi and Andrea del Sarto), or familiar types (such as Renaissance Italian dukes and bishops). The Brownings lived in Florence from 1846 until her death in 1861. Robert Browning then returned to England, where he was to spend most of his remaining days. He died in Venice, but the body was brought back to England and buried with honor in Westminster Abbey.

"Character" is the watchword for Browning's art, since he did not concern himself much with extended or complicated plots, and his ideas—like the ideas of most poets—were commonplace. But his insights into the depths and contradictions of human character were unmatched even by novelists of his day (such as Dickens, an exact contemporary). Another common feature of Browning's art is economy: how to find the one moment that defines a lifetime and then to cram all the details and nuances into one utterance. For the perfecting of the monologue as the ideal reflection of character, Browning should be honored as the great precursor of James Joyce and other writers who exploited the notion of the stream of consciousness or interior monologue. Many of the poems that T. S. Eliot and Ezra Pound turned out in their early years—between 1910 and 1920—were shaped by Browning's example. In some ways, Eliot's "The Love

Song of J. Alfred Prufrock" looks like a combination of what Browning achieved in "My Last Duchess" and what Arnold accomplished in "Dover Beach." Browning's long poem *The Ring and the Book* anticipates the modern stress on relativity of perspective, whereby a story changes according to the teller's experience and a single scene may be perceived and described very differently by different reporters. That may not sound so original now, but a hundred years ago it was quite an innovation. And Browning also set the stage for what was to happen in modern drama, in the hands of such masters as Shaw and O'Neill, although he died before the revolution in the theater really got going. But justice may prevail after all. A movie of *The Barretts of Wimpole Street* was made in 1934 (with Norma Shearer and Fredric March); Sir Terence Rattigan's play *The Browning Version* (1948), although not really about either Browning, at least keeps the name alive (and there have been two film versions, in 1951 and 1994).

Further Reading

Complete Works. Roma King, ed. Athens: Ohio University Press, 1969–continuing.

Bloom, Harold, ed. *Robert Browning*. New York: Chelsea House, 1985.

Irvine, William. *The Book, the Ring, and the Poet*. New York: McGraw-Hill, 1974.

⚘ *My Last Duchess*

Ferrara

That's my last Duchess painted on the wall,
Looking as if she were alive. I call
That piece a wonder, now: Frà Pandolf's hands
Worked busily a day, and there she stands.
Will't please you sit and look at her? I said
"Frà Pandolf" by design, for never read
Strangers like you that pictured countenance,
The depth and passion of its earnest glance,
But to myself they turned (since none puts by
The curtain I have drawn for you, but I)
And seemed as they would ask me, if they durst,

How such a glance came there; so, not the first
Are you to turn and ask thus. Sir, 't was not
Her husband's presence only, called that spot
Of joy into the Duchess' cheek: perhaps
Frà Pandolf chanced to say "Her mantle laps
Over my lady's wrist too much," or "Paint
Must never hope to reproduce the faint
Half-flush that dies along her throat": such stuff
Was courtesy, she thought, and cause enough
For calling up that spot of joy. She had
A heart—how shall I say?— too soon made glad,
Too easily impressed; she liked whate'er
She looked on, and her looks went everywhere.
Sir, 't was all one! My favor at her breast,
The dropping of the daylight in the West,
The bough of cherries some officious fool
Broke in the orchard for her, the white mule
She rode with round the terrace—all and each
Would draw from her alike the approving speech,
Or blush, at least. She thanked men,—good! but thanked
Somehow—I know not how—as if she ranked
My gift of a nine-hundred-years-old name
With anybody's gift. Who'd stoop to blame
This sort of trifling? Even had you skill
In speech—(which I have not)—to make your will
Quite clear to such an one, and say, "Just this
Or that in your disgusts me; here you miss,
Or there exceed the mark"—and if she let
Herself be lessoned so, nor plainly set
Her wits to yours, forsooth, and made excuse,
—E'en then would be some stooping; and I choose
Never to stoop. Oh sir, she smiled, no doubt,
Whene'er I passed her; but who passed without
Much the same smile? This grew; I gave commands;
Then all smiles stopped together. There she stands
As if alive. Will 't please you rise? We'll meet
The company below, then. I repeat,
The Count your master's known munificence

Is ample warrant that no just pretense
Of mine for dowry will be disallowed;
Though his fair daughter's self, as I avowed
At starting, is my object. Nay, we'll go
Together down, sir. Notice Neptune, though,
Taming a sea horse, thought a rarity,
Which Claus of Innsbruck cast in bronze for me!

COMPOSED AROUND 1840; PUBLISHED 1842. Browning was incapable of writing a successful full-length theatrical play, but he was an absolute master of concentrated dramatic poems in which characters in very limited circumstances reveal something very important about themselves that they may not even themselves be aware of. The soliloquy and epistle involve a single character speaking or writing a sustained utterance, and Browning wrote some excellent poems in both those formats. His genius, however, was most vividly brought out in the dramatic monologue. This kind of poem could conceivably be part of a much longer play, but the single monologue does all the work of telling a complete story. Typically, this sort of poem represents what a single character says to another in a situation that requires him or her to argue a case or make a point. By what they say and by how they say it, such characters reveal much about themselves—and with much more impact and surprise than could be delivered in a long leisurely play or movie. A dramatic monologue typically takes only a few minutes, but a whole human life can be distilled into that short expression.

In Browning's poem, the speaker is a sixteenth-century duke. (In most systems of nobility, dukes and duchesses rank just below princes and princesses. The Duke of Ferrara would rule a city-state of some size and importance; the city's present population is about 200,000.) The duke starts talking by pointing to something—"That"—and we soon perceive that he is talking to one other person, whom we can make out to be a representative from a neighboring count. Counts and countesses, placed over counties, ordinarily rank two grades below dukes and duchesses, but our duke seems to be anxious to please and impress his guest.

We can deduce that the duke is a widower now engaged in negotiations for the hand of his next duchess, and the daughter of the nearby count seems to be the chief candidate. The duke and the emissary seem to have been in an upstairs room discussing terms and are now on their way downstairs. The duke stops before a portrait of his last duchess, and as he talks about her we learn little by little that, because of her innocent manners and unwitting failure to be sub-servient to him alone, he has come to hate her and finally has gotten rid of her.

It seems to be a love story combined with a murder mystery, except that the duke loves only himself. The duke is dignified and cagey but not quite cagey enough. Some inner compulsion, probably an overwhelming sense of guilt, has compelled him to return to the scene and situation of his crime and to confess. His own language betrays him, since "my last duchess" can mean something besides "my most recent duchess": it can mean also "my final duchess," and if the count's representative has any sense at all the count's daughter will not become the "object" (another telling word) of the duke's affection.

FORM: Heroic couplets (pentameter couplets rhyming *aabbcc* etc.) With enjambment, the rhyming line-endings may be hard to detect, so that there is an element of deviousness and surprise in the partially hidden design.

✴ *Meeting at Night*

I

The gray sea and the long black land;
And the yellow half-moon large and low;
And the startled little waves that leap
In fiery ringlets from their sleep,
As I gain the cove with pushing prow,
And quench its speed i' the slushy sand.

2

Then a mile of warm sea-scented beach;
Three fields to cross till a farm appears;
A tap at the pane, the quick sharp scratch
And blue spurt of a lighted match,
And a voice less loud, through its joys and fears,
Than the two hearts beating each to each!

COMPOSED BY 1844; PUBLISHED 1845. In *Dramatic Romances* (1845) this poem
appeared as one part of a work called "Night and Morning." In a collection pub-
lished in 1849, however, the two parts appeared as separate poems, this one with
its present title and the other as "Parting at Morning." The latter poem is short
enough to reproduce in its entirety:

> Round the cape of a sudden came the sea,
> And the sun looked over the mountain's rim:
> And straight was a path of gold for him,
> And the need of a world of men for me.

(The "him" refers to the sun.) Forty years later Browning said that the two-part
poem is a man's "confession of how fleeting is the belief (implied in the first
part) that such raptures are self-sufficient and enduring—as for the time they
appear."

The drama is enhanced by the casting of "Meeting at Night" in the present tense, as though the reader were in the middle of the action, seeing, hearing, smelling the scene. "Parting at Morning" pulls back for a long shot in the past tense. This striking contrast in presentation may be what caused Browning to subdivide what had been a single poem.

FORM: Two tetrameter stanzas rhyming *abccba*.

I

Oh, to be in England
Now that April's there,
And whoever wakes in England
Sees, some morning, unaware,
That the lowest boughs and the brushwood sheaf
Round the elm-tree bole are in tiny leaf,
While the chaffinch sings on the orchard bough
In England—now!

II

And after April, when May follows,
And the whitethroat builds, and all the swallows!
Hark, where my blossomed pear-tree in the hedge
Leans to the field and scatters on the clover
Blossoms and dewdrops—at the bent spray's edge—
That's the wise thrush; he sings each song twice over,
Lest you should think he never could recapture
The first fine careless rapture!
And though the fields look rough with hoary dew,
All will be gay when noontide wakes anew
The buttercups, the little children's dower
—Far brighter than this gaudy melon-flower!

COMPOSED AROUND 1844; PUBLISHED 1845. Both this poem and its companion piece "Home-Thoughts, from the Sea" are spoken by an Englishman in southern Europe: probably Italy.

They say you never appreciate what you have at home until you spend some time away. The English may feel indifference or contempt toward the weather, plants, and animals of their damp and chilly northern home island, but their minds can be changed by living in the tropics, where birds and flowers and music can seem too loud and gaudy.

FORM: Irregular strophes mixing long and short rhymed lines with one set of lines not rhyming but ending in a repeated key word ("England").

Arthur Hugh Clough
(1819–1861)

As the son of a prosperous Liverpool cotton merchant, Clough enjoyed the educational advantage of spending some of his early years in South Carolina. He came back to England for school, and enjoyed yet another advantage: he was sent to Rugby School, where the headmaster was Thomas Arnold, with whose son, Matthew, Clough formed an enduring friendship. Like Matthew Arnold and Gerard Manley Hopkins, Clough went on to Balliol College, Oxford. His subsequent career in education and government was spotty, inconclusive, and—owing to his early death—all too short.

His writing is variegated and highly original. *The Bothie of Toper-na-Vuolich* (1848) has been called a novel in verse; "Amours de Voyage" is another verse tale, with the added novelty of being in the form of letters. "The Latest Decalogue" is flippantly light and may approach blasphemy. But Clough was also capable of writing the famous anthem of resolution and hope, "Say Not the Struggle Nought Availeth." Arnold addressed "To a Republican Friend, 1848" to Clough (who was hardly what Americans would call a Republican) and commemorated his old friend in "Thyrsis," one of the noblest pastoral elegies in English.

Further Reading

The Poems. F. L. Mulhauser, ed. Oxford: Clarendon, 1974.

Greenberger, Evelyn Barish. *Arthur Hugh Clough: The Growth of a Poet's Mind*. Cambridge: Harvard University Press, 1970.

Harris, Wendell V. *Arthur Hugh Clough*. New York: Twayne, 1970.

Thou shalt have one God only; who
Would be at the expense of two?
No graven images may be
Worshipped, except the currency:
Swear not at all; for, for thy curse
Thine enemy is none the worse:
At church on Sunday to attend
Will serve to keep the world thy friend:
Honour thy parents; that is, all
From whom advancement may befall:
Thou shalt not kill; but need'st not strive
Officiously to keep alive:
Do not adultery commit;
Advantage rarely comes of it:
Thou shalt not steal; an empty feat,
When it's so lucrative to cheat:
Bear not false witness; let the lie
Have time on its own wings to fly:
Thou shalt not covet, but tradition
Approves all forms of competition.

COMPOSED 1847; PUBLISHED 1862. Clough wrote this poem when he was young but withheld it from the public for many years.

It takes the idea of "What if?" and applies it to the actual conduct of hypocrites who are supposed to be following the Ten Commandments. Satire often pokes fun at wickedness and folly by asking such questions. What if the Ten Commandments were rewritten so that they said that people *ought* to act the way in which many people *do* act? The Victorians were particularly sensitive to religious hypocrisy, and the novels of George Eliot, Charles Dickens, and Thomas Hardy all contain examples of Christians who preach one thing—like love for your neighbor—while practicing the very opposite.

Scholars have established that Clough drafted another and later (and possibly sharper) version of the poem that was never published in his lifetime:

Thou shalt have one God only; who
Would tax himself to worship two?
God's image nowhere shalt thou see,
Save haply in the currency:
Swear not at all; since for thy curse
Thine enemy is not the worse:
At church on Sunday to attend
Will help to keep the world thy friend:
Honor thy parents; that is, all
From whom promotion may befall:
Thou shalt not kill; but needst not strive
Officiously to keep alive:
Adultery it is not fit
Or safe, for women, to commit:
Advantage rarely comes of it:
Thou shalt not steal; an empty feat,
When 'tis so lucrative to cheat:
False witness not to bear be strict;
And cautious, ere you contradict.
Thou shalt not covet; but tradition
Sanctions the keenest competition.

Some printings of the poem add the following four lines to the version published in Clough's lifetime:

The sum of all is, thou shalt love,
If any body, God above:
At any rate shall never labor
More than thyself to love thy neighbor.

FORM: Tetrameter couplets rhyming *aabbcc,* etc.

Julia Ward Howe

(1819–1910)

Julia Ward Howe may seem somewhat out of place in the company of poets whom one could consider more serious or professional or canonical. Like Francis Scott Key and Clement Moore, authors of "The Star-Spangled Banner" and "A Visit from Saint Nicholas," Julia Ward Howe is known for one poem that Americans associate with the celebrations and public events of childhood. Her battle hymn is included in some Protestant hymnals, and there have been best-selling recordings of it by performers from the Mormon Tabernacle Choir to Elvis. In the 1930s, John Steinbeck published a novel with a title taken from the battle hymn, *The Grapes of Wrath*. During the 1990s, John Updike published a novel called *In the Beauty of the Lilies*, about American social history since the Civil War.

Julia Ward Howe had the longest life of any poet in this collection, and she spent much of it in social and political activities. With her husband, Samuel G. Howe, she edited an antislavery paper, the Boston *Commonwealth*, and she was active in campaigns favoring the abolition of slavery and the granting of voting rights to women. From the perspective of the present, such causes look like self-evident human rights, but for much of the nineteenth century and even for some of the twentieth, wars were fought over these very issues.

Further Reading

Later Lyrics. Boston: Tilton, 1866.

Clifford, Deborah Pickman. *Mine Eyes Have Seen the Glory*. Boston: Little, Brown, 1979.

Hall, Florence Howe. *Julia Ward Howe*. New York: Arno, 1969.

Mine eyes have seen the glory of the coming of the Lord;
He is trampling out the vintage where the grapes of wrath are
    stored;
He hath loosed the fateful lightning of His terrible swift sword;
His truth is marching on.
    Glory! Glory! Hallelujah!
    Glory! Glory! Hallelujah!
    Glory! Glory! Hallelujah!
    His truth is marching on.

I have seen Him in the watch fires of a hundred circling camps;
They have builded Him an altar in the evening dews and damps;
I can read His righteous sentence by the dim and flaring lamps;
His day is marching on.
    Glory! Glory! Hallelujah!
    Glory! Glory! Hallelujah!
    Glory! Glory! Hallelujah!
    His day is marching on.

I have read a fiery gospel, writ in burnished rows of steel;
"As ye deal with my contemners, so with you my grace shall deal;
Let the Hero, born of woman, crush the serpent with his heel,
Since God is marching on."
    Glory! Glory! Hallelujah!
    Glory! Glory! Hallelujah!
    Glory! Glory! Hallelujah!
    Since God is marching on.

He has sounded forth the trumpet that shall never call retreat;
He is sifting out the hearts of men before His judgment seat;
Oh, be swift, my soul, to answer Him; be jubilant, my feet;
Our God is marching on.
    Glory! Glory! Hallelujah!
    Glory! Glory! Hallelujah!
    Glory! Glory! Hallelujah!
    Our God is marching on.

In the beauty of the lilies Christ was born across the sea,
With a glory in His bosom that transfigures you and me;
As He died to make men holy, let us die to make men free;
While God is marching on.
    Glory! Glory! Hallelujah!
    Glory! Glory! Hallelujah!
    Glory! Glory! Hallelujah!
    While God is marching on.

COMPOSED 1861; PUBLISHED 1862. Having seen Union soldiers camped near Washington, D.C., late in 1861, Julia Ward Howe wrote these words to the tune of a song popular among troops. James T. Fields, a poet and publisher, supposedly furnished the title, and the work was published in the *Atlantic Monthly* early in 1862.

Before the Civil War, there was a song celebrating John Brown (1800–1859), the militant abolitionist hanged after a violent uprising at Harper's Ferry, Virginia. The tune, which may have been composed by William Steffe, was given words by Edna Dean Proctor. Her version included such lines as "John Brown died on the scaffold for the slave," "John Brown's body through the world is marching on," and "John Brown's body lies mouldering in the grave; / John Brown lives in the triumph of the brave." Charles Sprague Hall adapted Proctor's text to a marching song, with stanzas beginning "John Brown's body lies a-mould'ring in the grave," "He's gone to be a soldier in the Army of the Lord," "John Brown's knapsack is strapped upon his back," "His pet lambs will meet him on the way," "They'll hang Jeff Davis on a sour apple tree," and "Now for the Union let's give three rousing cheers." Julia Ward Howe wrote her words for the same tune.

FORM: A stanza beginning with three rhymed heptameter lines followed by a trimeter line always ending with "marching on," then a refrain consisting of three repetitions of "Glory! Glory! Hallelujah!" and a repetition of line 4 with the "marching on" ending.

MATTHEW ARNOLD

(1822–1888)

MATTHEW ARNOLD was the son of the famous Dr. Thomas Arnold, head-master of Rugby and, toward the end of his life in 1842, professor of modern history at Oxford. Like another father-and-son team—James and John Stuart Mill—Thomas and Matthew Arnold exerted a potent influence over English cultural life for much of the nineteenth century. Matthew formed a lasting friendship with Arthur Hugh Clough while both were at Oxford and wrote a memorable elegy, "Thyrsis," when Clough died. In 1851 Arnold was appointed an inspector of schools, and for the next thirty-five years, on and off, traveled throughout England on inspection visits. Exposure to the daily life in many sorts of school made Arnold think deeply about the serious problems of education, culture, and society. Free universal public education had existed only since 1800, and the problems in Arnold's day were as complex and pervasive as our problems today—and in some cases are the same problems. Between 1857 and 1867, he occupied the Chair of Poetry at Oxford, and during this period produced his first books of literary criticism. In addition to his poetry, he wrote a substantial amount of important aesthetic and cultural criticism.

In essays, books, and public lectures—some of which he delivered in America during the 1880s—Arnold urged society to guide itself by constant reference to what he called "the best that is thought and known in the world." This high standard was best stated in the great texts of literature, philosophy, and religion. Walt Whitman, who heard Arnold lecture, dismissed him as a "literary dude," and some later writers seem to ridicule Arnold as a moral teacher. One of T. S. Eliot's early poems groups Arnold with Emerson as "Matthew and Waldo, guardians of the faith." Robert Frost's long poem "New Hampshire" presents a cowardly character who "stood on the safe side of the line talking; / Which is sheer Matthew Arnoldism." Despite such genial mockery, however, Arnold was an important and benevolent influence on both Eliot and Frost, and Eliot's "The Love Song of J. Alfred Prufrock" can be read as an extension of Arnold's "Dover Beach" into the modern world. In some ways, "Dover Beach" is the first significantly modern poem, and in 2022 the world will celebrate the 200th anniversary of the birth of a great man.

Further Reading

The Poems, 2nd ed. Miriam Allott, ed. New York: Longmans, 1965.

Honan, Park. *Matthew Arnold: A Life*. New York: McGraw-Hill, 1981.

Trilling, Lionel. *Matthew Arnold*. Enlarged ed. New York: Harcourt, 1977.

⚔ *Dover Beach*

The sea is calm tonight.
The tide is full, the moon lies fair
Upon the straits;—on the French coast the light
Gleams and is gone; the cliffs of England stand,
Glimmering and vast, out in the tranquil bay.
Come to the window, sweet is the night-air!
Only, from the long line of spray
Where the sea meets the moon-blanched land,
Listen! you hear the grating roar
Of pebbles which the waves draw back, and fling,
At their return, up the high strand,
Begin, and cease, and then again begin,
With tremulous cadence slow, and bring
The eternal note of sadness in.

Sophocles long ago
Heard it on the Aegean, and it brought
Into his mind the turbid ebb and flow
Of human misery; we
Find also in the sound a thought,
Hearing it by this distant northern sea.

The Sea of Faith
Was once, too, at the full, and round earth's shore
Lay like the folds of a bright girdle furled.
But now I only hear
Its melancholy, long, withdrawing roar,
Retreating, to the breath
Of the night-wind, down the vast edges drear
And naked shingles of the world.

Ah, love, let us be true
To one another! for the world, which seems
To lie before us like a land of dreams,
So various, so beautiful, so new,
Hath really neither joy, nor love, nor light,
Nor certitude, nor peace, nor help for pain;
And we are here as on a darkling plain
Swept with confused alarms of struggle and flight,
Where ignorant armies clash by night.

COMPOSED AROUND 1851; PUBLISHED 1867. A man is speaking to a
woman at night in a room from which Dover Beach can be seen. Dover, on the
southeast coast of England, is the closest point of approach to France, barely
twenty miles away across the English Channel. Lights from French lighthouses
and other sources are visible in England on a clear night. Dover is also where one
sees great white cliffs rising up out of the sea. Arnold and his wife stayed there
for a few days not long after their marriage in the summer of 1851.

The design of the poem is straightforward. The speaker describes the ele-
mentary physical setting, with a full moon, a high tide made even higher by the
gravitational pull of the moon, white cliffs against the darkness, and no sound
but the give and take of the sea on the pebble beach. Meditating on the scene,
the speaker recalls another description of the sea, maybe a passage in Sophocles'
play *Antigone*, where the threatened collapse of a royal family is suggested: "As
when a swelling wave, driven by Thracian sea blasts, rushes over the gloom
which lies beneath the sea, rolls up the dark shingle from the depth, and breaks
on the beach on which it resounds with a stormy moan." But this is a percussive
storm, not a question of "turbid ebb and flow." The thought moves on to fluc-
tuations in faith, also like the movement of tides in and out. In the midst of all
this uncertainty, the speaker asks his companion for the certainty, at least, of *their*
being true to each other. With the line endings going only from "tonight" to
"night," the poem may seem to end about where it began.

Eliot's "The Love Song of J. Alfred Prufrock" also involves a seaside medita-
tion on uncertainty and failure, although the speaker in that poem has no one to
propose being true to. Tennyson's "Break, Break, Break" involves a symbolic
interpretation of the behavior of the sea.

FORM: Irregular.

Emily Dickinson
(1830–1886)

DICKINSON WAS BORN in Amherst, Massachusetts, and spent most of her strange life there. She was the daughter of Edward Dickinson, a distinguished lawyer who served in the United States House of Representatives. He was also a judge and the treasurer of Amherst College. The middle child, with an older brother and a younger sister, Emily seems to have been an outgoing and gregarious young woman but became more reclusive as years passed. By about the age of thirty, she kept more and more to herself, seldom leaving her family's house and wearing white. Of her many poems—upward of 1800—only a few were published in her lifetime. In this respect she resembles Gerard Manley Hopkins. Since she was such a great and eloquent poet, people have naturally been interested in finding out more about her; but biographical speculations have run into many barriers, and her poetry itself continues to present enigmas, anomalies, and opacities. On the one hand, her poems reach back into prehistory and read like the ancient charms and riddles that are the earliest poetry. On the other hand, the poems reach into the future of deep psychological analysis that locates human life inside a vortex whirled by contradictory claims of love and death.

Whatever the truth about her life, she remains a poet of unmatched strength and vitality, and the primitive simplicity of her rhythm—consistently and almost monotonously iambic—is balanced by the audacious complexity of some of her rhymes. In some ways it is just impossible to imagine Emily Dickinson flourishing anywhere but the United States in the middle of the nineteenth century. Early collections of her poems were heavily—maybe impudently—edited with a lot of normalization and sanitizing; heroic work by Thomas Johnson from 1955 onward did something to establish a text more like what Dickinson actually wrote, with erratic capitalization and many peculiarities of punctuation.

Further Reading

The Complete Poems. Thomas J. Johnson, ed. Boston: Little, Brown, 1960.

Anderson, Cynthia Griffin. *Emily Dickinson's Poetry: Stairway of Surprise*. New York: Holt, 1960.

Wolff, Cynthia Griffin. *Emily Dickinson*. New York: Knopf, 1986.

✿ *Because I Could Not Stop for Death*

Because I could not stop for Death—
He kindly stopped for me—
The Carriage held but just Ourselves—
And Immortality.

We slowly drove—He knew no haste
And I had put away
My labor and my leisure too,
For His Civility—

We passed the School, where Children strove
At Recess—in the Ring—
We passed the Fields of Gazing Grain—
We passed the Setting Sun—

Or rather—He passed Us—
The Dews drew quivering and chill—
For only Gossamer, my Gown—
My Tippet—only Tulle—

We paused before a House that seemed
A Swelling of the Ground—
The Roof was scarcely visible—
The Cornice—in the Ground—

Since then—'tis Centuries—and yet
Feels shorter than the Day
I first surmised the Horses' Heads
Were toward Eternity—

COMPOSED AROUND 1863; PUBLISHED 1890. Most poems are spoken by a living person, but a few—like this one and "I Heard a Fly Buzz," and "The Death of the Ball Turret Gunner"—come to us as the utterances of those already dead. We are so attentive to survivors of near-death experiences, we would be doubly attentive to a voice from beyond the grave. And, as suits something close to church, the voice uses a measure common to the hymnal.

This poem valiantly seeks to domesticate death by personifying it as gentleman with good manners. "Ode to a Nightingale," with "easeful death," is not far away from this poem.

FORM: Ballad or common measure rhyming *abcb* with idiosyncratic rhymes.

✎ I Heard a Fly Buzz—When I Died

I heard a Fly buzz—when I died—
The Stillness in the Room
Was like the Stillness in the Air—
Between the Heaves of Storm—

The Eyes around—had wrung them dry—
And Breaths were gathering firm
For that last Onset—when the King
Be witnessed—in the Room—

I willed my Keepsakes—Signed away
What portion of me be
Assignable—and then it was
There interposed a Fly—

With Blue—uncertain stumbling Buzz—
Between the light—and me—
And then the Windows failed—and then
I could not see to see—

COMPOSED AROUND 1862; PUBLISHED 1896. Dickinson wrote almost 1800 short poems, but only a handful were published in her lifetime. Like "Because I Could Not Stop for Death" and many other of her poems, this one records the experience of death from beyond the grave. Dickinson lived at a time when conditions (health, sanitation, medicine, nutrition) favored large families, but illness and death were all around. Much of the illness afflicted the young, and infant mortality was much higher then than now. Dickinson, born in Massachusetts in 1830, surely had more firsthand experience of death than most women born in Massachusetts in 1930 and later.

Our fears may express themselves in dreams as dragons and other such huge and horrible monsters (the solemn side of "Jabberwocky"), but there may be more fear and horror in an ordinary thing like a housefly crawling on your face.

FORM: Ballad or common measure rhyming *abcb* with imperfect rhymes until the final pair (me/see) (the same effect is found in "A Narrow Fellow in the Grass").

A Narrow Fellow in the Grass

A narrow Fellow in the Grass
Occasionally rides—
You may have met Him—did you not
His notice sudden is—

The Grass divides as with a Comb—
A spotted shaft is seen—
And then it closes at your feet
And opens further on—

He likes a Boggy Acre
A Floor too cool for Corn—
Yet when a Boy, and Barefoot—
I more than once at Noon
Have passed, I thought, a Whip lash
Unbraiding in the Sun
When stooping to secure it
It wrinkled, and was gone—

Several of Nature's People
I know, and they know me—
I feel for them a transport
Of cordiality—

But never met this Fellow
Attended, or alone
Without a tighter breathing
And Zero at the Bone—

COMPOSED AROUND 1865; PUBLISHED 1866. Dickinson could make a poem out of the simplest materials lying around the kitchen or backyard, but, with the touch of her genius, domestic details took on the power of myth. She used ordinary verse techniques—here the ballad measure very common in hymns and other popular tunes—and repeated ancient conventions—here the riddle that describes something but does not name it. Readers like to figure things out for themselves, and it spoils the fun if somebody tells you all the answers.

As with many of Dickinson's best poems, we meet here a beguiling mix of the routine (especially in the steady iambic rhythms) and the outlandish (especially in the rhymes that do not quite rhyme, because of a deficiency in the vowel or consonant components, or both).

The rhymes are consistently inconsistent, so to speak, until the very last one, which is a perfect bass tone joining the syllables "-lone" and "bone." There is also a weird symmetry in the pattern of consonant sounds (not necessarily the letters) in the line "His notice sudden is." The outer syllables ("His" and "is") rhyme, and they frame a sentence that has this pattern: *h-z-n-d-s-s-d-n-z* (assuming a casual American sounding of "notice"). A reader may not consciously hear or see these patterns, but they do their work at an unconscious level. The effect is hypnotic and entrancing.

FORM: Ballad or common measure rhyming *abcb* with imperfect rhymes until the last stanza (alone/Bone).

Lewis Carroll
(Charles Lutwidge Dodgson)
(1832–1898)

To FORM HIS CELEBRATED PSEUDONYM, Dodgson dropped his last name, reversed the order of his first two names, and converted them from rather dense Northern forms to something more Latinate. He also transformed his complex personality, or personalities. He was an ordained minister and also an accomplished mathematician and classicist, but a deeper self communicated with children, mostly little girls. To amuse Alice Liddell, he wrote something first called "Alice's Adventures Underground," eventually published as *Alice's Adventures in Wonderland* (1865), followed by *Through the Looking Glass and What Alice Found There* (1871).

Dodgson has enjoyed immense worldwide success as a children's author with darker and more serious recesses in his character. In these ways he resembles Jonathan Swift and Edgar Allan Poe, who created permanently appealing works of the imagination that strike millions of readers and listeners as essential parables of the human condition, especially the human condition of children. Both Dodgson and Swift created characters whose size becomes a problem: Gulliver and Alice are, like children, either too big or too small. Both authors were brilliant men who never outgrew some of the capriciousness of childhood and who seemed so uncertain of their own identities that they often assumed made-up names. Along with Poe, they have kept an army of biographers and psychologists profitably busy.

As if all his intellectual and creative achievements were not enough, Dodgson was also a very fine photographer. One can still see many of his studies of children, including the remarkably beautiful Alice herself.

Further Reading

Complete Illustrated Works. Edward Guiliano, ed. New York: Avenel, 1982.
The Annotated Alice. Martin Gardner, ed. New York: Bramhall House, 1960.
Cohen, Morton N. *Lewis Carroll: A Biography*. New York: Knopf, 1995.

Jabberwocky

'Twas brillig, and the slithy toves
    Did gyre and gimble in the wabe;
All mimsy were the borogoves,
    And the mome raths outgrabe.

"Beware the Jabberwock, my son!
    The jaws that bite, the claws that catch!
Beware the Jubjub bird, and shun
    The frumious Bandersnatch!"

He took his vorpal sword in hand:
    Long time the manxome foe he sought—
So rested he by the Tumtum tree,
    And stood awhile in thought.

And as in uffish thought he stood,
    The Jabberwock, with eyes of flame,
Came whiffling through the tulgey wood,
    And burbled as it came!

One, two! One, two! And through and through
    The vorpal blade went snicker-snack!
He left it dead, and with its head
    He went galumphing back.

"And hast thou slain the Jabberwock!
    Come to my arms, my beamish boy!
O frabjous day! Callooh! Callay!"
    He chortled in his joy.

'Twas brillig, and the slithy toves
    Did gyre and gimble in the wabe;
All mimsy were the borogoves,
    And the mome raths outgrabe.

Composed by 1855; published (in different form) in 1871. This poem will be familiar to many readers. If you haven't read it already, it would be a good idea just to read through it before getting bogged down in commentary and annotation. An early version was titled "Stanza of Anglo-Saxon Poetry." Revised, it appears in *Through the Looking Glass*, where it is read by Alice and explained by Humpty Dumpty.

Stand back from the details and see an action-adventure cartoon about a youngster who, after being warned by a parent or other older person, goes off and slays a monster. He comes back to a celebration, and the last stanza repeats the first, as though the same thing were going to happen all over again.

Alice first reads the poem in a mirror-image version, which must be seen in a mirror to be restored to normal left-to-right print. Humpty's explanation has to do only with the meaning of hard words. Some are formed by a process called "portmanteau," in which elements of two words are packed together (as in a portmanteau or suitcase) to form a new blend. "Smog," (from "smoke" and "fog") and "motel," (from "motor" and "hotel") are examples. The word "chortle" from this poem has entered the language as an ordinary word for chuckling combined with snorting.

Form: Quatrains rhyming *abab*, all lines tetrameter except the fourth, which is trimeter.

Thomas Hardy
(1840–1928)

THOMAS HARDY WAS BORN on June 2, 1840, at Upper Bockhampton in Dorset. After several years as an apprentice in architecture, he began writing fiction and, over a thirty-year period, produced fourteen novels and a number of short stories. Then, from 1898, in another thirty-year career, he produced eight volumes of poetry as well as an epic drama, *The Dynasts*. Hardy is the only English-speaking writer who has any serious claim to superlative distinction in both fiction and poetry. At least five of his novels belong in the first rank: *Far from the Madding Crowd*, *The Return of the Native*, *The Mayor of Casterbridge*, *Tess of the d'Urbervilles*, and *Jude the Obscure*. Much of Hardy's writing in prose and poetry concerns the lives of the people of a region that Hardy liked to call Wessex, an old-fashioned name for the west Saxon realm of the Middle Ages, now the southwest portion of England, including Dorset, Somerset, and Wiltshire. Successive generations of poets on both sides of the Atlantic, including Ezra Pound, John Crowe Ransom, W. H. Auden, Dylan Thomas, and Philip Larkin, have recognized Hardy's preeminence as a versifier.

Externally, Hardy's life was uneventful. In 1874 he married Emma Lavinia Gifford, whom he had met while on an architectural assignment in Cornwall (the circumstances of their meeting and the general setting of the untamed Cornish coast are part of his early novel, *A Pair of Blue Eyes)*. Out of the thirty-eight years of their marriage, the last twenty were marked by a measure of estrangement. After her death in November 1912, he put aside any consideration of the bitterness and thought back instead to their earliest days together. A sequence of twenty-one extraordinary works called "Poems of 1912–1913" is a vivid record of his grief and their early love. In 1914 Hardy married his second wife, Florence Emily Dugdale, who lived with him until his death at the age of eighty-seven in 1928. He remained active and alert right to the end, continuing to produce strikingly original and touching poems even in his last year.

Further Reading

Complete Poetical Works. Samuel Hynes, ed. Oxford: Clarendon, 1982–1995.

Bailey, J. O. *The Poetry of Thomas Hardy: A Handbook and Commentary.* Chapel Hill: University of North Carolina Press, 1970.

Millgate, Michael. *Thomas Hardy: A Biography.* Oxford: Oxford University Press, 1982.

❧ The Darkling Thrush

I leant upon a coppice gate
    When Frost was specter-gray,
And Winter's dregs made desolate
    The weakening eye of day.
The tangled bine-stems scored the sky
    Like strings of broken lyres,
And all mankind that haunted nigh
    Had sought their household fires.

The land's sharp features seemed to be
    The Century's corpse outleant,
His crypt the cloudy canopy,
    The wind his death-lament.
The ancient pulse of germ and birth
    Was shrunken hard and dry,
And every spirit upon earth
    Seemed fervorless as I.

At once a voice arose among
    The bleak twigs overhead
In a full-hearted evensong
    Of joy illimited;
An aged thrush, frail, gaunt, and small,
    In blast-beruffled plume,
Had chosen thus to fling his soul
    Upon the growing gloom.

So little cause for carolings
    Of such ecstatic sound
Was written on terrestrial things
    Afar or nigh around,
That I could think there trembled through
    His happy good-night air
Some blessed Hope, whereof he knew
    And I was unaware.

COMPOSED AND PUBLISHED 1900. Hardy wrote this poem toward the end of 1900. When it was first published in a magazine dated December 29, 1900, the poem was called "By the Century's Deathbed," 1900 being the last year of the nineteenth century, not the first year of the twentieth. We tend to become reflective at the end of a year, and many make resolutions to turn over a new leaf. It's a multiple threshold when we have a time that is the end of a day, a month, a year, and a century. At the latitude of Hardy's native Dorset (51° north), sunset would come early on the last day of December, always a dark and cold time of year.

The speaker tells of being out alone at evening, looking through a thicket of small trees towards the declining sun in the west. Such sights are enough to cause sober meditation, made all the more solemn by the very special day.

In a bizarre overstatement, the poem turns the landscape into a corpse, with the clouds overhead as a crypt and the wind as a lament, accompanied by twisted stems that look like the broken strings of a lyre. Then the poem turns the landscape-corpse into the century's corpse, leaning out of its grave. From the "I" at the beginning of the poem to another "I" at the very middle, the poem gives a total picture of desolation and death.

Amazingly, just after this lifeless midpoint, the beginning of the seventeenth line introduces new music: a voice that sounds religious in an evensong or carol, an utter contrast to the broken music that has gone before. With this change of sound, the poet suggests a change of mood and perhaps a message of hope.

The situation of a bird's embodying a divine meaning also appears in Hopkins's "The Windhover" and Yeats's "Leda and the Swan." Other significant birds are in "The Eagle," "Ode to a Nightingale" (which also contains the rare word "darkling"), and "To a Skylark." Arnold's "Dover Beach" is another poem that contains "darkling." The word also appears in a similar poem by Coleridge, "Ode to the Departing Year" (1796).

FORM: Eight-line stanza equivalent to two ballad measures, alternating lines of tetrameter and trimeter rhyming *ababcdcd*.

GERARD MANLEY HOPKINS
(1844–1889)

HOPKINS WAS THE ELDEST of nine children born to a prosperous and cultivated Victorian family. He attended Oxford, where, under the influence of John Henry Newman, he converted from Anglicanism to Roman Catholicism. Two years later, in 1868, he entered the Society of Jesus (Jesuits), and was ordained a priest in 1877 after many years of hard study and discipline. There being fewer than 1000 Jesuits in England in Hopkins's lifetime, he was often moved from place to place to carry out burdensome duties of teaching, preaching, and pastoral care. When he joined the Jesuits, he gave up poetry, since it was too much of an indulgence and too much of a sensual pleasure for an ascetic, but in 1875, when the German ship *Deutschland* ran aground in a storm, causing the deaths of five Franciscan nuns, a church superior asked Hopkins for a memorial poem. He complied, in a sense: "The Wreck of the Deutschland" is an audaciously experimental poem with many unprecedented novelties of diction and versification and with much agitation of spirit as the priest struggles with the problem of explaining why bad things happen to good people. Despite the lukewarm reception of this poem, Hopkins resumed the writing of verse on a limited basis, producing few poems and publishing none.

He had the good fortune to know Robert Bridges, an exact contemporary who had been with him at Oxford and with whom he corresponded for many years. After Hopkins's early death in 1889, Bridges came into possession of all the poems, with which he was clearly at something of a loss. Although he was an experimental poet himself, Bridges, like many others, had trouble understanding exactly what Hopkins had been up to, especially in his innovations with rhythm and rhyme. Eventually, Bridges became Poet Laureate and in 1918 brought out an edition of Hopkins's poems. From then on, Hopkins gained a reputation as a poet of much interest, although the eccentricities continued to keep many readers away. Little by little, common readers began responding to the passionate poems of religious vision, and now, more than a hundred years after his death, Hopkins is receiving the attention that he deserves. Even now we are still learning to catch up with his innovations, which are testimony to the authenticity of Hopkins's enormous feeling—ecstasy in many cases, desperation in a few. He has come more and more to resemble Milton: a poet of outlandish idiosyncrasies who possessed a many-sided genius for the language and music of poetry and who combined a cosmic religious vision with attention to minute details of the English countryside.

Further Reading

Poems, 4th ed. G. H. Gardner and Norman MacKenzie, eds. London: Oxford University Press, 1970.

Roberts, Gerald. *Gerard Manley Hopkins: A Literary Life*. New York: St. Martin's, 1994.

Sulloway, Alison G. *Critical Essays on Gerard Manley Hopkins*. Boston: G. K. Hall, 1990.

Pied Beauty

Glory be to God for dappled things—
   For skies of couple-colour as a brinded cow;
     For rose-moles all in stipple upon trout that swim;
Fresh-firecoal chestnut-falls; finches' wings;
   Landscape plotted and pieced—fold, fallow, and plough;
     And áll trádes, their gear and tackle and trim.
All things counter, original, spare, strange;
   Whatever is fickle, freckled (who knows how?)
     With swift, slow; sweet, sour; adazzle, dim;
He fathers-forth whose beauty is past change:
     Praise him.

COMPOSED 1877; PUBLISHED 1918. Hopkins wrote this poem in a Welsh village during the summer of 1877, one of his best years for writing poetry.

Hopkins, born an Anglican, converted to Roman Catholicism and became a Jesuit priest. He was a thoughtful scholar but also a passionate observer of the details of nature, and many of his shorter poems concentrate on the smallest items of ordinary life, leaving the abstractions to others. It was typical of Jesuits to frame their academic paperwork with the initials of two governing mottoes: A.M.D.G. (*Ad Majorem Dei Gloriam*: "To the Greater Glory of God") and L.D.S. (*Laus Deo Semper*: "Praise to God Always"). And those sentiments mark the beginning and end of this poem of praise for the changeless God whose creation is full of change. The poem is an inventory of a variety of things, from the large (like the sky) to the tiny (spots on a fish), along with a variety of traits all in one way or another involving variation, difference, oddity. Most celebrations of the divine involve abstraction and uniformity: "Jesus Christ is the same yesterday and today and for ever"—Hebrews 13:8. Hopkins emphasizes that for us, with our limited but enjoyable physical senses, the Creator's creation is never the same, always changing. Much of philosophy wants to pigeonhole everything and everybody. Since no real thing or person exactly fits the ideal pigeonhole, bureaucrats ruthlessly distort and trim and stretch until we do fit, but only at the sacrifice of detail, warmth, and soul. Hopkins, a supreme individualist who took idiosyncrasy almost to the extreme point, struggled against the impulse to pigeonhole and sang aloud for a world of change and variety.

Wordsworth's sonnet "Composed upon Westminster Bridge, September 3, 1802" also finds beauty in an unexpected place, although Wordsworth seems to prefer things bare and smokeless, whereas Hopkins favors the mixed and messy. The enjoyment of strangeness resembles the sentiment in Herrick's "Delight in Disorder." But nothing resembles one Hopkins poem quite so much as another Hopkins poem: much as "Pied Beauty" puts changeable nature, freckled and fickle, in the place of a spotlessly remote ideal, "The Windhover" puts a dappled and dangerous predator in the place of the meek dove and lamb of conventional Christian symbolism. "God's Grandeur" is yet another detailed Gloria ("Glory to God in the Highest") that finds God in small ordinary things. All three poems take advantage of the rhyme between "thing" and "wing," as though to repeat that, even in common objects, there dwells the capacity for flight.

FORM: Curtal sonnet, form invented by Hopkins with six-line beginning and four-and-a-fraction-line conclusion, rhyming *abcabcdbcdc*.

🪶 *Spring and Fall*

TO A YOUNG CHILD

Márgarét, áre you gríeving
Over Goldengrove unleaving?
Leáves, líke the things of man, you
With your fresh thoughts care for, can you?
Ah! ás the heart grows older
It will come to such sights colder
By and by, nor spare a sigh
Though worlds of wanwood leafmeal lie;
And yet you *will* weep and know why.
Now no matter, child, the name:
Sórrow's springs áre the same.
Nor mouth had, no nor mind, expressed
What heart heard of, ghost guessed:
It ís the blight man was born for,
It is Margaret you mourn for.

COMPOSED 1880; PUBLISHED 1918. Hopkins wrote this poem in September, the time of year in which Keats wrote "To Autumn" and Shelley wrote "Ode to the West Wind." Since the poem is about fall and nothing else, it is hard to see why the title should contain "Spring"—until you read the chilling line "Sorrow's springs are the same." Not "spring" the season but "spring" the source and origin and also the machine. (One word means a season, a body of water, and a mechanical device—all involving some kind of beginning.)

The poet addresses a child of unspecified age as she seems to be mourning the losses that come each fall. He adds a few vivid details and then lets her know the truth (he is a preacher): we see only ourselves in nature, and when we mourn nature we mourn ourselves.

The language is unusually austere: of the ninety-odd words, only three ("Margaret," "matter," "expressed") are not Germanic. The use of alliteration throughout adds to the drumming effect of monosyllables.

FORM: Tetrameter couplets rhyming *aabbcc* etc.

⚔ The Windhover

To Christ Our Lord

I caught this morning morning's minion, king-
    dom of daylight's dauphin, dapple-dawn-drawn Falcon,
       in his riding
Of the rolling level underneath him steady air, and striding
High there, how he rung upon the rein of a wimpling wing
In his ecstasy! then off, off forth on swing,
    As a skate's heel sweeps smooth on a bow-bend: the hurl and
      gliding
    Rebuffed the big wind. My heart in hiding
Stirred for a bird,—the achieve of, the mastery of the thing!

Brute beauty and valour and act, oh, air, pride, plume, here
    Buckle! AND the fire that breaks from thee then, a billion
Times told lovelier, more dangerous, O my chevalier!

    No wonder of it: shéer plód makes plough down sillion
Shine, and blue-bleak embers, ah my dear,
    Fall, gall themselves, and gash gold-vermilion.

COMPOSED 1877; PUBLISHED 1918. Hopkins wrote this sonnet in May 1877 as one more expression of his priestly labors to connect the material world to the divine will. It is a sacramental effort, finding an outward and visible symbol for an inward and invisible spiritual truth. Much as Blake's "The Tyger" and Tennyson's "The Eagle" convert a powerful animal into an equally powerful emblem, Hopkins converts a predatory bird into an emblem of Christ, to whom the poem is dedicated and addressed.

The poet begins by reporting what he has seen: the amazing sight of a small creature seeming to defy gravity and to resist the pressure of the wind by hovering far above the earth. Predators and scavengers need altitude to search for food. Once they spot something (windhovers, or kestrels, specialize in rodents, of which they eat as many as 300 a year), they "stoop" or dive downward and catch their prey. A relative of the windhover, the peregrine falcon, diving in such a hunting attack becomes the fastest animal on earth. The bird hovers, then swoops down, and both the hovering and the swooping are exciting to see.

After a detailed and ecstatic description of the bird, the poet turns to Christ, whom he credits with even more splendor than the bird. Last, in a dramatic descent from the divine to the mundane, the poet says that, despite all the wonders he has evoked, there is no real wonder in finding illumination in a bird and in God, for even the commonest activities—such as plowing—and the commonest objects—such as the remains of a fire in a fireplace—can radiate with divine meaning. The gold-vermilion color scheme of the end takes the appearance of a fire as a further sacrament: the gold is like the bread that symbolizes the flesh of Christ; the vermilion is like the wine that symbolizes his blood.

"Ah my dear" is borrowed from Herbert's "Love III," another poem that ends with a symbolic meal. "The Windhover" can also be compared with Hardy's "The Darkling Thrush": Hopkins's poem is a spring morning vision of a bird that suggests Christ, Hardy's a winter evening vision of a bird that suggests hope. "The Windhover" also has much in common with Yeats's "Leda and the Swan": in both, a powerful bird becomes the enigmatic symbol of a supreme deity, and both repeat the same three elements in the same order—"master," "brute," "air." And both poems are sonnets. Hopkins's begins in the past and ends in the present, while Yeats's begins in the present and ends in the past.

FORM: Italian sonnet rhyming *abbaabba cdcdcd* with feminine rhymes in the *b* and *d* positions.

William Butler Yeats
(1865–1939)

Yeats's life was neatly divided into a nineteenth-century half and a twentieth-century half; he was both an impractical dreamer and a hardheaded practical man of affairs; he was a Theosophist and a Rosicrucian but also a Senator in the government of the new Irish republic in the 1920s. In some ways he was the most Irish of Irishmen, but his family was Protestant and he never mastered the Irish language. His father, John Butler Yeats, was a celebrated painter, and Yeats himself studied art. He soon turned to literature, however, and produced a succession of lovely works in many modes: romantic lyric, political satire, mythic metamorphosis (transforming one of his great loves, Maud Gonne, into a Helen), verse drama, aesthetic criticism, visionary history, and some of the deepest and most entertaining autobiographical writing of the age.

Yeats was active in the Rhymer's Club (with Dowson) and later with the Abbey Theater, and he kept up a robust interactive friendship with Ezra Pound for many years. In his youth he happened to meet Gerard Manley Hopkins, and he was acquainted in various ways with Thomas Hardy, George Bernard Shaw, Oscar Wilde, James Joyce, Sean O'Casey, and Lady Gregory. As a critic and as the editor of the influential *Oxford Book of Modern Verse*, Yeats situated himself in the context of his own immediate generations, shouldering aside the Thomas Hardy whose "work lacked technical accomplishment" and ignoring Wilfred Owen entirely but making room for W. H. Auden and many younger writers. By the middle of the twentieth century, Dylan Thomas was saying that, although Yeats *was* probably the greatest poet of the age, he still considered Hardy his favorite; Philip Larkin transformed his own career into a cautionary tale, with his earlier verse affected and infected by Yeats's mannerisms ("pervasive as garlic"), which could not be dislodged and exorcised by anything but Hardy's severe idiom, to which Larkin turned after the "Celtic fever" had abated.

Yeats remained single until his fifties, when he married a young woman named Georgie Hyde Lees, with whom he had a son and a daughter, for both of whom he wrote engaging poetic prayers.

Further Reading

Poems. Richard Finneran, ed. New York: Macmillan, 1983.

Donoghue, Denis. *William Butler Yeats*. New York: Ecco Press, 1989.

Ellmann, Richard. *The Identity of Yeats*. New York: Oxford University Press, 1964.

✺ *The Second Coming*

Turning and turning in the widening gyre
The falcon cannot hear the falconer;
Things fall apart; the center cannot hold;
Mere anarchy is loosed upon the world,
The blood-dimmed tide is loosed, and everywhere
The ceremony of innocence is drowned;
The best lack all conviction, while the worst
Are full of passionate intensity.

Surely some revelation is at hand;
Surely the Second Coming is at hand.
The Second Coming! Hardly are those words out
When a vast image out of *Spiritus Mundi*
Troubles my sight: somewhere in sands of the desert
A shape with lion body and the head of a man,
A gaze blank and pitiless as the sun,
Is moving its slow thighs, while all about it
Reel shadows of the indignant desert birds.
The darkness drops again; but now I know
That twenty centuries of stony sleep
Were vexed to nightmare by a rocking cradle,
And what rough beast, its hour come round at last,
Slouches towards Bethlehem to be born?

COMPOSED 1919; PUBLISHED 1921. Yeats wrote these words immediately after the end of the First World War that devastated much of Europe and the Middle East, and also at the time of bloody conflicts in Ireland. Such catastrophes cause the poet to think back to those parts of the Bible that deal with the end of the world: Daniel, chapter 9; Matthew, chapter 24; and all of the Apocalypse (Revelation). The poem could have been called "Apocalypse Now." Like those biblical visions and prophecies, this vision puts the end in the form of symbols. The falcon and the desert birds resemble the eagles or vultures in Matthew 24:28. The rough beast sounds like the sphinx of Egypt, on his way to Bethlehem for another birth.

Nowadays, every war and natural disaster is interpreted by somebody as evidence that the end of the world is at hand. Yeats's words have stayed on people's minds. This poem is quoted in Norman Mailer's *Armies of the Night* and Mary Karr's *The Liars' Club*, and there have been books entitled *Slouching Toward Kalamazoo* and *Slouching Toward Gomorrah*.

FORM: Blank verse.

✺ The Lake Isle of Innisfree

I will arise and go now, and go to Innisfree,
And a small cabin build there, of clay and wattles made:
Nine bean-rows will I have there, a hive for the honey-bee,
And live alone in the bee-loud glade.

And I shall have some peace there, for peace comes dropping slow,
Dropping from the veils of the morning to where the cricket sings;
There midnight's all a glimmer, and noon a purple glow,
And evening full of the linnet's wings.

I will arise and go now, for always night and day
I hear lake water lapping with low sounds by the shore;
While I stand on the roadway, or on the pavements gray,
I hear it in the deep heart's core.

COMPOSED AROUND 1890; PUBLISHED 1892. This poem came to Yeats one day while he was standing on the pavement of Fleet Street in London. A little fountain in a shop window reminded him of the waters of a lake back home in Ireland and also of the peaceful pond in Thoreau's *Walden*. The poem seems to be spoken at such a moment by someone longing to escape the pressures of the city and to find rest in the simpler occupations of the country, in the midst of healing waters.

Yeats's rather ingenuous lyric provoked two responses by Ezra Pound (in "Mauberley" and "The Lake Isle"), one by William Carlos Williams ("These"), and one by Wallace Stevens ("Page from a Tale").

FORM: Quatrains rhyming *abab*, three hexameter lines followed by one tetrameter; same six-word passage begins first and third stanzas.

✴ Leda and the Swan

A sudden blow: the great wings beating still
Above the staggering girl, her thighs caressed
By the dark webs, her nape caught in his bill,
He holds her helpless breast upon his breast.

How can those terrified vague fingers push
The feathered glory from her loosening thighs?
And how can body, laid in that white rush,
But feel the strange heart beating where it lies?

A shudder in the loins engenders there
The broken wall, the burning roof and tower
And Agamemnon dead.
                            Being so caught up,
So mastered by the brute blood of the air,
Did she put on his knowledge with his power
Before the indifferent beak could let her drop?

COMPOSED AROUND 1920; PUBLISHED 1924. This poem, so violent and
immediate, is also somewhat distanced and remote: a poem about a painting of
a myth. Leda was one of many human women loved by the Greek father-god
Zeus (Roman Jupiter). Since he was too splendid to appear in his own form to
mortal view, he had to disguise himself, in this case as a swan. The encounter has
inspired sculptors and painters for centuries, including some who present the
swan as beautiful and benevolent. But the painting that Yeats had in mind, by
Michelangelo or one of his followers, is enigmatic and vivid, with powerful con-
trast of light and dark and with turbulent shapes interacting awkwardly, one
large wing outspread to match the gesture of an arm flung back. The bizarre
scene is so interesting because it accounts for the otherworldly power of Helen,
who was the chief cause of the Trojan War. Helen was one of four children born
from the union of Zeus and Leda. The others were her sister Clytemnestra and
their brothers Castor and Pollux, twin gods of war. In some versions of the
myth, Helen and Pollux were the immortal members of the quartet, while
Clytemnestra and Castor, begotten by Leda's husband Tyndareus, were mortal.

In whatever shape, however, all the children were vitally important in Greek history. And they have remained important in the literature of the West. In astronomy, Jupiter is a planet, and one of its many satellites is named Leda. The Swan is the constellation Cygnus (Latin for "swan"), and Castor and Pollux are Gemini (the twins).

Like "The Second Coming," "Leda and the Swan" tries to get at the meaning of the terror of modern history. Yeats proposes repeated patterns of violations of boundaries, whereby divine forces in animal form enter the human realm and produce offspring of supernatural beauty but at the same time of supernatural evil. The Zeus-Leda-Helen pattern was repeated, for Yeats, in the Jehovah-Mary-Christ pattern (with a dove as intermediary instead of a swan) two thousand years later, and we are now about two thousand more years along the line of history. In another poem Yeats asks, "What theme had Homer but original sin?" The problem of what makes bad things happen is linked to the question of whether the same things keep repeating themselves age after age. "Leda and the Swan" faces the issues, offering a structure of statement-question in the present and statement-question in the past.

Probably Yeats had Hopkins's "The Windhover" much in his mind. In the first version of his poem, Yeats even had the swan hovering. Both poems are sonnets, and they have many words and images in common. Yeats's line "So mastered by the brute blood of the air" repeats three elements from "The Windhover" and in the same order: *mastery, brute, air.* Both poems take a lovely but dangerous bird and make it a manifestation of the divine.

Donne's "Batter My Heart, Three-Personed God" is another poem about enigmatic ravishment by a divine principle.

FORM: Anglo-Italian sonnet rhyming *ababcdcd effefg.*

Sailing to Byzantium

I

That is no country for old men. The young
In one another's arms, birds in the trees
—Those dying generations—at their song,
The salmon-falls, the mackerel-crowded seas,
Fish, flesh, or fowl, commend all summer long
Whatever is begotten, born, and dies.
Caught in that sensual music all neglect
Monuments of unageing intellect.

II

An aged man is but a paltry thing,
A tattered coat upon a stick, unless
Soul clap its hands and sing, and louder sing
For every tatter in its mortal dress,
Nor is there singing school but studying
Monuments of its own magnificence;
And therefore I have sailed the seas and come
To the holy city of Byzantium.

III

O sages standing in God's holy fire
As in the gold mosaic of a wall,
Come from the holy fire, perne in a gyre,
And be the singing-masters of my soul.
Consume my heart away; sick with desire
And fastened to a dying animal
It knows not what it is; and gather me
Into the artifice of eternity.

IV

Once out of nature I shall never take
My bodily form from any natural thing,
But such a form as Grecian goldsmiths make
Of hammered gold and gold enamelling
To keep a drowsy Emperor awake;
Or set upon a golden bough to sing
To lords and ladies of Byzantium
Of what is past, or passing, or to come.

COMPOSED AROUND 1925; PUBLISHED 1927. When young, Yeats wrote poems like "The Lake Isle of Innisfree" about longing to be away from the busy world of affairs and to escape to the peaceful life of rural simplicity. Then, from about 1925, when he turned sixty, Yeats wrote poems like "Sailing to Byzantium" about longing to be away from everything in the present world and to escape to an idealized past. Here an old man tells of his discontent with the summer world of youthful creatures (human or otherwise) in their sensual music of loving and singing. For all its warmth and pleasure, that world is an unending cycle of biology: begetting, bearing and being born, dying. Since in that changeful world of the body, the mind and spirit have no place, an old person can find some comfort only in the idea of a good place in the past. This ideal place is a three-thousand-year-old city that, with three names in succession, has been a symbol of unity and community. It lies at the crossroads of Europe and Asia, north and south, east and west. It has belonged to Thracians, Greeks, Romans, Crusaders, and Turks, and it contains monuments of many sects of pagan religions, Christianity, and Islam. According to Yeats, it was possible in such a place fifteen hundred years ago to find unity of art, religion, philosophy, and daily life.

FORM: Ottava rima (pentameter stanzas rhyming *abab](abc*).

ERNEST DOWSON
(1867–1900)

DOWSON, BORN IN KENT, was schooled for a couple of years at Oxford, but he left the university to pursue the literary life in London and Paris, where he fell in with members of the Rhymers' Club, including William Butler Yeats, and got to know Oscar Wilde and his circle of brilliant dissolutes. Dowson lacked Wilde's iron constitution and soon gave in to dissipation and disease. He spent much of his short life in France, the unhappy incarnation of decadence. He was consumptive and made his condition worse by drinking. While living in the slummy East End of London, he met his "Cynara," a café-owner's daughter who was to marry a waiter.

In the early 1890s, at the urging of his friend Lionel Johnson, he converted to Roman Catholicism, but he drifted away from the Church after both parents committed suicide during 1894. Amid the gloom and squalor of his blighted life, Dowson was given a few shining moments of genius.

Further Reading

Poetical Works. Desmond Flower, ed. London: Cassell, 1967.
Dowling, Linda. *Language and Decadence in the Victorian Fin de Siècle*.
    Princeton: Princeton University Press, 1986.
Swann, Thomas Burnett. *Ernest Dowson*. New York: Twayne, 1964.

Last night, ah, yesternight, betwixt her lips and mine
There fell thy shadow, Cynara! thy breath was shed
Upon my soul between the kisses and the wine;
And I was desolate and sick of an old passion,
    Yea, I was desolate and bowed my head:
I have been faithful to thee, Cynara! in my fashion.

All night upon mine heart I felt her warm heart beat,
Night-long within mine arms in love and sleep she lay;
Surely the kisses of her bought red mouth were sweet;
But I was desolate and sick of an old passion,
    When I awoke and found the dawn was gray:
I have been faithful to thee, Cynara! in my fashion.

I have forgot much, Cynara! gone with the wind,
Flung roses, roses riotously with the throng,
Dancing, to put thy pale, lost lilies out of mind;
But I was desolate and sick of an old passion,
    Yea, all the time, because the dance was long:
I have been faithful to thee, Cynara! in my fashion.

I cried for madder music and for stronger wine,
But when the feast is finished and the lamps expire,
Then falls thy shadow, Cynara! the night is thine;
And I am desolate and sick of an old passion,
    Yea, hungry for the lips of my desire:
I have been faithful to thee, Cynara! in my fashion.

COMPOSED 1891; PUBLISHED 1896. The title of this poem, which is a line
from one of the odes of the Roman poet Horace, means "I am not what I was
under the rule of the kind Cynara." The woman's name seems to be related to a
Greek word for "puppy" or "small dog" and also to "cynic" (a cynic believes that
people are motivated by self-interest). The attitude of the speaker certainly qual-

ifies as cynical, as does his ironic warping of "faithful." We use "in my fashion" or "after a fashion" as a polite way of confessing something negative. To say "I studied—after a fashion" probably means "I didn't study much at all."

The poem seems modest, but it has inspired a Broadway song by Cole Porter ("Always true to you, darlin', in my fashion"), and the phrase "gone with the wind" turns up in James Joyce's *Ulysses* and provides the title of Margaret Mitchell's best-selling novel that was turned into a most celebrated movie.

In some ways the poem is an aubade, but the woman addressed is not the same as the woman whom the speaker has been with. The speaker, hungover and remorseful, imagines a good woman whose memory interferes with his sensual pleasures. Being so haunted by her in a way means, after a fashion, that he is faithful to her.

FORM: Four six-line stanzas rhyming *abacbc*, all lines hexameter except the fifth, which is pentameter; fourth line always ends with "passion" and the sixth line is the same in each stanza, acting as a refrain.

Edwin Arlington Robinson
(1869–1935)

ROBINSON BEGAN OBSCURELY, born and reared in Maine and educated for two years at Harvard. He lived much of his life in New York City, where he worked at odd jobs, including a time with the subway authority. Later, when his poems began to receive sympathetic notice from critics and readers (including President Theodore Roosevelt), his poverty was alleviated but his solitude and reclusiveness continued. He never married and had few friends. For his earliest poems, written during the 1880s, he fell under the influence of Thomas Hardy's rather gloomy novels of individual tragedy (none of Hardy's poetry was published in book form until 1898, by which time Robinson's style was already formed). Robinson's early books were not successful, but for the last twenty years of his life he was among the most honored American poets, receiving three Pulitzer Prizes. The two poems in this collection are typical of Robinson's strongest sort of verse: quick, incisive sketches of the blighted lives of those who may once have had some promise of talent or enterprise but who wind up doomed to small-town misery.

Robinson also wrote ambitious philosophical poems and, in his last years, specialized in Arthurian narratives, including *Merlin, Lancelot*, and *Tristram*. After his death, Robinson's reputation suffered something of an eclipse, but many older and younger poets—including Robert Frost, James Dickey, and James Wright—have borne witness to Robinson's continuing power. Although nothing of his in this collection is a sonnet, it ought to be mentioned that he was one of the best American sonnet writers, forming a bridge between Longfellow and Frost in a continuous tradition of sonnets peculiarly suited to the idiom and landscape of New England.

Further Reading

Collected Poems. New York: Macmillan, 1930.

Bloom, Harold, ed. *Edwin Arlington Robinson: Modern Critical Views*. New York: Chelsea House, 1988.

Winters, Yvor. *Edwin Arlington Robinson*. New York: New Directions, 1971.

Miniver Cheevy, child of scorn,
    Grew lean while he assailed the seasons;
He wept that he was ever born,
    And he had reasons.

Miniver loved the days of old
    When swords were bright and steeds were prancing;
The vision of a warrior bold
    Would set him dancing.

Miniver sighed for what was not,
    And dreamed, and rested from his labors;
He dreamed of Thebes and Camelot,
    And Priam's neighbors.

Miniver mourned the ripe renown
    That made so many a name so fragrant;
He mourned Romance, now on the town,
    And Art, a vagrant.

Miniver loved the Medici,
    Albeit he had never seen one;
He would have sinned incessantly
    Could he have been one.

Miniver cursed the commonplace
    And eyed a khaki suit with loathing;
He missed the medieval grace
    Of iron clothing.

Miniver scorned the gold he sought,
    But sore annoyed was he without it;
Miniver thought, and thought, and thought,
    And thought about it.

Miniver Cheevy, born too late,
    Scratched his head and kept on thinking;
Miniver coughed, and called it fate,
    And kept on drinking.

COMPOSED AROUND 1905; PUBLISHED 1910. Robinson wrote these sarcastic stanzas just before World War I blasted everybody's notions of chivalry to smithereens. Up to about 1915, however, a certain sort of sensitive person could meet disappointment in the everyday world, retreat or escape into some Never Never Land of romance and adventure, then become demoralized and start drinking.

This is a generalized sketch of a life, not a single telling episode like "Mr. Flood's Party," another poem by Robinson featuring a caricature of a lonely man driven to drink by disappointment.

Like Don Quixote, who was deranged by reading chivalric romances, Miniver Cheevy is thrown into ridiculous attitudes, made vivid by the irony in such ideas as "the medieval grace / Of iron clothing." There are some similarities between this poem and Eliot's "The Love Song of J. Alfred Prufrock," which also dates from about 1910. Both works exhibit an isolated man pathetically out of place in the modern world and desperately trying to find something to connect himself to.

FORM: Quatrains rhyming *abab* with feminine rhymes in all the even-numbered lines; three lines of tetrameter followed by one of dimeter, a pattern that recalls the stanza in Keats's "La Belle Dame sans Merci."

Mr. Flood's Party

Old Eben Flood, climbing alone one night
Over the hill between the town below
And the forsaken upland hermitage
That held as much as he should ever know
On earth again of home, paused warily.
The road was his with not a native near;
And Eben, having leisure, said aloud,
For no man else in Tilbury Town to hear:

"Well, Mr. Flood, we have the harvest moon
Again, and we may not have many more;
The bird is on the wing, the poet says,
And you and I have said it here before.
Drink to the bird." He raised up to the light
The jug that he had gone so far to fill,
And answered huskily: "Well, Mr. Flood,
Since you propose it, I believe I will."

Alone, as if enduring to the end
A valiant armor of scarred hopes outworn,
He stood there in the middle of the road
Like Roland's ghost winding a silent horn.
Below him, in the town among the trees,
Where friends of other days had honored him,
A phantom salutation of the dead
Rang thinly till old Eben's eyes were dim.

Then, as a mother lays her sleeping child
Down tenderly, fearing it may awake,
He set the jug down slowly at his feet
With trembling care, knowing that most things break;
And only when assured that on firm earth
It stood, as the uncertain lives of men
Assuredly did not, he paced away,
And with his hand extended paused again:

"Well, Mr. Flood, we have not met like this
In a long time; and many a change has come
To both of us, I fear, since last it was
We had a drop together. Welcome home!"
Convivially returning with himself,
Again he raised the jug up to the light;
And with an acquiescent quaver said:
"Well, Mr. Flood, if you insist, I might.

"Only a very little, Mr. Flood—
For auld lang syne. No more, sir; that will do."
So, for the time, apparently it did,
And Eben evidently thought so too;
For soon amid the silver loneliness
Of night he lifted up his voice and sang,
Secure, with only two moons listening,
Until the whole harmonious landscape rang—

"For auld lang syne." The weary throat gave out,
The last word wavered; and the song being done,
He raised again the jug regretfully
And shook his head, and was again alone.
There was not much that was ahead of him,
And there was nothing in the town below—
Where strangers would have shut the many doors
That many friends had opened long ago.

COMPOSED AROUND 1915; PUBLISHED 1920. Robinson wrote many
poems about the sad people in a small place in Maine he called Tilbury Town.
Whereas Robinson's "Miniver Cheevy" is a generalized sketch of a life, "Mr.
Flood's Party" is a single telling episode; even so, both poems feature caricatures
of desperately lonely men driven to drink by disappointment. Both the "Mr."
and the "Party" of the title are ironic, since Eben Flood is by himself.

The viewpoint is somewhat detached and disinterested, but the poet con-
tributes some tender touches here and there. By simply asserting the presence of
"two moons" (instead of belaboring the point that drunkenness caused Flood to

see double), the poem enters into the character's consciousness. The comparisons to a mother and the heroic knight Roland (recounted in the kind of medieval poem that Miniver Cheevy and maybe Mr. Flood would have liked) also add sympathy to the sketch of Mr. Flood. His besotted state is hardly defended or justified, but neither is it condemned as a moral flaw too awful to forgive.

FORM: Eight-line pentameter stanza rhyming *abcbdefe*.

Walter de la Mare
(1873–1956)

WALTER DE LA MARE, who was born in Kent, was too poor to go to school beyond adolescence. He worked for many years as a bookkeeper for a petroleum conglomerate—Anglo-American Oil Company, at the time a branch of Standard Oil—and it was not until he was in middle age that he was free to spend all his time as a writer. He is best known for his poetry, but he also wrote fiction, including the celebrated *Memoirs of a Midget* (1931).

Like much of English poetry all the way back to the Middle Ages, de la Mare's goes beyond the daily scene of empirical objects perceived by practical adults, which, as everybody must admit, is only a small portion of the real world. Instead, de la Mare concentrates on the nocturnal dreams of children with visits to realms just out of reach of the conscious mind. Accordingly, the poems tease us with a convincing but vague aura of reality and unreality mixed. To offset the hazards of cuteness and vagueness, de la Mare exercised a most definite technical control of his verse with carefully calibrated musical effects. De la Mare's poetry was prized and praised by Thomas Hardy, T. S. Eliot, and W. H. Auden.

As is noted in the commentary on de la Mare's "The Listeners," that poem was one of the last that Thomas Hardy requested to hear on his deathbed. Ten years after Hardy's death, de la Mare published a poem called "Thomas Hardy" that ends with a ghostly vision of the dead poet:

> Stooping and smiling, he questioned, "No birdnotes myself do I hear?
> Perhaps 'twas the talk of chance farers, abroad in the hush with us
> here—
>   In the dusk-light clear?"
> And there peered from his eyes, as I listened, a concourse of women and
> men,
> Whom his words had made living, long-suffering—they flocked to
>   remembrance again;
> "O Master," I cried in my heart, "lorn thy tidings, grievous thy song;
> Yet thine, too, this solacing music, as we earthfolk stumble along."

Further Reading

The Complete Poems. New York: Knopf, 1970.

Duffin, Theresa. *Walter de la Mare: A Study of His Poetry*. Freeport, NY: Books for Libraries Press, 1969.

Whistler, Theresa. *Imagination of the Heart: The Life of Walter de la Mare*. London: Duckworth, 1994.

"Is there anybody there?" said the Traveler,
    Knocking on the moonlit door;
And his horse in the silence champed the grasses
    Of the forest's ferny floor:
And a bird flew up out of the turret,
    Above the Traveler's head:
And he smote upon the door again a second time;
    "Is there anybody there?" he said.
But no one descended to the Traveler;
    No head from the leaf-fringed sill
Leaned over and looked into his gray eyes,
    Where he stood perplexed and still.
But only a host of phantom listeners
    That dwelt in the lone house then
Stood listening in the quiet of the moonlight
    To that voice from the world of men:
Stood thronging the faint moonbeams on the dark stair,
    That goes down to the empty hall,
Hearkening in an air stirred and shaken
    By the lonely Traveler's call.
And he felt in his heart their strangeness,
    Their stillness answering his cry,
While his horse moved, cropping the dark turf,
    'Neath the starred and leafy sky;
For he suddenly smote on the door, even
    Louder, and lifted his head:—
"Tell them I came, and no one answered,
    That I kept my word," he said.
Never the least stir made the listeners,
    Though every word he spake
Fell echoing through the shadowiness of the still house
    From the one man left awake:
Ay, they heard his foot upon the stirrup,
    And the sound of iron on stone,
And how the silence surged softly backward,
    When the plunging hoofs were gone.

Walter de la Mare 225

COMPOSED AROUND 1910; PUBLISHED 1912. No one can say for sure what this poem is all about. It is set at night and takes place in the past, when people rode horses and houses had turrets. Someone has come on a quest or mission. All we know of him is the capitalized designation, the Traveler, and his purpose seems so serious and urgent that we may recall the link between "travel" and "travail"—hard work. With its haunted house, moonlight, phantoms, nameless character, and archaic forms like "spake," the poem seems to be a parable or dream vision.

Thomas Hardy, according to his widow's account of his last days early in 1928, at the end "could no longer listen to the reading of prose, though a short poem now and again interested him. In the middle of one night he asked his wife to read aloud to him 'The Listeners' by Walter de la Mare."

FORM: Four-line units rhyming *abcb* with irregular pentameter and hexameter lines alternating with tetrameter and trimeter lines.

ROBERT FROST
(1874–1963)

IT IS ANOMALOUS (but maybe peculiarly American) that Frost should be so strongly associated with the idiom and landscape of New England, since he was born in California (west of the Mississippi River, like the birthplaces of Ezra Pound, Marianne Moore, and T. S. Eliot) and named for Robert E. Lee, the Confederate general. But Frost was raised a New Englander and the titles of many of his books insist on the identification: *North of Boston* obviously, *A Boy's Will* more subtly (the phrase comes from a poem by Longfellow, who was born in Maine), *New Hampshire* undeniably. Frost lived mostly in New Hampshire and Vermont but also spent significant periods in Michigan and Florida, as well as a crucial two years in England just before the First World War. His first two books were published in England, and one of Frost's first reviewers was his enthusiastic fellow American, Ezra Pound.

Frost was unique in his power to combine a modernist sensibility and learning with a knack for the truly popular. In "Mending Wall" he became the only modern poet who could genuinely be said to have written a proverb: "Good fences make good neighbors." Biographical revelations after Frost's death showed how false had been the image of a gentle rustic philosopher. Frost was a genius of his art, and he was cunning and crafty, writing mostly poems of bitterness, estrangement, terror, solitude, and desolation but projecting the façade of a humorist. In person he could be generous—if that was his mood—but he could as easily turn jealous, spiteful, and cruel. Of his six children, only one turned out really well.

Further Reading

Collected Poems, Prose, and Plays. New York: Library of America, 1995.

Poirier, Richard. *Robert Frost: The Work of Knowing*. New York: Oxford University Press, 1977.

Pritchard, William H. *Robert Frost: A Literary Life Reconsidered*. Amherst: University of Massachusetts Press, 1993.

⚞ *Stopping by Woods on a Snowy Evening*

Whose woods these are I think I know.
His house is in the village, though;
He will not see me stopping here
To watch his woods fill up with snow.

My little horse must think it queer
To stop without a farmhouse near
Between the woods and frozen lake
The darkest evening of the year.

He gives his harness bells a shake
To ask if there is some mistake.
The only other sound's the sweep
Of easy wind and downy flake.

The woods are lovely, dark and deep,
But I have promises to keep,
And miles to go before I sleep,
And miles to go before I sleep.

COMPOSED ABOUT 1922; PUBLISHED 1923. Frost claimed to have stayed up all one night writing his long poem "New Hampshire" and then to have written "Stopping by Woods on a Snowy Evening" the following morning. Both poems are in Frost's fourth book, *New Hampshire* (1923).

The words represent the present-tense inner meditations of someone in the middle of a paradox. With things to do and places to go—and, above all, promises to keep—the speaker nonetheless pauses just to watch snow falling. It is the kind of thought that could pass through your head in a few seconds. Here I am, the poem suggests, with pressing obligations making me go to all the trouble of harnessing my horse and going out on a winter night with snow falling, on a rural road away from a village. The words are little and clear, but the outlines of the poem remain indefinite. Is this "darkest evening" the winter solstice, around December 21, when the daylight hours are shortest and night-time hours longest? If so, the poem is connected to Hardy's "The Darkling Thrush." The darkest evening could also be January 20, traditionally the coldest night of the year. Or this could just be literally the darkest night the speaker has seen thus far. Equally indefinite is the cause of the speaker's concern about being seen and about what seems bizarre: his horse's opinion! Frost's fifth line weirdly echoes the beginning of an old political ballad: "My little lord, methinks 'tis strange. . . ." Isolated people often create someone to talk to and treat as though a human being. The experience here seems so elementary that it has been given a psychiatric interpretation: the speaker finds loveliness in the dark and deep woods because he has a death wish. But, if your name is Frost and you live in New England in the winter, it may be enough just to find loveliness in falling snow because it is lovely. Frost's other poem in this collection, "Mending Wall," is another present-tense meditation on why we do what we do.

FORM: Tetrameter quatrains; interlocking rhyme in an adaptation of terza rima: *aaba bbcb ccdc dddd*.

Mending Wall

Something there is that doesn't love a wall,
That sends the frozen-ground-swell under it
And spills the upper boulders in the sun,
And makes gaps even two can pass abreast.
The work of hunters is another thing:
I have come after them and made repair
Where they have left not one stone on a stone,
But they would have the rabbit out of hiding,
To please the yelping dogs. The gaps I mean,
No one has seen them made or heard them made,
But at spring mending-time we find them there.
I let my neighbor know beyond the hill;
And on a day we meet to walk the line
And set the wall between us once again.
We keep the wall between us as we go.
To each the boulders that have fallen to each.
And some are loaves and some so nearly balls
We have to use a spell to make them balance:
"Stay where you are until our backs are turned!"
We wear our fingers rough with handling them.
Oh, just another kind of outdoor game,
One on a side. It comes to little more:
There where it is we do not need the wall:
He is all pine and I am apple orchard.
My apple trees will never get across
And eat the cones under his pines, I tell him.
He only says, "Good fences make good neighbors."
Spring is the mischief in me, and I wonder
If I could put a notion in his head:
"*Why* do they make good neighbors? Isn't it
Where there are cows? But here there are no cows.
Before I built a wall I'd ask to know
What I was walling in or walling out,
And to whom I was like to give offense.
Something there is that doesn't love a wall,

That wants it down." I could say "Elves" to him,
But it's not elves exactly, and I'd rather
He said it for himself. I see him there,
Bringing a stone grasped firmly by the top
In each hand, like an old-stone savage armed.
He moves in darkness as it seems to me,
Not of woods only and the shade of trees.
He will not go behind his father's saying,
And he likes having thought of it so well
He says again, "Good fences make good neighbors."

COMPOSED AROUND 1912; PUBLISHED 1914. "Mending Wall" is the
lead-off poem in Frost's second book, whose title, *North of Boston*, suggests the
world of northern New England, an austere and rocky region. New Hampshire
is called the Granite State, and the settlers who cleared its land for agriculture
built up piles of loose stones into walls. Every year, winter frosts bring new
stones up to the surface.

This poem presents a picture of two rural New Englanders working together
to restore a wall that has been damaged by winter. The speaker is the wiser of the
two, since his neighbor is presented as a rustic with no depth. He has no origi-
nal thought but accepts what he heard his father say: "Good fences make good
neighbors."

The rustic New England farmer acts as though it is worth his while to keep a
wall where none is really needed. Words like "good" may mislead readers into
thinking that the poem is about being a good neighbor in the biblical or even
the sociopolitical sense: helping, caring, sharing, loving. But a good fence is a
strong barrier to keep people apart; the better the fence, the less you see of your
neighbor. The American phrase "spite fence" is eloquent testimony to a spirit far
from good and neighborly. And people still say, "I need my space."

The sentiment about good neighbors being made by efficient barriers
appears in *Poor Richard's Almanac*, but the precise wording belongs to Frost, as
does the rare honor of being one of the few modern writers to compose a gen-
uine proverb.

FORM: Blank verse (unrhymed iambic pentameter).

T.S. Eliot
(1888–1965)

THOMAS STEARNS ELIOT was born in St. Louis, Missouri, on the banks of the Mississippi River, and later spoke of his background as, variously, Southwestern or Midwestern (not very precise terms); even so, his deeper loyalty seems to have been to New England, where he was a Harvard student and where his family had a summer home, and later to Old England, to which he emigrated in 1914 and where he stayed, becoming a British subject in 1927. He took advantage of his complex background to present himself as a mixed person; some even said that he was evasively "playing possum" (hence the nickname given to him by Ezra Pound, resulting in a lighthearted book called *Old Possum's Book of Practical Cats*, which, long after the poet's death, was to give the musical comedy stage its all-time longest-running hit).

His first marriage, to Vivienne Haigh-Wood, began happily enough but in time turned into a tragic mismatch still not understood, either by advocates or by enemies. Michael Hastings's controversial play *Tom and Viv* makes an effort to get to the bottom of the predicament, by which Vivienne suffered physical ailments that caused her to become dependent on drugs that brought on different physical ailments that caused her to become dependent on yet other drugs—all this in a person of extraordinary sensitivity and imagination. No one has yet settled to question of how Eliot dealt with all these vexing problems. He and she were legally separated in the early 1930s; she was committed to a private mental hospital in 1937 and died there ten years later. They were never divorced, and Eliot did not remarry until 1957, ten years after his first wife's death.

His education was more in philosophy than in literature, and he all but finished the work for a doctorate at Harvard. He worked as an officer of Lloyds Bank for quite a few years, and then became a valued member of the directorate of the publishing firm Faber and Faber. During the 1920s he established a potent reputation as a poet and as a critic, also editing the influential magazine *The Criterion* (1922–39). Like Thomas Hardy, he was given the rare and coveted Order of Merit; like William Butler Yeats, he was awarded the Nobel Prize for Literature—the only American-born poet to be so honored.

Further Reading

Complete Poems and Plays. London: Faber, 1973.

Ackroyd, Peter. *T. S. Eliot: A Life*. New York: Simon and Schuster, 1984.

Smith, Grover. *T. S. Eliot's Poetry and Plays: A Study in Sources and Meaning*.
   Chicago: University of Chicago Press, 1974.

✄ *The Love Song of J. Alfred Prufrock*

> *S'io credessi che mia risposta fosse*
> *a persona che mai tornasse al mondo,*
> *questa fiamma staria senza più scosse.*
> *Ma per ciò che giammai di questo fondo*
> *non tornò vivo alcun, s'i' odo il vero,*
> *senza tema d'infamia ti rispondo.*

Let us go then, you and I,
When the evening is spread out against the sky
Like a patient etherised upon a table;
Let us go, through certain half-deserted streets,
The muttering retreats
Of restless nights in one-night cheap hotels
And sawdust restaurants with oyster-shells:
Streets that follow like a tedious argument
Of insidious intent
To lead you to an overwhelming question . . .
Oh, do not ask, "What is it?"
Let us go and make our visit.

In the room the women come and go
Talking of Michelangelo.

The yellow fog that rubs its back upon the window-panes,
The yellow smoke that rubs its muzzle on the window-panes,
Licked its tongue into the corners of the evening,
Lingered upon the pools that stand in drains,

Let fall upon its back the soot that falls from chimneys,
Slipped by the terrace, made a sudden leap,
And seeing that it was a soft October night,
Curled once about the house, and fell asleep.

And indeed there will be time
For the yellow smoke that slides along the street
Rubbing its back upon the window-panes;
There will be time, there will be time
To prepare a face to meet the faces that you meet;
There will be time to murder and create,
And time for all the works and days of hands
That lift and drop a question on your plate;
Time for you and time for me,
And time yet for a hundred indecisions,
And for a hundred visions and revisions,
Before the taking of a toast and tea.

In the room the women come and go
Talking of Michelangelo.

And indeed there will be time
To wonder, "Do I dare?" and, "Do I dare?"
Time to turn back and descend the stair,
With a bald spot in the middle of my hair—
(They will say: "How his hair is growing thin!")
My morning coat, my collar mounting firmly to the chin,
My necktie rich and modest, but asserted by a simple pin—
(They will say: "But how his arms and legs are thin!")
Do I dare
Disturb the universe?
In a minute there is time
For decisions and revisions which a minute will reverse.

For I have known them all already, known them all—
Have known the evenings, mornings, afternoons,
I have measured out my life with coffee spoons;
I know the voices dying with a dying fall

Beneath the music from a farther room.
    So how should I presume?

And I have known the eyes already, known them all—
The eyes that fix you in a formulated phrase,
And when I am formulated, sprawling on a pin,
When I am pinned and wriggling on the wall,
Then how should I begin
To spit out all the butt-ends of my days and ways?
    And how should I presume?

And I have known the arms already, known them all—
Arms that are braceleted and white and bare
(But in the lamplight, downed with light brown hair!)
Is it perfume from a dress
That makes me so digress?
Arms that lie along a table, or wrap about a shawl.
    And should I then presume?
    And how should I begin?

. . . . . .

Shall I say, I have gone at dusk through narrow streets
And watched the smoke that rises from the pipes
Of lonely men in shirt-sleeves, leaning out of windows? . . .

I should have been a pair of ragged claws
Scuttling across the floors of silent seas.

. . . . . .

And the afternoon, the evening, sleeps so peacefully!
Smoothed by long fingers,
Asleep . . . tired . . . or it malingers,
Stretched on the floor, here beside you and me.
Should I, after tea and cakes and ices,
Have the strength to force the moment to its crisis?
But though I have wept and fasted, wept and prayed,

Though I have seen my head (grown slightly bald) brought in
    upon a platter,
I am no prophet—and here's no great matter;
I have seen the moment of my greatness flicker,
And I have seen the eternal Footman hold my coat, and snicker,
And in short, I was afraid.

And would it have been worth it, after all,
After the cups, the marmalade, the tea,
Among the porcelain, among some talk of you and me,
Would it have been worth while,
To have bitten off the matter with a smile,
To have squeezed the universe into a ball
To roll it towards some overwhelming question,
To say: "I am Lazarus, come from the dead,
Come back to tell you all, I shall tell you all"—
If one, settling a pillow by her head,
    Should say: "That is not what I meant at all.
    That is not it, at all."

And would it have been worth it, after all,
Would it have been worth while,
After the sunsets and the dooryards and the sprinkled streets,
After the novels, after the teacups, after the skirts that trail along
    the floor—
And this, and so much more?—
It is impossible to say just what I mean!
But as if a magic lantern threw the nerves in patterns on a screen:
Would it have been worth while
If one, settling a pillow or throwing off a shawl,
And turning toward the window, should say:
    "That is not it at all,
    That is not what I meant, at all."

 . . . . . .

No! I am not Prince Hamlet, nor was meant to be;
Am an attendant lord, one that will do

To swell a progress, start a scene or two,
Advise the prince; no doubt, an easy tool,
Deferential, glad to be of use,
Politic, cautious, and meticulous;
Full of high sentence, but a bit obtuse;
At times, indeed, almost ridiculous—
Almost, at times, the Fool.

I grow old . . . I grow old . . .
I shall wear the bottoms of my trousers rolled.

Shall I part my hair behind? Do I dare to eat a peach?
I shall wear white flannel trousers, and walk upon the beach.
I have heard the mermaids singing, each to each.

I do not think that they will sing to me.

I have seen them riding seaward on the waves
Combing the white hair of the waves blown back
When the wind blows the water white and black.

We have lingered in the chambers of the sea
By sea-girls wreathed with seaweed red and brown
Till human voices wake us, and we drown.

Composed around 1909; published 1917. Eliot wrote many poems of many sorts while still an adolescent, and the Prufrock who repeats "I grow old" was invented by a poet of twenty. The setting seems to be Boston and Cambridge, where Eliot spent several years while attending Harvard.

In dramatic monologues like Browning's "My Last Duchess" and Tennyson's "Ulysses," a speaker in a dramatic situation talks aloud in a single sustained utterance to somebody else. Prufrock, in an indefinite situation, addresses a "you," but we cannot be sure who that is. Forty years after the poem was written, Eliot rather evasively suggested that Prufrock is talking to an "unidentified male companion." The internal evidence of the poem itself, however, suggests that the poem is addressed to no one but the speaker himself, who may not even be speaking aloud. The structure of the poem is more like a meditation, reverie, or dream than any kind of dramatic utterance. What seems likely is that this so-called love song is not a love song, it is not a song, and it is not about love. It is a nonsong about nonlove and is probably a soliloquy, which is the outward expression of a dramatic character's inward thoughts not addressed to any other character but only overheard by the audience. Another feature of the soliloquy, such as those in Shakespeare's plays, is that it truly represents the actual thoughts of the character.

As with Yeats's "The Lake Isle of Innisfree," the poem begins with a speaker who wants to go: Yeats's voice says, "I will arise and go now, and go to Innisfree"; Eliot's says, "Let us go then, you and I . . . Let us go . . . Let us go . . ." but it is improbable that either speaker is going anywhere. The poems are soliloquies spoken by isolated men living in a busy city that cuts them off from nature and from other people.

Wilfred Owen
(1893–1918)

THE STORY OF WILFRED OWEN'S LIFE seems short, sad, and simple. He was born in Shropshire in a family of very modest means. His father worked for the railway, and his mother was pious and thrifty with the limited resources available to her. Owen had a scrappy education at Shrewsbury Technical School and University College, Reading, with an aborted term at the University of London, from which poverty forced him to withdraw. He wound up teaching for two years at a Berlitz language school in Bordeaux.

Owen enlisted in the army during the first year of the First World War. For the first half of 1917 he was on the Western Front. In June, he became ill and was moved to a hospital in Edinburgh, where he had the good luck to meet Siegfried Sassoon, already a famous war poet. Owen went back to France at the end of August 1918 and was killed on November 4, exactly one week before the war ended. Sassoon edited Owen's collected poems in 1920.

He was only twenty-five, but he had had time to produce an impressive variety of poems, most of them dealing with war. He was also a notable technical innovator, especially in rhyming.

Further Reading

Poems. Jon Stallworthy, ed. New York: Norton, 1986.
Kerr, Douglas. *Wilfred Owen's Voices*. New York: Oxford University Press, 1993.
Stallworthy, Jon. *Wilfred Owen*. London: Oxford University Press, 1974.

Strange Meeting

It seemed that out of battle I escaped
Down some profound dull tunnel, long since scooped
Through granites which titanic wars had groined.
Yet also there encumbered sleepers groaned,
Too fast in thought or death to be bestirred.
Then, as I probed them, one sprang up, and stared
With piteous recognition in fixed eyes,
Lifting distressful hands as if to bless.
And by his smile, I knew that sullen hall,
By his dead smile I knew we stood in Hell.
With a thousand pains that vision's face was grained;
Yet no blood reached there from the upper ground,
And no guns thumped, or down the flues made moan.
"Strange friend," I said, "here is no cause to mourn."
"None," said that other, "save the undone years,
The hopelessness. Whatever hope is yours,
Was my life also; I went hunting wild
After the wildest beauty in the world,
Which lies not calm in eyes, or braided hair,
But mocks the steady running of the hour,
And if it grieves, grieves richlier than here.
For of my glee might many men have laughed,
And of my weeping something had been left,
Which must die now. I mean the truth untold,
The pity of war, the pity war distilled.
Now men will go content with what we spoiled,
Or, discontent, boil bloody, and be spilled.
They will be swift with swiftness of the tigress.
None will break ranks, though nations trek from progress.
Courage was mine, and I had mystery,
Wisdom was mine, and I had mastery:
To miss the march of this retreating world
Into vain citadels that are not walled.
Then, when much blood had clogged their chariot-wheels,
I would go up and wash them from sweet wells,

Even with truths that lie too deep for taint.
I would have poured my spirit without stint
But not through wounds; not on the cess of war.
Foreheads of men have bled where no wounds were.
I am the enemy you killed, my friend.
I knew you in this dark: for so you frowned
Yesterday through me as you jabbed and killed.
I parried; but my hands were loath and cold.
Let us sleep now. . . ."

COMPOSED 1918; PUBLISHED 1920. Owen wrote this nightmarish poem not long before he was killed, aged twenty-five, right at the end of World War I.

The speaker imagines that he has gone from war into a vision of hell, where he meets another man, whom he had killed in battle. This friendly enemy turns out to have been a poet like the speaker himself.

FORM: Except for the truncated last line, the poem is in iambic pentameter. The units are couplets except for one triplet (the lines ending "hair," "hour," "here"). Instead of conventional rhyme, the lines are joined by a strange device like the strangeness of the meeting. As with "hall" and "hell," for example, the syllables begin and end with the same consonants but have different vowels. This combination of alliteration and consonance is sometimes called "pararhyme."

W.H. Auden

(1907–1973)

GERTRUDE STEIN, EZRA POUND, and T. S. Eliot, among many others, were American-born writers who emigrated to Europe and spent much of their adult lives in exile. Wystan Hugh Auden, with characteristic audacity, reversed the trend. Even after spectacular success as the leader of a generation who emerged strongly and brilliantly in England in the 1930s, Auden moved to the United States in 1939 and became a citizen in 1946. (In 1935, in a generous gesture, Auden had married Thomas Mann's daughter Erika so that she could have a British passport and escape Hitler's Germany. Auden, a homosexual, had never met his bride before the day of the wedding, and they seldom saw each other afterward, though they did remain friends.) Only at the very end of his life did he move back to England.

He was thoroughly modern. Born in the twentieth century, he was at home with science, technology, and engineering; his father was a physician, and Auden claimed to have entertained childhood ambitions of becoming a mining engineer. Auden also took to modernist psychology (represented by Freud and by Homer Lane as well) and modernist economics (represented by Marx). Friendships were extremely important to him: he knew such members of the older generation as E. M. Forster and T. S. Eliot, and he was the center of a lively group of writers that included Christopher Isherwood and Louis MacNeice (with both of whom Auden collaborated), Stephen Spender, C. Day-Lewis, and Rex Warner. In America, he befriended many of his seniors (such as Robert Frost), contemporaries (such as Kenneth Rexroth), and juniors (such as Richard Howard and John Hollander).

Auden, a chameleon of idioms and tones, probably commanded a greater range of forms and styles than any other twentieth-century poet. He was also a notable essayist, critic, teacher, and editor.

His poetry enjoyed new celebrity when one of his works was quoted in the 1994 movie *Four Weddings and a Funeral*.

Further Reading

Collected Poems. Edward Mendelson, ed. London: Faber, 1976.

Carpenter, Humphrey. *W. H. Auden: A Biography*. Boston: Houghton Mifflin, 1981.

Hecht, Anthony. *The Hidden Law: The Poetry of W. H. Auden*. Cambridge: Harvard University Press, 1993.

Musée des Beaux Arts

About suffering they were never wrong,
The Old Masters: how well they understood
Its human position; how it takes place
While someone else is eating or opening a window or just walking
    dully along;
How, when the aged are reverently, passionately waiting
For the miraculous birth, there always must be
Children who did not specially want it to happen, skating
On a pond at the edge of the wood:
They never forgot
That even the dreadful martyrdom must run its course
Anyhow in a corner, some untidy spot
Where the dogs go on with their doggy life and the torturer's
    horse
Scratches its innocent behind on a tree.

In Breughel's *Icarus*, for instance: how everything turns away
Quite leisurely from the disaster; the plowman may
Have heard the splash, the forsaken cry,
But for him it was not an important failure; the sun shone
As it had to on the white legs disappearing into the green
Water; and the expensive delicate ship that must have seen
Something amazing, a boy falling out of the sky,
Had somewhere to get to and sailed calmly on.

COMPOSED 1938; PUBLISHED 1940. Auden wrote this poem at a time when he was giving up political arguments that some critics condemned as propagandistic. Turning instead to personal matters of life and art, he wrote several poems about artists (including William Butler Yeats and Henry James) and the significance of art.

If you approach this poem as a lecture in art history, you will feel disappointed. The first sentence is inverted; it would be clearer to state, "The Old Masters were never wrong about suffering." But the painting that Auden cites— Brueghel's *Landscape with the Fall of Icarus*—is hardly a typical work. The Old Masters did not agree about anything, including the placement of the main event right in the middle of a painting. (The Brueghel painting, by the way, is also the subject of a poem by William Carlos Williams, and Auden's poem itself is the subject of a poem by Randall Jarrell called "The Old and New Masters.")

This poem is not a lesson in art history. It is, rather, a glimpse into the mind of a suffering person. Someone tormented by suffering seeks consolation in an art museum. After that twisted start—"About suffering they were never wrong"—the speaker discovers something about suffering. One person's grief does not affect the whole world. The speaker ultimately arrives at a point of acceptance and something like calm.

FORM: Irregular rhymed strophes with lines of varying length.

Theodore Roethke
(1908–1963)

THEODORE ROETHKE WAS BORN in Michigan and spent much of his mature life in the Northwest, teaching at the University of Washington. In the barest externals, his career resembles that of Kenneth Rexroth, who was born in Indiana in 1905 and spent much of his mature life in California. Theirs was a generation of true heartland German-Americans who could start in the Midwest (like Eliot) and (unlike Eliot) keep moving west, seeking the authentic American soil and idiom. In Roethke's poetry, you cannot avoid the vegetable kingdom in many manifestations, from weeds to roses, from germination to fermentation. Roethke came from a long line of foresters and nurserymen, and every time he heard the word "horticulture" he reached for his typewriter.

Roethke's generation came along about twenty years after the great masters of modern poetry (such as Wallace Stevens, William Carlos Williams, Ezra Pound, and T. S. Eliot); and all of them—W. H. Auden and Rexroth as well as Roethke—seem to represent an oasis of consolidation in a luxuriant desert of expansion and experimentation. Roethke, at any rate, certainly took fewer chances than his immediate forebears—fewer, even, than the slightly more remote Thomas Hardy and W. B. Yeats. He was studious and sensitive, with verses that work as homage to many of his honored predecessors, including William Blake, Gerard Manley Hopkins, and Yeats. Roethke was a vigorous and faithful inheritor and conservator of the great tradition.

Further Reading

The Collected Poems. New York: Doubleday, 1966.
Blessing, Richard Allan. *Theodore Roethke's Dynamic Vision*. Bloomington: Indiana University Press, 1974.
Sullivan, Rosemary. *Theodore Roethke: The Garden Master*. Seattle: University of Washington Press, 1975.

My Papa's Waltz

The whiskey on your breath
Could make a small boy dizzy;
But I hung on like death:
Such waltzing was not easy.

We romped until the pans
Slid from the kitchen shelf;
My mother's countenance
Could not unfrown itself.

The hand that held my wrist
Was battered on one knuckle;
At every step you missed
My right ear scraped a buckle.

You beat time on my head
With a palm caked hard by dirt,
Then waltzed me off to bed
Still clinging to your shirt.

COMPOSED AROUND 1945; PUBLISHED 1948. Theodore Roethke, Kenneth Rexroth (1905–1982), and several other American writers of the same generation grew up during Prohibition (1920–1933), when alcoholic beverages were illegal, and had a love-hate relation with drink and drunkenness, parental or personal or both. One of Rexroth's poems remembers his father with "breath smelling richly/Of whiskey and cigars." Rexroth sprang from a Germanic heritage in Indiana, Roethke from a very similar heritage in neighboring Michigan. Here he remembers his father in a most memorable scene, probably repeated many times. This Prussian papa is a complex peasant, for whom the kitchen is still the center of family life. "Waltz" is a German word, and for much of its history the dance was associated with Germany and Austria. This Old World father with battered knuckles and dirt-caked palms seems like a primitive earth spirit joyously celebrating with such force that the child speaks the poem dramatically *to* the father, not just *about* him.

FORM: Trimeter quatrains rhyming *abab*. As John Frederick Nims has pointed out, the three-beat lines preserve the spirit of the waltz, which is in 3/4 time.

Randall Jarrell
(1914–1965)

JARRELL IS THE YOUNGEST American poet in this collection, and, with the exception of Dylan Thomas, the youngest of any nationality. He was born in Tennessee and died in North Carolina, but significant parts of his life were spent outside the South—childhood in California, World War II in the Army Air Corps, some teaching time at Kenyon College in Ohio and elsewhere. He was a student, colleague, or friend of John Crowe Ransom and Cleanth Brooks, and he can be grouped as a younger member of the Fugitive-Agrarian group and the New Critics. In writing fiction and criticism as well as poetry, Jarrell resembles his somewhat older contemporary, Robert Penn Warren. Jarrell was a bold and witty critic who could appreciate Walt Whitman, Robert Frost, and William Carlos Williams at a time when such appreciation was somewhat out of fashion. His poetry is marked by strong feeling and accurate observation of the technology of the modern world. Even though we know that people have been dying horribly in war for thousands of years, modern warfare has brought new and deeper horrors, of which Jarrell was peculiarly, eloquently cognizant. It was thoroughly modern of Jarrell to take a modern mechanized horror, flak (and the German name is perfect), and join it with fundamental images involving both Karl Marx and Sigmund Freud: "From my mother's sleep I fell into the State"— an image that also joins this gunner to William Blake's "hapless soldier" whose sigh "Runs in blood down palace walls."

Further Reading

The Complete Poems. New York: Farrar, Straus & Giroux, 1969.

Ferguson, Suzanne, ed. *The Poetry of Randall Jarrell.* Baton Rouge: Louisiana State University Press, 1971.

Pritchard, William H. *Randall Jarrell: A Literary Life.* New York: Farrar, Straus & Giroux, 1990.

❧ The Death of the Ball Turret Gunner

From my mother's sleep I fell into the State
And I hunched in its belly till my wet fur froze.
Six miles from earth, loosed from its dream of life,
I woke to black flak and the nightmare fighters.
When I died they washed me out of the turret with a hose.

COMPOSED AROUND 1944; PUBLISHED 1945. Jarrell served in the Army Air Corps during World War II. He was not a flier, but he was familiar with bombers like the B-17 and B-24 that had a spherical rotating plexiglass turret mounted on the underside for protection against attacks from below. "I hunched in its belly" describes the ironically fetal posture of the person in the turret: probably a small man. The hose, according to Jarrell, was a steam-hose.

The dead gunner speaks the poem from beyond the grave. The phrase "When I died" occurs also in another American poem: Dickinson's "I Heard a Fly Buzz."

FORM: Four pentameter lines and one of heptameter. The second and fifth lines rhyme.

Dylan Thomas
(1914–1953)

Dylan Thomas was a fully mature poet while still an adolescent and published his first book, *18 Poems*, before his twenty-first birthday. Like T. S. Eliot, Hart Crane, and several other modern poets, Thomas began as an extraordinarily complex writer and, by terrific suffering and discipline, struggled through to achieve a breathtaking clarity and simplicity.

Born in Swansea, Wales, son of a schoolteacher, Thomas skipped college, working instead as a writer from the age of twenty until his death, not yet forty years old, in New York. He excelled in both poetry and prose, and he was by far the greatest reader and performer of the modern poets. His flourishing, around 1950, happened to coincide with the emergence of the long-playing phonograph record, and many who would not otherwise have experienced any poetry were privileged to hear Thomas read aloud, either in person or on record.

He was in some ways alien to the austerities of the modernists before him and the postmodernists after, but one would have to be totally deaf and ice-cold not to respond to Thomas's magnificent voice. As his three poems in this collection attest, Thomas belonged in a great tradition that includes William Blake, John Keats, Thomas Hardy, Gerard Manley Hopkins, and William Butler Yeats—poets who sang ecstatically and wisely of birth, love, death, and glory.

Further Reading

The Poems. Daniel Jones, ed. New York: New Directions, 1971.
Ferris, Paul. *Dylan Thomas.* New York: Dial, 1977.
Olson, Elder. *The Poetry of Dylan Thomas.* Chicago: University of Chicago Press, 1954.

ᛉ *Do Not Go Gentle into That Good Night*

Do not go gentle into that good night,
Old age should burn and rave at close of day;
Rage, rage against the dying of the light.

Though wise men at their end know dark is right,
Because their words had forked no lightning they
Do not go gentle into that good night.

Good men, the last wave by, crying how bright
Their frail deeds might have danced in a green bay,
Rage, rage against the dying of the light.

Wild men who caught and sang the sun in flight,
And learn, too late, they grieved it on its way,
Do not go gentle into that good night.

Grave men, near death, who see with blinding sight
Blind eyes could blaze like meteors and be gay,
Rage, rage against the dying of the light.

And you, my father, there on the sad height,
Curse, bless, me now with your fierce tears, I pray,
Do not go gentle into that good night.
Rage, rage against the dying of the light.

COMPOSED 1951; PUBLISHED 1952. Thomas addressed this poem to his own dying father. The sentiment seems to be the opposite of the feeling in Thomas's "A Refusal to Mourn the Death, by Fire, of a Child in London," but both poems show that Thomas wrote about birth, love, and death in one of the oldest traditions in the world. It may have to be a losing battle in the long run, but refusing to accept your fate may have more honor than passively giving in. This poem has an important function in the 1996 film *Dangerous Minds*.

FORM: Villanelle.

Fern Hill

Now as I was young and easy under the apple boughs
About the lilting house and happy as the grass was green,
   The night above the dingle starry,
    Time let me hail and climb
   Golden in the heydays of his eyes,
And honored among wagons I was prince of the apple towns
And once below a time I lordly had the trees and leaves
    Trail with daisies and barley
   Down the rivers of the windfall light.

And as I was green and carefree, famous among the barns
About the happy yard and singing as the farm was home,
   In the sun that is young once only,
    Time let me play and be
   Golden in the mercy of his means,
And green and golden I was huntsman and herdsman, the calves
Sang to my horn, the foxes on the hills barked clear and cold,
    And the sabbath rang slowly
   In the pebbles of the holy streams.

All the sun long it was running, it was lovely, the hay
Fields high as the house, the tunes from the chimneys, it was air
   And playing, lovely and watery
    And fire green as grass.
   And nightly under the simple stars
As I rode to sleep the owls were bearing the farm away,
All the moon long I heard, blessed among stables, the nightjars
   Flying with the ricks, and the horses
    Flashing into the dark.

And then to awake, and the farm, like a wanderer white
With the dew, come back, the cock on his shoulder: it was all
   Shining, it was Adam and maiden,
    The sky gathered again
   And the sun grew round that very day.

So it must have been after the birth of the simple light
In the first, spinning place, the spellbound horses walking warm
　　Out of the whinnying green stable
　　　　On to the fields of praise.

And honored among foxes and pheasants by the gay house
Under the new made clouds and happy as the heart was long,
　　In the sun born over and over,
　　　　I ran my heedless ways,
　　My wishes raced through the house high hay
And nothing I cared, at my sky blue trades, that time allows
In all his tuneful turning so few and such morning songs
　　Before the children green and golden
　　　　Follow him out of grace,

Nothing I cared, in the lamb white days, that time would take me
Up to the swallow thronged loft by the shadow of my hand,
　　In the moon that is always rising,
　　　　Nor that riding to sleep
　　I should hear him fly with the high fields
And wake to the farm forever fled from the childless land.
Oh as I was young and easy in the mercy of his means,
　　　　Time held me green and dying
　　　　Though I sang in my chains like the sea.

COMPOSED 1945; PUBLISHED 1946. The British give names to houses
more often than Americans do. "Fern Hill" is the name of a country house that
belonged to Thomas's aunt when he was growing up in Wales. (Ferns are prim-
itive plants that once covered much of the earth: petroleum deposits are the fos-
sil remains of great fern forests.) Thomas spent summer holidays there, and this
poem is a fond act of remembering the glories of youth and springtime. The
poem resembles Shelley's "Ode to the West Wind," another ecstatic celebration
of the whole of nature. Both poems recognize that birth is one part of life, and
that death is another, but the poets suggest that we love life all the more because
we know about death, just as we appreciate spring more because we have been
through a winter. In the usual style of children, the speaker is the only human

presence in the poem and seems to be the only person in the warm world.

Along with the rebirth and renewal of the world of nature, Thomas celebrated also a renewal of the world of language. Instead of the outworn "once upon a time" we hear the newly minted "once below a time" (which may be more accurate); instead of the automatic "all day long" we hear "All the sun long," which is much fresher.

FORM: A nine-line stanza with first, second, sixth, and seventh lines in irregular hexameters; the third and fifth in irregular tetrameters; the fourth in irregular trimeters; and the eighth and ninth either trimeter-tetrameter or tetrameter-trimeter. Either full rhyme or repetition of stressed vowels between the ends of the first and sixth lines (boughs/towns), the second and seventh (green/leaves), the third and eighth (starry/barley), and the fourth, fifth, and ninth (climb/eyes/light).

A Refusal to Mourn the Death, by Fire, of a Child in London

Never until the mankind making
Bird beast and flower
Fathering and all humbling darkness
Tells with silence the last light breaking
And the still hour
Is come of the sea tumbling in harness

And I must enter again the round
Zion of the water bead
And the synagogue of the ear of corn
Shall I let pray the shadow of a sound
Or sow my salt seed
In the least valley of sackcloth to mourn

The majesty and burning of the child's death.
I shall not murder
The mankind of her going with a grave truth
Nor blaspheme down the stations of the breath
With any further
Elegy of innocence and youth.

Deep with the first dead lies London's daughter,
Robed in the long friends,
The grains beyond age, the dark veins of her mother,
Secret by the unmourning water
Of the riding Thames.
After the first death, there is no other.

Composed 1945; published 1946. Early in World War II, London was bombed nightly by German planes that could not choose their targets very accurately, so that innocent civilians, including children, were as likely to be killed as military combatants.

Thomas's refusal to mourn resembles Donne's "A Valediction: Forbidding Mourning": in both, a clear occasion for mourning is denied. In Donne's poem, however, the mourning is caused merely by temporary separation. Here the refusal is more an admission that mourning is really impossible. How can one speak of the unspeakable? There is nothing to say, when human plotting causes the most innocent of victims to die in the most agonizing way. When the first death is so atrocious, there is little consolation in the point that there is no second.

The first thirteen lines—more than half the poem—are a single sentence. The Welsh Thomas, like devotional poets of the seventeenth century, such as John Donne, the Welsh-born George Herbert, and the Welsh Henry Vaughan, sends the mind back to the beginning of life ("the first dead") and forward to the end of time.

FORM: Four six-line stanzas rhyming *abcabc*; the first, third, fourth, and sixth lines are long (tetrameter or pentameter), the second and fifth short (dimeter or trimeter).

Notes on the Poems

Anonymous, *"Sir Patrick Spens"* (page 1)

Dunfermline: town on the east coast of Scotland
skeely: skillful
braid: broad, imposing
Noroway: Norway, 400 miles to the northeast
hame: home
neist: next
e'e: eye
tauld: told
weet: wet
faem: foam
Monenday, Wodensday: Monday, Wednesday (the earlier forms suggest the pagan origins of day-names from celestial bodies like the moon and gods like Woden)
hae: have
a': all
gude: good
alack: alas
hoysed: hoisted, raised
yestreen: yesterday evening
auld: old (a phenomenon in which the moon's disk is dark except for a thin bright crescent on one edge)
league: about three miles
lift: sky
gurly: growly, rough
ankers brak: anchors broke (probably means the lines or cables holding the anchors broke and the anchors were carried away)
lap: sprang
sic: such

cam owre: came over

claith: cloth

wap: wrap, bind

laith: unwilling

cork-heel'd shoon: shoes with cork heels, a sign of smart comfort

lang or a': long before all

wat: wet

aboon: above

mony: many

mair cam haim: more came home

flatter'd: floated, tossing

gowd: gold

kames: combs

nae mair: no more

Half-owre: halfway over: the ship came within ten miles of getting back home, evidently finishing 790 miles of an 800-mile round trip

Aberdour: town near Dunfermline

fathoms: a fathom is six feet

ANONYMOUS, *"Edward, Edward"* (page 5)

brand: sword

go: walk, conduct yourself

red-roan: bay mixed with white or grey. A bay is a handsome reddish-brown horse with black mane and tail, once favored by cavalry soldiers.

steed: a horse used for riding, as in the hunt or warfare

dole: sorrow, grief. The word is related to *dolor*.

dree: suffer

woe is me: an old dative formation: woe is to me

penance: a punishment in consequence of a sin; a voluntary act performed to express sorrow for sins; also a sacrament that includes contrition and remorse for sin, with confession to a priest, acceptance of a punishment, and absolution or forgiveness

dree: perform

towers: on a castle

hall: large room for gatherings of people

bairns: children

the world's room: the world is roomy

ANONYMOUS, *"Western Wind"* (page 8)

the small rain: in order that the rain can fall. Small here means in fine drops, not coarse.

if: if only

Sir Thomas Wyatt, *"They Flee from Me That Sometime Did Me Seek"* (page 10)

forsaken: abandoned, deserted

stalking: stepping softly

danger: related to domination: control. Middle English *daunger* meant both power and peril. This danger in connection with wild birds persists through centuries, right up to the "dangerous" in Hopkins's "The Windhover."

To take bread: a running image here of birds that may feel safe eating from one's hand; also other people who run away when once they sought one out

range: to wander freely in all directions

Busily seeking with: as with "busy" in "busybody" or in Donne's "The Sun Rising" (Busy old fool), this is more than busy activity: it is restlessly looking after one's own pleasure in an unending round of novelties.

Twenty times better: more than twenty times

thin array: light clothing

after a pleasant guise: (1) in a pleasant way, (2) after a pleasant masquerade (in disguise)

small: slender

therewithal: therewith, with that

broad waking: wide awake

thorough: through, because of

have leave to go of her goodness: have permission to go (1) away from the goodness of her presence (2) because of her goodness

newfangleness: newfangledness: being crazy about the latest thing in fashion or elsewhere

kindly: after the fashion of her kind (womankind) with play on kindness and kindliness

served: treated

fain: eagerly, gladly: I would really like to know.

Sir Walter Ralegh, *"The Nymph's Reply to the Shepherd"* (page 13)
(See Marlowe's *"The Passionate Shepherd to His Love"*)

from field to fold: that is, from summer to winter quarters

Philomel: the nightingale

wanton: overabundant, with a play on connotations of immorality

heart of gall: Gall, another name for bile, is the bitter opposite of honey.

fancy's spring, but sorrow's fall: That is, sweet talk is the springtime of the imagination but the unavoidable autumn of sorrow.

kirtle: a long dress

folly: foolishness

posies: as in Marlowe's original, both bunches of flowers and collections of poems

In folly ripe, in reason rotten: From the viewpoint of folly, all right; but from the viewpoint of reason, not all right.

no means: by no means

no date: no term or time of ending

SIR PHILIP SIDNEY, *"With How Sad Steps, O Moon"* (page 16)

sad: the usual meaning of mournful and unhappy, also with overtones of weight and density

wan: off-color; sickly pale; earlier used for pale light from the moon and stars

archer: Cupid, often portrayed with a bow (the arrows still show up piercing Valentine hearts)

tries: tries out, tests

if that: if

languished: weakened; earlier applied to moonlight that is diminished

descries: reveals, discloses: Your weakened grace reveals your condition to me.

even of fellowship: since we are alike

deemed: considered

want of wit: lack of intelligence

Do they call virtue there ungratefulness?: That is, Do they call ungratefulness a virtue there?

CHRISTOPHER MARLOWE, *"The Passionate Shepherd to His Love"* (page 19)

prove: try, test, experience, establish. "The exception proves the rule" means "The exception tests the rule."

madrigals: Lyrical love poem; also songs for several unaccompanied voices with elaborate counterpoint

posies: bunches of flowers. The word comes from "poesy" and also has meant a poem, a line of verse (used as a motto), and an anthology.

kirtle: old word for a gown

myrtle: an evergreen shrub with fragrant leaves and flowers

Fair-lined: possibly a variant of vair-lined, vair being the name of a fine fur
much in vogue for slippers at one time. (Probably Cinderella's slipper was
of *vair*—same in French and English—and not of *verre*, "glass" in French.
Vair and *verre* sound very much alike; besides, fur is a much more practical
material for footwear than glass.)

swain: country worker or worker's helper; also meant shepherd

WILLIAM SHAKESPEARE, *"Fear No More the Heat o' the Sun"*
(page 23)

Home art gone, and ta'en thy wages: you have gone home and your wages have
been taken (paid to you).

As chimney sweepers: like chimney sweepers, who work in dust. The critic
Hugh Kenner has reported hearing people in Shakespeare's native War-
wickshire call dandelion flowers "golden" and the same flowers when gone
to seed "chimney sweepers" (they look like chimney sweepers' brushes).

clothe: dress in clothing

scepter: government

physic: medicine

thunder stone: thunderbolt or meteorite

Consign to thee: agree to the same terms or suffer the same fate as you

exorciser: magician, conjurer, exorcist

Ghost unlaid forbear thee: "unlaid" refers to a ghost that has not been formally
driven away; may any unlaid ghost leave you alone

consummation: perfection, fulfillment (in death)

renowned: made famous, celebrated

WILLIAM SHAKESPEARE, *"When to the Sessions of Sweet Silent
Thought"* (page 25)

sessions: literally, sittings: when a court of law is in order

summon: to call up or beckon

dear: expensive

drown an eye, unus'd to flow: weep with eyes unaccustomed to weeping

cancell'd: past and almost forgotten (also with the sense in which a debt or
mortgage is canceled)

th' expense: loss

foregone: postponed or given up

tell . . . account: ordinary words but also terms in banking, a profession with
tellers (who tell in the sense of counting) and accountants (who give an
accounting: tellers who tell stories give an *account*)

WILLIAM SHAKESPEARE, *"Let Me Not to the Marriage of True Minds"* (page 26)

true: faithful, constant
an ever-fixed mark: a landmark, something to steer by
every wand'ring bark: vessels at sea
Whose worth's unknown: the height may refer to the star (which would have a measurable altitude or elevation) or to the bark (which would be of a certain height)
fool: clown or jester
his bending sickle's compass: vulnerable to time's destruction (Shakespeare uses "his" for "its")
his brief hours: time's
writ: wrote
nor no: such double negatives were allowed four centuries ago

WILLIAM SHAKESPEARE, *"Shall I Compare Thee to a Summer's Day?"* (page 27)

more lovely and more temperate: than summer
lease hath all too short a date: expires too soon
eye of heaven: the sun
every fair from fair declines: through decay, every fair thing quits being fair
untrimm'd: stripped of beautiful trimming
thou ow'st: you own (the words "owe," "own," and "ought" are all related)

WILLIAM SHAKESPEARE, *"The Expense of Spirit in a Waste of Shame"* (page 28)

expense: spending, expenditure
waste of shame: shameful waste
perjured: guilty of perjury: lying under oath
not to trust: not to be trusted
straight: right away
laid: placed in one's way
in possession so: mad also in possession
extreme: going to extremes, overboard
in proof: in the process of being tested
proved: having been tested
very: true
Before . . . behind: when it is in front of one . . . when it is behind one

WILLIAM SHAKESPEARE, *"That Time of Year Thou Mayst in Me Behold"* (page 29)

or none, or few: either none or few

ruin'd choirs: Trees where birds were singing recently ("late") and which are now bare of leaves are likened to choirs, which here means places in a church set apart for singers. Typically such a choir would have pillars like tree trunks branching into intertwining ribs in the ceiling overhead. This image may have something to do with the despoiling of the monasteries during the reign of Henry VIII.

death's second self: That is, night is another form of death.

Consum'd with that which it was nourished by: The ashes are left after the fire has done its work. At first, by making the fire burn in lively flames, the wood was nourishment, but it was consumed and left only ashes, which in turn consume (put out) the fire.

WILLIAM SHAKESPEARE, *"When Icicles Hang by the Wall"* (page 30)

bears: carries, hauls

ways: paths, roads

keel: stir something to cool it ("keel" and "cool" are related)

saw: wise saying; also droning sound

crabs: crab apples

JOHN DONNE, *"Death, Be Not Proud"* (page 32)

dreadful: inspiring dread

pictures: emblems or representations

Much pleasure: that is, "Much pleasure flows"

poppy or charms: sleep-inducing extract of the opium poppy, or a verbal formula or physical object given powers to make one sleep

why swell'st thou: why are you puffed up with conceit

One short sleep past: that is, "Once a short period of sleep is over"

JOHN DONNE, *"Batter My Heart, Three-Personed God"* (page 33)

three-personed: the Trinity of Christian theology: God as Father, Son, and Holy Ghost

bend: direct or apply

usurped: wrongfully taken

to another due: belonging to someone else
admit: let in
to no end: with no purpose
viceroy: second-in-command to a king
me should defend: should defend me
captived: put in captivity
fain: gladly
betrothed: engaged
enthrall: enslave

JOHN DONNE, *"At the Round Earth's Imagined Corners"* (page 34)

corners: Revelations 7 and 8 include four angels standing at the four corners of
  the earth and seven angels equipped with trumpets. Maps showed the four
  winds stationed at four corners.
scattered bodies: scattered over the earth and also scattered from their original
  integral form
flood did, and fire shall o'erthrow: "o'erthrow" understood after "did," elemen-
  tary destruction reaching from the flood of the Old Testament to the final
  conflagration of the New
dearth: scarcity, famine
agues: acute fevers ("ague" and "acute" are related)
hath slain: has killed
never taste death's woe: tasting death recurs in the New Testament (John 8:52,
  Hebrews 2:9); in Luke 9:27, Christ promises his disciples, "But I tell you
  truly, there are some standing here who will not taste death before they see
  the kingdom of God."
a space: a short time
this lowly ground: the earth before the Apocalypse
sealed my pardon: guaranteed my salvation

JOHN DONNE, *"The Good Morrow"* (page 35)

Good-morrow: good morning
by my troth: by my faith, a way of expressing strong feeling ("troth" and
  "truth" are related)
country pleasures: simple rustic life
snorted: snored
seven sleepers: a Christian legend about seven Ephesians, victims of persecution,
  who hid in a cave and slept safely for 187 years
but this, all pleasures fancies be: all pleasures but this one are fantasies
For love, all love of other sights controls: For love controls all love of other sights.

one little room: Christopher Marlowe's play *The Jew of Malta* (produced around 1592, published in 1633) contains the line "Infinite riches in a little room."

My face in thine eye: a reflection of my face in the mirror of your eye

sharp north . . . declining west: cold north, sunset west

JOHN DONNE, *"The Sun Rising"* (page 37)

Busy: not just active but also prying and meddlesome, like a busybody

seasons run: that is, follow the sun's course as the earth does through the changing seasons

Saucy: impertinent; for Americans, the meaning has largely been taken over by the variant "sassy"

pedantic: like a teacher in checking the time

chide: scold

prentices: apprentices; junior workers learning a trade

court-huntsmen: court hangers-on hunting for advantage by joining the King in his enthusiasm for hunting

harvest offices: duties, jobs associated with harvest; it is also possible that "to harvest" is a verb here, so that the line means (1) summon country workers to their harvest work, and (2) summon petty officials to reap little jobs.

all alike: uniform, consistent, the same all the time

clime: climate

Thy beams: a contorted sentence: Why shouldst thou think thy beams so reverend and strong? Why should you consider your beams so reverend and strong?

But that: except that, with eyes shut, I could not see her

th'Indias of spice and mine: the East Indies (including what was once called the Spice Islands) provided spice, the West Indies gold from mines. These groups of islands in the western Atlantic and southwestern Pacific were called Indias or Indies by explorers who thought they had found India. The same error led to calling Native Americans "Indians."

hear, All here: a pun on words that sound the same

She'is: printed thus, this is pronounced and scanned as one syllable

play: imitate

mimic: hollow sham, imitation

alchemy: the general name for chemical research up through about 1600, mostly devoted to the transformation of base metal into gold; the specific reference here is to a substance, which was mainly brass, that was offered as a substitute for gold: hence, debased, inferior, false

contracted thus: reduced to the size of our bed

thine age asks ease: your being old makes you need easy work

sphere: imagined circular orbit around the earth

JOHN DONNE, *"A Valediction: Forbidding Mourning"* (page 39)

Valediction: farewell. In North America, school graduation ceremonies often include a valedictory address delivered by a valedictorian: literally "one who says farewell."

profanation: cheapening; treating something holy as though it were not holy

laity: people outside our charmed circle

Moving of th'Earth: earthquake

trepidation of the spheres: a technical concept from medieval astronomy: Thabet ben Korrah's theory that vibrations in the celestial sphere caused such apparent irregularities as the precession of the equinoxes (actually caused by movement of the earth's axis)

sublunary: under the moon: ordinary, subject to change

elemented: made it up, provided elements for it

Inter-assurèd: mutually assured

gold: gold beaten into thin foil

compass: a wooden or metal instrument for drawing circles, with a fixed pointed leg and an adjustable leg with a pencil or other marking device. In this poem, with so much imagery from astronomy, it could matter that there is a constellation called the Compass (Circinus), although this is another sense of the word, meaning a device for computing directions.

obliquely: at an angle

just: complete, perfect

JOHN DONNE, *"Go and Catch a Falling Star"* (page 41)

mandrake: A plant (*Mandragora officinarum*) known as a poison and a narcotic. Its forked root may look like a human body, so that many superstitions attach themselves to it. The word, related to mandragora, has been fancifully interpreted as a combination of "man" and "drake" (meaning "dragon").

cleft: the devil is said to have cloven hooves, like the god Pan's or a goat's or a pig's

mermaids singing: related to the legend of the sirens and lorelei whose beautiful singing was so irresistible that mariners were lured onto rocks. The phrase also appears in Eliot's "The Love Song of J. Alfred Prufrock."

Serves to advance: works to make something succeed

born to: born with the power to do something

befell thee: happened to you

true: constant, faithful

Such a pilgrimage were sweet: such a ritual journey to a sacred place would be sweet

BEN JONSON, *"On My First Son"* (page 44)

child of my right hand: One meaning of "Benjamin" is "child of the right hand," a sign of good fortune.

I thee pay: I give you back

the just day: the boy's birthday

lose all father: lose all qualities attached to being a father

lament: mourn

envy: accented on the second syllable and pronounced to rhyme with "why" (this sounding persists in certain British dialects)

'scaped: escaped

yet age: the child escaped the usual miseries of life, and, if nothing else were to come as a misery, age would remain. The point here is like that in Shakespeare's "Fear No More the Heat o' the Sun."

Jonson his: that is, Jonson's (the possessive formed by an apostrophe followed by *s* was erroneously thought to be a contraction of "his")

poetry: "poem" means "something created," so that the child is a poem created by his parents

henceforth: from this time on

his vows: the father's vows

BEN JONSON, *"Song: To Celia"* (page 45)

pledge: offer a toast

but: only

Jove's nectar: Jove, or Jupiter, was the chief god of the Romans. The gods of classical antiquity lived on a diet of nectar and ambrosia (both words mean "conferring immortality").

sup: drink little by little (sip is a variant of sup)

I would not change: probably "would not take in exchange"

late: lately, recently

BEN JONSON, *"Still to Be Neat"* (page 46)

neat . . . dressed: Here "neat" means "elegantly clothed" and "dressed" means "all dressed up."

As: as though

hid: hidden

found: found out, revealed

taketh: captivates

adulteries: adulterations, cheapening modifications

ROBERT HERRICK, *"To the Virgins, to Make Much of Time"*
(page 48)

succeed: follow

former: earlier

coy: possibly quiet and modest, but usually with a suggestion of feigned or
affected reluctance

prime: springtime

tarry: delay, wait, postpone

ROBERT HERRICK, *"Upon Julia's Clothes"* (page 49)

Whenas: When

methinks: it seems to me

liquefaction: changing state from solid to liquid (we still speak of watered
silk); also, in Herrick's day, the melting of the soul in religious enthusiasm

cast: direct

mine eyes: my eyes

brave vibration: "brave" here (as in the "brave new world" in Shakespeare's *The
Tempest*) means "spectacular, splendid"

ROBERT HERRICK, *"Delight in Disorder"* (page 50)

wantonness: here an appealing capriciousness, not necessarily with the modern
connotations of lewdness

lawn: a shawl made of lawn, which is a fine linen originally produced in Laon,
France

Enthralls: subjugates: the lace (as in "shoelace") is a cord keeping the stom-
acher in place

stomacher: a triangular panel set into the open front of a dress and held in
place (over the chest and stomach) by cords

thereby: beside the cuff

wild civility: an example of oxymoron, since wildness and civility are usually
opposite

art: the use of artifice in grooming and other activities, not necessarily a fine
art; the same sense of art is at work in Jonson's "Still to Be Neat"

GEORGE HERBERT, *"Love III"* (page 52)

lacked: Two meanings here: a dutiful host might ask, "Do you lack any-
thing?"—that is, "Is everything all right with your room?" But it could also
mean, "Is your character lacking anything?" Love means the first, the
speaker means the second.

Ah my dear: This commonplace but touching phrase also appears in Hopkins's

"The Windhover." Hopkins loved Herbert's poetry and used it more than once as the source of words and images.

Who made the eyes: One of Herbert's earlier poems called "Love" ends with a reference to "him who did make and mend our eyes."

where it doth deserve: that is, not heaven

meat: food or nourishment in general, a meal, not necessarily the flesh of an animal. Suggesting both the Communion meal and the symbolic Marriage Feast of the Lamb in Revelations. Louis L. Martz has noted that this passage in Herbert's poem takes words and images from Christ's words in Luke 12:37: "Blessed are those servants, whom the lord when he cometh shall find watching: verily I say unto you, that he shall gird himself, and make them to sit down to meat, and will come forth and serve them."

GEORGE HERBERT, *"The Pulley"* (page 54)

Pulley: a simple device in which a rope led over a grooved wheel lifts weights: the religious meaning—that negative restlessness has a positive effect—is parallel to the physical motion of pulling downward on a rope to make an object move upward. The word "pulley" is not related to "pull" but to the "pole" that means "axis, pivot."

standing by: in a state of readiness

dispersed: (pronounced as three syllables) scattered

Contract: be reduced, concentrated

span: the distance from the tip of the thumb to the tip of the little finger when the hand is extended: about nine inches

made a way: flowed, ran (like "standing by" above, this phrase was originally nautical)

stay: pause

Rest: In the story of Pandora, after all troubles had been emptied from her box, only hope remained; here rest or repose remains.

rest in Nature: be content with

keep the rest: "rest" meaning "repose" and "rest" meaning "remainder" are different words from different roots, but the poet uses both senses

repining: not satisfied

GEORGE HERBERT, *"Virtue"* (page 55)

sweet: Although now mostly an affair of taste, "sweet" can also apply to sound (as in John Newton's "Amazing grace, how sweet the sound") and touch (as in the sweet spot of a tennis racket or golf club). The wasted sweetness of some flowers is a common theme in Waller's "Go, Lovely Rose" and Gray's "Elegy Written in a Country Churchyard."

bridal: wedding

angry: red, like an angry face

brave: splendid, fine. The same (now obsolete) sense of the word persists in the "brave new world" in Shakespeare's *The Tempest* and the "brave vibration" in Herrick's "Upon Julia's Clothes."

ever: forever, always

box where sweets compacted lie: petals are crushed together to release their fragrance

closes: closes of musical phrases, cadences, examples of the dying fall, as in Shakespeare's *Twelfth Night* and Eliot's "The Love Song of J. Alfred Prufrock."

gives: gives way, yields

coal: cinder

THOMAS CAREW, *"Ask Me No More Where Jove Bestows"* (page 57)

Jove: the chief Roman god, same as Jupiter, corresponding to the Greek Zeus. His wife was his sister Juno, the goddess for whom June is named.

bestows: stows or stores

orient deep: "orient" means "rising" and here seems to mean "emerging"; "deep" is a noun meaning "depth"

causes: a thing sleeps in its causes by being implicit in the forces that bring it about: purpose, form, matter, and source or maker. From Aristotle and other ancient Greek philosophers we get the idea that a given thing is what it is because of the principles or causes that determine its nature. A tin cup, for example, is what it is because it has the purpose of holding liquids and other things (the final cause); it has a size and a shape that make the holding possible (the formal cause); it is made of tin (the material cause); and it was made by some person or process (the efficient cause).

golden atoms: sunlight imagined as particles; "atom" means "indivisible" and was used in Carew's time for the smallest component of matter

powders: cosmetic powders have been put on hair or wigs, but here the term seems to mean highlights

dividing: performing a division; an obsolete musical term for dividing one long note into many small ones, somewhat like a bird's song

light: a witty combination of two distinct meanings of "light": to land (alight) and to give light

Fixed . . . as in their sphere: the fixed stars, unlike the planets, keep the same relative position in the firmament. The celestial sphere was imagined as a sphere in which the stars were placed.

phoenix: the fabled bird that, after living for centuries, burns itself to death and then rises anew from the ashes

EDMUND WALLER, *"Go, Lovely Rose"* (page 60)

wastes: two senses: she fritters her time away and devastates me
resemble: liken, compare
shuns to have: avoids having
sprung: grown, bloomed
abide: live
uncommended: unpraised
retired: hidden
Bid: tell
Suffer: permit
And not blush so: and not blush so much when she is admired
common fate: the destiny that all (rare) things have in common
wondrous: wondrously

JOHN MILTON, *"Lycidas"* (page 64)

Monody: Strictly, a lament in which a single mourner expresses grief; the word
  means singing alone, as distinguished from singing in a chorus. The last
  eight lines of "Lycidas," however, seem to be sung or spoken by a second
  voice.
Yet once more: the poet has written laments before
Laurels: sacred to Apollo, god of learning and poetry (hence "laureate" for
  someone honored for poetry or intellectual achievement)
Myrtles brown: dark myrtle, sacred to Venus, goddess of love and beauty
Ivy never sere: evergreen ivy, sacred to Bacchus, god of wine; also associated
  with learning, as in the Ivy League; "sere" means withered, dried up
crude: unripe
mellowing year: King drowned in August, just before the onset of autumn
  (called by Keats "Season of mists and mellow fruitfulness" in "To
  Autumn")
dear: important, also dire
dead ere his prime: dead before his prime (ere = before); King died at twenty-
  five
hath not left his peer: no one left behind is his equal
he knew / Himself to sing: he himself was a singer (poet)
bier: tomb, grave
welter: writhe, twist in pain
meed: worthy reward
melodious tear: elegy
Sisters of the sacred well: the Muses, nine daughters of Jove and Mnemosyne
  (Memory), who inspire artists in many fields. They are identified with vari-

ous streams and fountains that could be called a sacred well: Hippocrene, Aganippe, Pieria.

beneath the seat of Jove: the throne or altar of Jove

some gentle Muse: a poet

lucky: unsought, propitious

my destin'd Urn: the funeral inscription for his coming death

sable: mournful

nurst: The idea of a school as nurse or nourisher persists in such terms as *alma mater* (nourishing mother) and *alumnus* or *alumna* (male or female nursling).

Lawns: clearings (this sense of the word also appears in Gray's "Elegy Written in a Country Churchyard")

the Gray-fly winds her sultry horn: noise of summer at midday (wind = blow)

Batt'ning: feeding, fattening

th'Oaten flute: pastoral song

Satyrs: goatlike woodland creatures devoted to pleasure

Fauns: rural deities, usually shown with goat's ears, tail, and legs

Damaetas: evidently one of the teachers at Cambridge University

now thou art gone: here, as at the end of the poem, the speaker addresses Lycidas

gadding: straggling

Copses: thickets with trees designated for cutting (like the coppice in Hardy's "The Darkling Thrush")

lays: verses

Canker: cankerworm, a destructive insect larva

Taint-worm: intestinal worm

weanling: newly weaned calf

White-thorn blows: hawthorn blossoms

Nymphs: mythological maidens specifically identified with features of nature, such as mountains, woodlands, fresh water, salt water

steep: the east end of Anglesey is a steep mountain

Bards, the famous Druids: ancient officials whose duties combined religion, government, literature, and education. The bards have become known mostly as poets, the druids as priests.

Mona the island of Anglesey, near which King died

Deva: the Dee, a western river, by which Chester is situated

her wizard stream: prophetic

fondly: foolishly

that Orpheus bore: Calliope, who bore (gave birth to) Orpheus; she was the muse of epic poetry

the rout: "rout" means "mob." Thracian women (Bacchantes) in a frenzy dismembered Orpheus.

gory visage: Orpheus's head

Hebrus: a river

Lesbian shore: the island of Lesbos

What boots it: what good does it do

uncessant: incessant, unceasing

homely: unsophisticated, domestic

slighted: paid little attention

thankless: one who inspires works that earn no thanks

as others use: as others are accustomed to do

sport with Amaryllis: conventional female name in pastoral romance

Neaera: another stereotyped name. Tangled hair also appears in Lovelace's "To Althea, from Prison" and also in his "Song: To Amarantha, That She Would Dishevel Her Hair."

last infirmity: the last weakness to be overcome by nobility

Guerdon: reward

the blind Fury with th'abhorred shears: this is Atropos (the name means "Inexorable"), not technically a Fury but one of the Fates, with shears for cutting the thread of fate

Phoebus: Apollo

glistering foil: the setting of a jewel

broad rumor: rumor noised around

Arethuse: both a fountain and a nymph of Diana; a type of pastoral muse

Mincius: stream near Mantua, where Virgil was born; a city associated with poetry and prophecy

the Herald of the Sea: Triton, also mentioned in Wordsworth's "The World Is Too Much with Us"

Neptune's plea: a plea of innocence in the death of Lycidas

beaked Promontory: craggy headland

Hippotades: Aeolus, son of Hippotas, was god of the winds, sometimes credited with the invention of navigation.

not a blast: according to some accounts, the day of the shipwreck was calm

Panope: one of the Nereids, sea nymphs

fatal and perfidious Bark: the ship itself is accused of treachery

Built in th'eclipse: the contamination caused by being built during an eclipse sounds like a sailors' superstition

Camus: the River Cam, that gives the town and university of Cambridge their name, is here transformed into a river god (rather like Old Man River in *Show Boat*) wearing academic regalia with different colors: dark like reeds but also red like the hyacinth

reverend Sire: honored father

footing: moving

His Mantle hairy: his cloak both fuzzy, like some plants, and furry, like some academic robes

Inwrought: decorated

sanguine flower inscrib'd with woe: Greek legend imagined that markings on the hyacinth spelled out something woeful like *ai ai* or *io* (in Greek script).

reft: bereft

The Pilot: probably St. Peter

Two massy Keys: possibly the keys of heaven

of metals twain: of two metals: gold and iron

amain: with force

Mitred locks: wearing a bishop's mitre (headgear)

stern bespake: sternly spoke

Enow: enough

reck'ning: consideration

bidden: invited

Blind mouths: a much disputed phrase: possibly a conversion of those who should be seers and feeders into blind creatures reduced to nothing but hungrily open mouths

What recks it them?: what difference does it make to them?

They are sped: they speed along prosperously, they are advanced speedily

list: like, please

scrannel: feeble

swoln: swollen

draw: inhale

the grim Wolf: some corrupt church, such as the Roman Catholic or the High Anglican Church

privy paw: by stealth or secrecy

apace: rapidly

two-handed engine: an instrument of punishment

Alpheus: river-god in love with Arethuse; also referred to in Coleridge's "Kubla Khan"

dread: fearful

Sicilian Muse: associated with Theocritus and other Greek poets living on Sicily

Vales: valleys

hither cast: throw here

Flowrets: little flowers

wanton winds: playful, mischievous

swart Star: Sirius, the Dog Star that presides over the Dog Days when vegetation turns dark (swart or swarthy) and dies

quaint enamell'd eyes: many-colored

rathe: early. This is the obsolete positive form of which "rather" is the comparative.

Crow-toe: wild hyacinth

Jessamine: jasmine

Pink: a white or pink flower

freakt with jet: flecked, streaked

Musk-rose: also in Keats's "Ode to a Nightingale"

well-attir'd Woodbine: bindweed

Cowslips wan: pale flowers

Amaranthus: the unfading (deathless) flower of paradise

Lycid: a shortened form of Lycidas; modern names are often derived by dropping a suffix from classical ancestors, such as Mark and Luke from Marcus and Lucas

sounding Seas: repeated in one version of Poe's "Annabel Lee"

Hebrides: Milton seems to have been consulting a map. North from the scene of the drowning of Lycidas lie the Hebrides, islands off the west and northwest coast of Scotland.

whelming: covering or subduing

monstrous world: the undersea world with monsters

Bellerus: south from the scene of drowning lies Cornwall, the extreme southwest tip of Great Britain. Bellerus was a giant supposedly buried at Land's End, just west of Penzance. (The north-to-south scope of Great Britain is still called from John o' Groat's to Land's End—with the former being the northern extreme of Scotland.)

the guarded Mount: St. Michael's Mount is an island in Mount's Bay just off the Cornish coast near Penzance, facing toward the South. This mountain named in honor of Saint Michael the Archangel strikingly resembles Mont-Saint-Michel on the French coast. Michael Drayton's fascinating *Poly-Olbion* (1612), published while Milton was a child, begins with a survey of geography from the south:

The sprightly muse her wing displays
And the French islands first surveys,
Bears up with Neptune, and in glory
Transcends proud Cornwall's promontory;
There crowns Mount Michael, and discries
How all those riverets fall and rise.

Namancos and Bayona's hold: These are places in Catholic Spain, southward from Cornwall.

Look homeward Angel: the source of the title of Thomas Wolfe's first novel

ruth: pity

Dolphins: thought to save lives, as in the myth of Arion

hapless: luckless

your sorrow: for whom you sorrow

day-star: the sun

anon soon tricks: repairs, adjusts

new-spangled Ore: gold with renewed luster

him that walk'd the waves: Christ

Nectar: sustenance of the gods (the word means "overcoming death")

his oozy locks he laves: washes his slimy hair

unexpressive: inexpressible

nuptial song: the Lamb's marriage in Revelation 19

thou art the Genius: in a bold turn, the poem again addresses the dead Lycidas, who has become the spirit attending the shore

recompense: compensation

perilous: the word is repeated in Keats's "Ode to a Nightingale"

uncouth Swain: unknown rustic

stops: holes in a flute

Quills: reeds of a pipe

Doric: dialect of ancient pastoral poets; regarded as simple, plain, and rustic. The Doric column is known to be the simplest and sturdiest.

stretch't out: cause the shadows of the hills to lengthen at evening

SIR JOHN SUCKLING, *"Why So Pale and Wan, Fond Lover?"* (page 72)

Wan: means both pale and of a sickly color. The phrase "pale and wan" was used by Chaucer and Shakespeare.

Fond: both fond in the regular sense and foolish. The earlier form "fonned" came from "fon," a verb meaning "to make a fool of." The modern sense is more polite.

Prithee: I pray thee; please

prevail: work

do 't: do it

Quit: stop, leave off; also abandon the project

This cannot take her: this "take" means "win"; the later "take" means "take." Saying things like "take the trick" is a reminder that Suckling was a gambler sometimes credited with inventing the popular card game cribbage.

RICHARD LOVELACE, *"To Lucasta, Going to the Wars"* (page 75)

arms: weapons

fly: both "to move quickly" and "to flee"

mistress: many meanings, all the way from goddess or muse who controls and governs a man to woman not one's wife with whom one maintains a sexual relationship—all meanings seem to be at work here

chase: pursue in general but probably with an additional connotation of hunting on horseback (as in steeplechase). Also echoes "chaste" two lines before, which in turn translates the "casta" element in the name Lucasta.

the field: specifically, a battlefield

embrace: many meanings: mechanical bracing involving swords, shields, and the equipment of horseback riding; to hold in general; to hold in the arms affectionately (with sexual overtones); to perceive, comprehend, cultivate, believe, support

RICHARD LOVELACE, *"To Althea, from Prison"* (page 76)

Love: the god Cupid, usually portrayed with wings

Althea: object of "brings"

fetter'd: tied

wanton: The verb generally means "to play or frolic," but specifically it suggests amorous play.

gods: some seventeenth-century texts read "birds"

no allaying Thames: no diluting water

health: toasts

draughts: (pronounced "drafts") swallows or drinks

tipple: the rare general sense is "drink"; the much commoner specific sense connotes alcoholic beverages

committed: caged

linnets: small songbirds

shriller throat: it was thought that caged birds were better singers

Enlarged: liberated

hermitage: place of escape and refuge

ANDREW MARVELL, *"To His Coy Mistress"* (page 79)

were: would be

Ganges' side: river in India

Humber: estuary in Marvell's home region in northeast England

complain: sing a song of plaintive love

the Flood: Noah's flood

conversion of the Jews: either never or at the end of time

vegetable: not modern "plant-like" but an older meaning: "living, lively, capable of growth"

Deserts: wildernesses

marble vault: tomb

try: test, probe

quaint honor: both words, as nouns, have meant female genitalia. For such a use of "quaint," see Chaucer's "The Miller's Tale." "Her honor was violated" has a concrete as well as an abstract sense.

glew: plant gum, aromatic and lustrous. Other manuscripts justify variant readings here: "Now, therefore, while the youthful glue / Sits on thy skin like morning dew;" "Now, therefore, while the youthful hue / Sits on thy skin like morning dew."

slow-chapped: chaps or chops are jaws

ANDREW MARVELL, *"The Garden"* (page 81)

amaze: bewilder, perplex, confuse (put themselves into a maze: mazes are usu- ally made of tall hedges in a garden)

palm . . . oak . . . bays: symbols of success in various fields of competition: warfare, civic duty, poetry

narrow-verged: confined

upbraid: chastise

Quiet . . . Innocence: By personification these qualities are given human form. In a figure called apostrophe that often goes with personification, they are addressed as though they could hear.

companies: crowds

all but rude: nothing but rude

No white nor red: floral colors often associated with Venus; also the colors of the symbolic roses in the Wars of the Roses (white for York, red for Lancaster)

mistress' name: sweetheart's name

passions' heat: "heat" as in track competition

Apollo . . . Daphne: The nymph Daphne was turned into a laurel tree so that she could escape the god Apollo; her name is the Greek word for laurel.

Pan . . . Syrinx: Syrinx became a reed to escape the god Pan; her name is relat- ed to "syringe" and "syringa."

curious: unusual, strange, rare; also excellent

that ocean: that is, a place where each object is matched by a mental image (its own resemblance)

various light: changing light, as if reflected from iridescent plumage

Garden-State: Adam's condition before Eve

help . . . meet: Because of a misunderstanding of God's words in Genesis 2:18 ("I will make him an help meet for him"), we have wound up with two new terms. In the scripture, the sentence means, "I will make for him a helper suitable for him." Both "help" and "meet" as used here became obsolete in time, so that late in the seventeenth century John Dryden could write "help-meet" for "man." Eventually, the hyphen dropped out and "helpmeet" was established as a distinct word; since it didn't clearly make sense, some speakers touched it up and made "helpmate." Marvell seems to have the older senses in mind, and his statement is a rhetorical question: When you have everything, what else do you need?

'twere: it would be

dial: clock face or sundial

zodiac: A complicated joke is at work here, since "zodiac" comes from the Greek for animal and most of the signs of the zodiac are creatures like rams, bulls, fish, crabs, scorpions, and human beings.

HENRY VAUGHAN, *"The Retreat"* (page 85)

Retreat: means both a backward movement and a place of refuge

second race: life is compared to a race in Hebrews 12:1

to fancy ought: to care for anything

above / a mile or two: more than a mile or two

first love: that is, Christ. The phrase "first love" appears in Revelation 2:4.

short space: across that short time

his bright face: Christ's

gilded: made golden by sunlight or coloration

sev'ral: separate, distinctive

shoots of everlastingness: "shoot" has meant both the rising of sap and the putting out of new growth

track: path

train: a succession: here both a way of life and an angelic company

city of palm trees: used in the Old Testament for Jericho but also the Promised Land or Heavenly City (Deuteronomy 34:1–4).

stay: delay

in the way: on the path

return: This word connects the poem to the ancient tradition of the *nostos* or story of homecoming. The word "nostalgia" literally means "sickness to return home." The *Odyssey* tells the story of Odysseus's return to his old home after the Trojan War; the *Aeneid* describes Aeneas's search for a new home after the same war. The last word of Milton's *Paradise Regained* is "returned."

THOMAS GRAY, *"Elegy Written in a Country Churchyard"* (page 88)

Elegy: a mournful poem, especially one for the dead

curfew: curfew bell, which originally signaled the time in the evening when fires were to be covered or put out (the word comes from French *couvrefeu*, "cover fire")

lea: grassland, pasture

folds: enclosures for livestock; here cows with cowbells

bower: enclosure

yew: an evergreen, formerly planted in graveyards so that the poisonous berries would not be eaten by livestock

cell: grave

rude: rustic

clarion: a loud trumpet or its sound

echoing horn: hunting horn

ply: work at

glebe: earth

jocund: cheerful

stroke: of an axe

Ambition. . . Grandeur: a vivid example of personification

boast of Heraldry: belonging to a family, usually royal or noble, entitled to display a coat of arms

paths of glory: The phrase provided the title for Humphrey Cobb's antiwar novel *Paths of Glory*, which was one inspiration for William Faulkner's *A Fable*; Cobb's novel was also the basis of Stanley Kubrick's film *Paths of Glory* (1957).

fretted: decorated

urn: a funerary container ornamented with pictures

animated: lifelike

its mansion: that is, the body

provoke: call forth

Hands that the rod of empire might have swayed: that might have influenced the course of imperial government

spoils: things that have been acquired or learned

Penury: poverty

genial current: warm stream

purest ray serene: Thomas Hardy surmised that the phrase "pure serene" in Keats's "On First Looking into Chapman's Homer" was indebted to this line from Gray. The image of undersea jewels reaches back to Shakespeare's *Richard III* (1:4:9–33) and *The Tempest* ("Full Fathom Five": 1:2:397–405) and forward to Hardy's poem "The Convergence of the Twain."

Hampden: John Hampden (1594–1643), Member of Parliament, opposed King Charles I, killed in the Civil Wars

dauntless: fearless

Milton: John Milton, 1608–1674, a poet clearly glorious and far from mute; a mute inglorious Milton would be a great poet whom circumstances keep in silence and obscurity

Cromwell: Oliver Cromwell, 1599–1658, soldier and statesman, leader of the Puritan forces in the Civil War, governed as Lord Protector from 1653 until his death

circumscribed: limited

ingenuous: innocent

madding: milling (this line is the source of the title of Hardy's novel *Far from the Madding Crowd*)

ignoble: base, not noble

sequestered: set apart

tenor: usual condition

uncouth: uncultivated

th' unlettered Muse: a muse who sponsors humble writing. "Unlettered" is literally "illiterate."

Nor cast: and not cast

wonted: accustomed

If chance: if it should happen

Haply: maybe

hoary-headed swain: rustic with grey or white hair

lawn: untilled ground, sometimes between woods; a glade; the same use as in Milton's "Lycidas"

pore: study carefully

hard by: close to

woeful wan, like one forlorn, / Or crazed with care, or crossed in hopeless love: Notable passage for subtle musical effects, especially alliteration. Note also the subdued pun on "wan" and "one." To be crazed with care is to be damaged or impaired by worries.

customed: accustomed

heath: rough uncultivated land, sometimes with heather and other such hardy plants

rill: brook

dirges due: suitable mournful verses

lay: poem

thorn: thorn tree

Science: learning or knowledge in general

melancholy: sadness

bounty: generosity of spirit

dread abode: feared home (the grave)

they alike: both merits and frailties

trembling hope: both terms reappear at the end of Hardy's "The Darkling Thrush"

THOMAS GRAY, *"Ode on the Death of a Favorite Cat, Drowned in a Tub of Gold Fishes"* (page 93)

azure flowers: blue floral designs, still popular on porcelain, especially that from China

Demurest: modest and serious, sometimes with overtones of affectation or artificiality

pensive: thoughtful. This passage seems to owe something to Milton's "Il Penseroso," which contains this couplet: "Come pensive nun, devout and pure, / Sober, steadfast, and demure."

lake: water in the vase

conscious tail: her moving tail expresses her feelings

tortoise: a tortoiseshell cat has a coat that combines black, brown, red, and yellow

vies: competes

jet: black

She saw: that is, she saw her own reflection in the water

Still had she gazed: these terms also occur in a slightly later poem, Oliver Goldsmith's "The Deserted Village": "And still they gazed. . . ."

Genii: geniuses: resident or guardian spirits, as used in Milton's "Lycidas"

Tyrian: purple (dye from Tyre). The original color was crimson, later enlarged to include many shades of red, violet, and purple.

Betray'd: disclosed, revealed

hapless: unlucky

Nymph: in antiquity, a female spirit inhabiting a stream, wood, or mountain; later a beautiful girl

averse: opposed

Presumptuous: too confident

verge: margin

beguil'd: fooled, misled

Eight times: exploiting the notion that a cat has nine lives

Dolphin: thought in antiquity to come to the aid of drowning victims (some people today still think so)

Nereid: a sea-nymph, one of the daughters of Nereus, a sea-god

stirr'd: moved, acted

Tom . . . Susan: common names for servants

Fav'rite: capitalized in this way, the word suggests an earlier meaning: "A chosen intimate companion of a monarch or other person in power, especially when unduly favored" (*New Shorter Oxford English Dictionary*).

retriev'd: taken back

heedless: thoughtless, reckless

lawful prize: legitimate loot

glisters: glistens, glitters

William Blake, *"The Tyger"* (page 96)

burning bright: The tiger is yellow or orange with dark stripes that look like flames.

forests of the night: nocturnal predators, tigers hunt by night

deeps: depths of water, like an ocean

sinews: Images here describing the creation of the Tyger come from various kinds of work important in early manufacturing: framing a house, working iron with a forge and anvil, twisting fibers into threads and ropes.

When the stars threw down their spears: recalls the legend of the rebellion of Satan and other angels, before the creation of humankind. It is typical of Blake's genius that the poem avoids delivering itself of polysyllabic statements about high and mighty abstractions. Instead, Blake frames his questions around vivid concrete things from the real world in words of one syllable.

William Blake, *"London"* (page 98)

thro': through

charter'd: mapped; granted special rights; hired out (as in a "chartered" jet: here everything is for sale)

and mark: and remark, notice

ban: a call to arms (archaic); a formal curse or denunciation. A related word, "banns," means an announcement of plans for a marriage.

mind-forg'd manacles: handcuffs, here representing any restraint; social restraints are forged (both created and faked) by the mind and are not necessarily a part of the world

Chimney-sweepers: Young boys, the smaller the better, were used for this dirty work.

blackning: (1) becoming literally black because of air polluted by the burning of soft coal and figuratively black because of moral pollution; (2) causing other things and institutions to become dark

appalls: related to pale and pallor: here the word means "causes to turn pale, shock, scandalize"

hapless: luckless

curse: both the profane utterance and the curse of disease

plagues: venereal disease, specifically syphilis that causes babies to be born already sick

hearse: weddings look like funerals, and both may use a ceremonial vehicle; "hearse" has also meant any religious ceremony

WILLIAM BLAKE, *"And Did Those Feet in Ancient Time"* (page 100)

those feet: Christ's
Mills: probably grain mills, with stones for grinding; generally, places for labor, which is a punishment for sin

WILLIAM BLAKE, *"The Lamb"* (page 102)

mead: meadow
vales: valley
He calls himself a Lamb: Christ is called the Lamb of God

WILLIAM BLAKE, *"Auguries of Innocence"* (page 103)

Shudders hell: makes hell shudder
Predicts: is an omen of
misus'd: abused, whipped
for Human blood: in divine retribution
Cherubim: usually, "cherubim" is the plural of "cherub"; cherubim are customarily placed in the second angelic rank, below seraphim and above thrones
Game Cock: rooster used in the blood sport of cockfighting, sometimes armed with sharp-edged metal spurs
Bat: here the animals are not actual victims of abuse but symbols, the bat equated with insanity (battiness)
Owl: saying what sounds like who
wanton Boy: echoes a passage in Shakespeare's *King Lear*, with Gloucester saying, "As flies to wanton boys are we to th' gods; / They kill us for their sport." This use of wanton means "childishly cruel."
Chafer's sprite: beetle's soul
Bower: dwelling
pass the Polar Bar: get past the barrier to heaven
Bags: moneybags
pine: suffering; related to "pain, penalty, punish," and the second element in "subpoena"
Rod: cane of punishment
Palsied: afflicted with palsy (related to paralysis but also involving tremors)
Farthing: obsolete small coin, worth a fourth of a penny
Afric: Africa, specifically the Gold Coast
Laurel Crown: or wreath, a sign of honor from ancient Rome through today
Emmet: ant
winding Sheet: shroud, garment of death
With not thro' the Eye: to see *with* the eye is to limit vision to what is in front

of the physical senses; to see *through* the eye is to get beyond the merely physical to spiritual vision. Later Blake wrote, " 'What,' it will be Question'd, 'When the Sun rises, do you not see a round disk of fire somewhat like a Guinea?' O no, no, I see an Innumerable company of the Heavenly host crying, 'Holy, Holy, Holy is the Lord God Almighty.' I question not my Corporeal or Vegetative Eye any more than I would Question a Window concerning a Sight. I look thro' it & not with it."

ROBERT BURNS, *"A Red, Red Rose"* (page 108)

Luve: Love
bonnie lass: pretty girl
a' the seas gang dry: all the seas go dry (an image from the Apocalypse— Revelation 21:1); also combines all four traditional elements, with the water becoming air and earth becoming fire
wi': with
sands o' life: suggests the running sand in an hourglass
weel: well
Tho' it were: even though it were

WILLIAM WORDSWORTH, *"She Dwelt Among the Untrodden Ways"* (page 112)

untrodden ways: paths and byways seldom used
Dove: a small stream (there are several with this name)
maid: young woman

WILLIAM WORDSWORTH, *"The World Is Too Much with Us"* (page 113)

sordid boon: that is, giving our hearts is a terrible price to pay for what little we have received
This Sea . . . the winds . . . .: these elements of nature are given some kind of living form, as human beings, animals, or plants
Pagan suckled in a creed outworn: again, even an inanimate creed receives living form, capable of suckling a child
lea: open land
Proteus: in Greek myth, a sea god able to change shape
Triton: another sea god from Greek myth (his name survives as that of Ariel's father in *The Little Mermaid*)
wreathed horn: a conch-shell horn decorated with sea plants

WILLIAM WORDSWORTH, *"The Solitary Reaper"* (page 114)

Reaper: one who cuts grain in harvest time

Highland Lass: a young woman from the mountainous area of the center and north of Scotland

strain: passage of music

Vale: valley

Hebrides: islands off the coast of Scotland; the Outer Hebrides lie to the northwest

plaintive numbers: sad measures of music

lay: a song or poem. Sir Walter Scott's narrative *The Lay of the Last Minstrel* was published in 1805.

o'er the sickle bending: echoes a line from Shakespeare's "Let Me Not to the Marriage of True Minds": "Within his bending sickle's compass come" (but also very close to the wording of Wilkinson's book)

bore: carried

WILLIAM WORDSWORTH, *"Composed upon Westminster Bridge, September 3, 1802"* (page 116)

like a garment: as in "The World Is Too Much with Us," the poet relies on personification to humanize a scene

Ships, towers, domes, theatres, and temples: Today, two centuries later, the view from Westminster Bridge is much the same: ships and barges are still tied up at Westminster Pier, the Houses of Parliament and Westminster Abbey are nearby, and many steepled churches and the dome of St. Paul's Cathedral can be seen.

steep: saturate

sweet will: Other poets named William have used "sweet will": the phrase occurs in Shakespeare's Sonnet 135 and Yeats's "A Prayer for My Daughter."

WILLIAM WORDSWORTH, *"A Slumber Did My Spirit Seal"* (page 117)

diurnal: daily. This word comes from the same root as "journal." The appearance of a rather technical word in an otherwise plain setting resembles the flash-bulb of "liquefaction" in Herrick's "Upon Julia's Clothes."

SAMUEL TAYLOR COLERIDGE, *"Kubla Khan"* (page 120)

Xanadu: Coleridge's spelling of Xamdu, Xaindu, or Xandu, which are old versions of the name of the city now called Shangtu, in Inner Mongolia.

Kubla Khan: Kublai Khan (1216–1294), grandson of Genghis Khan, was the first Mongol emperor of China.

Alph: The Greek river Alpheus flows through Elis and beside the sacred plain of Olympia, site of the original Olympian or Olympic games. It was also the location of a sacred area called the Altis, which was a walled enclosure with towers, gardens, and temples. The river was thought to run underground and even under the ocean.

girdled round: surrounded

sinuous rills: small streams with curving paths

athwart a cedarn cover: at an angle to a patch of ground covered with vegetation, including cedars

momently: an adverb with many meanings: "from moment to moment, every moment, at any moment, for the moment, for a single moment." Possibly also a compressed "momentously" reinforcing the meaning of "every moment"

the thresher's flail: an agricultural implement with a handle attached to a loosely swinging club

a lifeless ocean: like the ocean under which the Alpheus was supposed to flow

the mingled measure: melodies mixed together

rare device: unusually distinguished craft or devising

damsel with a dulcimer: a young unmarried woman with a metal-stringed instrument that one plays by striking the strings with a hammer

Abyssinia: earlier name of Ethiopia

Mount Abora: Probably Mount Amara in Abyssinia, another sacred precinct associated with classical pictures of Paradise (and mentioned in Book IV of Milton's *Paradise Lost*)

Her symphony: "Sounding together" is the root-meaning of "symphony," which here means "harmony, concord."

thrice: three is a sacred number often found in charms and oaths

honey-dew: a sweet substance like nectar or honey

the milk of Paradise: Descriptions of the Promised Land involve a diet of milk and honey.

GEORGE GORDON BYRON, 6TH BARON BYRON, *"She Walks in Beauty"* (page 126)

aspect: facial expression, countenance

gaudy: tastelessly showy

Had half impaired: would have impaired by half

serenely: calmly

dwelling-place: biblical term for home, as in the beginning of one translation of Psalm 84: "How lovely is your dwelling place, O Lord of Hosts!"

eloquent: expressive

PERCY BYSSHE SHELLEY, *"Ode to the West Wind"* (page 129)

hectic: flushed with fever; red
Pestilence-stricken: suffering a very bad disease
Thine azure sister: wind of spring
clarion: a trumpet with a rousing sound
Spirit: the word literally means "breath"
thine aery surge: turbulence in the air
Maenad: frenzied woman dedicated to the service of Dionysus, god of wine
sepulchre: tomb
pumice: a type of volcanic glass
Baiae's bay: near Naples
Cleave: split
sea-blooms and oozy woods: submarine vegetation
bear: carry
impulse: literally, drive or push
skiey: of, in, or like the sky: a rare word seldom found outside poetry (used
    also by Shakespeare, Coleridge, and Keats)
sore: severe, painful
lyre: Eolian lyre or harp, supposedly played by the wind, in the manner of
    wind chimes
quicken: animate
incantation: chanting

PERCY BYSSHE SHELLEY, *"Ozymandias"* (page 133)

Ozymandias: One of the many Greek forms of one of the many names of
    Rameses II, who ruled Egypt for almost seventy years (1304–1237 B.C.).
    Also called Rameses the Great, he was probably the Pharaoh who first per-
    secuted the Israelites. His mummy still exists.
trunkless: that is, the legs stand alone, with no body above them
visage: a human face; also (an older meaning) an image of face
hand that mocked: the sculptor's hand: the mocking has two senses: aesthetic
    copying and ridiculing, as though the sculptor knew exactly what he was
    doing
heart: the king's
king of kings: Ozymandias ruled a large empire. The phrase, also sometimes
    applied to Christ, is used in Yeats's "Among School Children," referring to
    Alexander the Great.
beside: besides, else

PERCY BYSSHE SHELLEY, *"To a Skylark"* (page 134)

blithe: merry, lighthearted

full heart: this fullness echoes the full-throated in Keats's "Ode to a Nightingale" and is in turn echoed by the "full-hearted" in Hardy's "The Darkling Thrush."

profuse: plentiful

blue deep: of the sky

sunken sun: just before sunrise

even: evening

silver sphere: either the moon or the morning star

measures: musical passages

Thy skill to poet were: your skill would be to a poet

JOHN KEATS, *"To Autumn"* (page 141)

maturing sun: On the autumnal equinox around September 21, day and night are about equal. Throughout the autumn, the days become shorter and the nights longer, until the winter solstice, around December 21, when the day is at its shortest and the night its longest. The sun can be said to die at this point and be reborn the next day, when the days gradually become longer, the nights shorter. The sun is also maturing in the sense of causing things on the earth to mature.

thatch-eves: eaves of a thatched roof, made of straw or other materials, still used in rural England

plump the hazel shells: make the hazelnuts grow large and round

clammy cells: compartments in a beehive, formed out of wax to hold the larvae; often moist and cool

oft amid thy store: "oft" (often) attaches itself to "seen" and to "amid," as though to suggest "who has not often seen you often in the midst of what you have produced?"

granary: a place where threshed grain is stored

winnowing: the action of separating the lighter chaff from grain by letting the wind blow through it as it is lifted with a special shovel or fan

the fume of poppies: A field of opium poppies can make you drowsy, as happened most memorably in *The Wizard of Oz.*

hook: scythe or sickle

swath: the track left behind by a scythe, as in "cut a swath"

gleaner: one who gathers up a crop that has been reaped

laden: loaded with a burden

sallows: willows

borne aloft: carried up into the air

bourn: the boundary separating two fields; sometimes used to mean a general area or domain. Here, also an echo of "borne" two lines earlier.

treble soft: "treble" means "triple" (so that "treble soft" means "three-times soft"); it also means the highest-pitched singing voice, appropriate here for a songbird. In musical notation, where "piano" means "soft," "treble soft" could be *ppp*, which is one way to represent pianissimo (very soft).

garden-croft: a plot of land attached to a house

JOHN KEATS, *"La Belle Dame sans Merci"* (page 143)

sedge: a marsh plant

Knight at arms: a warrior of high rank, usually called "Sir," typically riding a horse and carrying heavy weapons

woe begone, woe-begone: beset by misfortune. Now usually one word, "woebegone"; an archaic form revived in the nineteenth century but now so grotesque that it is seldom used seriously. Garrison Keillor's Lake Wobegon is the latest appearance of the lugubrious word.

granary: literally a storehouse for grain; here the squirrel's hoard of food

a lily on thy brow: a pale forehead

fever dew: perspiration

Meads: meadows

faery's child: the set of words including "fay", "fairy," and "faery" has had a most complex history. Not all fairies are little people. Tooth fairies and the like are a modern survival of a race of supernatural beings once thought to inhabit a beautiful realm of enchantment. In some mythological systems, the fairies are not gods but superhuman representations of forces, like the Graces or the Fates (the latter word is in fact related to "fay" and "fairy").

Zone: girdle or belt

steed: horse used for riding, especially a warhorse. This word has the same root as "stud."

relish sweet: strongly flavored condiment or other food

manna dew: food like that miraculously provided for the Israelites on their way from Egypt to the Promised Land

elfin grot: Elves resemble fairies in most respects nowadays; formerly, elves may have counted as masculine and wicked, unlike fairies who were feminine and good. "Elfin" here means "enchanting." "Grot" is an archaic or poetic form of "grotto," meaning "cave," with overtones of the picturesque and the exotic.

full sore: as bitterly as could be

Woe betide: archaic for "may woe befall you" (a curse) or "woe may befall you" (a warning); the latter is the sense in the poem *lulled:* pronounced as two syllables, as is also the case with "gaped" and "sighed." If lulled were to be sounded in the usual way, it would be spelled lull'd. This is a general but not consistent practice in printing poetry up to about 1900.

latest: last

in thrall: enslaved by enchantment

gloam: twilight

sojourn: tarry, stay for a while

wight: person, usually male. The word is now literary only.

JOHN KEATS, *"On First Looking into Chapman's Homer"* (page 146)

in fealty to Apollo: "Fealty" and "fidelity" come from the same source and mean much the same thing; Apollo was the ancient sun-god associated with music, poetry, prophecy, medicine, light, and clarity.

demesne: domain, realm

pure serene: Thomas Hardy believed that Keats had borrowed this combination of words from Gray's "Elegy Written in a Country Churchyard" ("purest ray serene").

Darien: in Panama

JOHN KEATS, *"Ode to Nightingale"* (page 148)

hemlock: a poisonous herb (not the American hemlock), traditionally the means of the execution of Socrates

opiate: narcotic

Lethe-wards: toward the river of forgetfulness in Hell

thy happy lot: your happy condition

Dryad: tree nymph

beechen: of a tree with smooth bark and glossy green leaves

a draught of vintage: a drink of wine

Flora: Roman goddess of flowers

Provençal song: the medieval Troubadours lived in Provence, in the south of France

Hippocrene: the Muses' fountain on Mount Helicon

spectre-thin: ghostlike

but to think: just to think

Bacchus and his pards: god of wine and revelry, whose chariot was drawn by leopards

viewless: invisible

Poesy: poetry

tender is the night: This is the source of the title of one of F. Scott Fitzgerald's novels. Fitzgerald said that he learned to write prose by reading Keats's poetry, with its emphasis on verbs and concreteness. Early in Fitzgerald's *The Great Gatsby*, a Keatsian nightingale makes a surprise appearance on Long Island. A distraught Daisy says, "I looked outdoors for a minute, and it's very romantic outdoors. There's a bird on the lawn that I think must be a nightingale come over on the Cunard or White Star Line."

haply: by chance, perhaps

Queen-Moon: the virgin goddess (Greek Artemis or Roman Diana) associated with the moon

Fays: fairies

verdurous: green as lush vegetation

embalmed: balmy

each sweet: each plant

eglantine: a hedge shrub, related to honeysuckle

Darkling: in darkness. This rare word reappears in Arnold's "Dover Beach" and Hardy's "The Darkling Thrush."

mused: pondered or murmured

abroad: away

ecstasy: the same word or related forms appear in Hopkins's "The Windhover" and Hardy's "The Darkling Thrush"

high requiem: dirge, funeral music

clown: a rustic peasant

Ruth: A noble Moabite widow who accompanied her mother-in-law Naomi who returned to her native Judah, which was alien to Ruth. The idea that she was homesick is Keats's contribution to the story. Once in Judah, Ruth married Boaz, and they became parents of Obed, eventually the grandfather of David.

corn: any grain; here, probably barley

casements: windows

perilous seas: possibly the inspiration for "desperate seas" in Poe's "To Helen"

faery: an enchanted world, like that in Edmund Spenser's *The Faerie Queene*.

fancy: imagination

cheat: deceive

plaintive: mournful

ELIZABETH BARRETT BROWNING, *"How Do I Love Thee? Let Me Count the Ways"* (page 154)

feeling out of sight: passing beyond the range of physical experience

to the level: up to the limit

passion: suffering as well as strong feeling

The repetitions of "I love thee" are an example of anaphora.

EDGAR ALLAN POE, *"To Helen"* (page 156)

Helen: a woman of superlative beauty and power. The most famous Helen
was one of the children born from the union described in Yeats's "Leda
and the Swan." Although married to King Menelaus of Sparta, she was
given to Paris, youngest son of King Priam of Troy, whereupon began the
decades of bitter conflict known as the Trojan War.

Nicéan: Related to one of several places named Nicaea or Nicea, such as Iznik
in Turkey (ancient Nicea), Nikaia in Greece, and Nice in France. All derive
their names from "Nike," Greek for victory in general and the famous
winged goddess in particular. Nicean barks accordingly could be sailing
ships bringing tired and wandering warriors home after a victory. Nicean
may also echo Nyseian (Milton, *Paradise Lost*, book 4, line 275), referring
to the island of Nysa, one home of the wanderer Bacchus.

wanderer: no specific identity has been established: possibly Bacchus, as
above; or Ulysses (arriving home in Ithaca after decades away, soon to
leave again in the episode described in Tennyson's "Ulysses"); or Menelaus,
Helen's first husband

bore: carried, transported

desperate seas: echoing the "perilous seas" in Keats's "Ode to a Nightingale"

long wont: accustomed for a long time

hyacinth: The name of various gemstones and flowers, both of which could
relate to hair. The color of the stone is given as golden or (in heraldry)
tawny, in which case the hair would be red or reddish gold. Homer's
Odyssey uses "hyacinthine" for hair whereof the color seems to mix silver
and gold. But also perhaps "in many close curls," like the flower-clusters of
the hyacinth. Milton applies Homer's descriptive word to Adam's hair:
"Hyacinthine Locks / Round from his parted forelock manly hung /
Clust'ring" (*Paradise Lost*, book 4, lines 301–3, not far from the reference to
Nysa noted above).

Naiad airs: manners like those of a naiad, a nymph associated with fresh water

glory: these famous lines live on, somewhat varied, in the introduction of the
popular song "I Left My Heart in San Francisco": "The loveliness of Paris
seems somehow sadly gay; / The glory that was Rome was of another day."

window-niche: a recessed opening in a wall

agate: translucent stone of many colors

Psyche: Greek for "soul." In Greek myth, Psyche was the beloved of Eros
(Cupid).

Holy Land: strictly, places associated with the Bible, especially West Palestine
and Judea; broadly, any sacred place to which pilgrimages are made. In
one sense, the poem here returns to its phonemic home, since "Holy

Land" (*h-l-l-nd*) has almost the same pattern of consonants as "Helen" (*h-l-n*), an effect to which Poe would have been alert.

EDGAR ALLAN POE, *"Annabel Lee"* (page 158)

Coveted: envied
bore: carried
sepulchre: tomb
dissever: separate
night-tide: night time

ALFRED, LORD TENNYSON, *"Break, Break, Break"* (page 162)

I would: I wish
haven: harbors are often sheltered by surrounding hills. "Under" here means "down from," not "underneath."

ALFRED, LORD TENNYSON, *"The Eagle"* (page 164)

crag: steep mass of rock, projecting from a cliff
azure: intense blue, especially of the tropical sky
falls: the eagle, which is a predator and scavenger, looks for food from a great height and then flies down

ALFRED, LORD TENNYSON, *"Ulysses"* (page 165)

mete and dole: measure and hand out
lees: sediment of wine
Hyades: a group of stars the springtime rising of which was thought to foretell rain (the name has been fancifully associated with the Greek for rain or water—as in "hydrant"—but probably is more akin to "hyena" and means "piglets"; the rare word "hyetal" does mean "rainy")
cities of men / And manners: echoes the beginning of Homer's *Odyssey*
I am a part: echoes another restless traveler: "I live not in myself, but I become / Portion of that around me" (Byron, *Childe Harold's Pilgrimage*, III, lxxii)
margin: horizon
scepter: a staff held by a ruler, emblem of sovereignty
offices: works, jobs
Meet: appropriate
wrought: worked, created
that strove with Gods: gods and goddesses took part in the Trojan War

the slow moon climbs: the full moon rises at sunset (as in Arnold's "Dover Beach" and Sidney's "With How Sad Steps, O Moon, Thou Climb'st the Skies"). When the moon is full, high tides are at their highest, normally the best time for getting a sailing ship underway.

the Happy Isles: dwelling place of dead heroes

Achilles: most powerful of the Greek warrior-kings, killed at the end of the Trojan War (by an arrow in the heel, near the Achilles tendon). In Homer's *Odyssey*, book XI, Odysseus travels to the abode of the dead in search of prophecy, and he meets Achilles there.

ROBERT BROWNING, *"My Last Duchess"* (page 170)

My . . . me: These first and last words of the poem clearly indicate the scope of the duke's sympathies.

Fra Pandolph: Not a historical figure. "Frà" is an abbreviation of Italian *frate*, "brother," used as the title of a monk or friar, in this case a court painter or painter employed by the court.

durst: archaic past tense of "dare"

Her mantle: Frà Pandolph very politely uses the third person with a woman of rank, instead of "Your." A mantle is a loose sleeveless cloak, associated with authority and rank.

laps: folds, falls, overlaps

favor: a gift, probably a piece of jewelry or a flower

officious: meaning "carrying out an office," but with various overtones and connotations. Earlier, the word could just mean "obliging" or "kind," but those meanings have now given way to senses of unduly aggressive or intrusive carrying out of official duties.

lessoned: taught, schooled, lectured to

nor plainly set: and not put

forsooth: indeed

This grew; I gave commands: a vague passage about the worsening situation. The commands are unspecified, and some have imagined that the last duchess was removed from the court but not from mortal life. That now impresses most readers as naive.

munificence: generosity

ample warrant: sufficient guarantee, assurance

pretense: simply a claim, not necessarily false (a pretender to a throne may be a just claimant)

dowry: money given by a bride or her family to a prospective husband

Neptune: Roman sea god, here represented in a posture of domination that the duke regards as aesthetically pleasing

Claus of Innsbruck: another imaginary artist. Innsbruck is in the Tyrol region of what is now Austria. There were counts of Tyrol, and the duke may be pointing out that he is not only a patron and connoisseur of fine sculpture but also a friend of the count's home region.

ROBERT BROWNING, *"Meeting at Night"* (page 174)

half-moon large and low: this would occur around midnight
gain: reach
cove: small bay
prow: projecting front part of a boat
thro': through (here meaning "because of")

ROBERT BROWNING, *"Home-Thoughts, from Abroad"* (page 176)

brushwood sheaf: bundle of cut or broken twigs
bole: trunk
chaffinch: a finch
whitethroat: a warbler
spray's edge: edge of small twigs or shoots
hoary: white as though from age
dower: a gift from nature

ARTHUR HUGH CLOUGH, *"The Latest Decalogue"* (page 179)

Decalogue: the Ten Commandments (Exodus 20). The commandments, briefly, are these: 1. Thou shalt have no other god before me. 2. Thou shalt not make unto thee any graven image. 3. Thou shalt not take the name of the Lord thy God in vain. 4. Remember the Sabbath day, to keep it holy. 5. Honor thy father and thy mother. 6. Thou shalt not kill. 7. Thou shalt not commit adultery. 8. Thou shalt not steal. 9. Thou shalt not bear false witness. 10. Thou shalt not covet that which belongs to thy neighbor.
for, for: because despite your curse
Officiously: busily, with a show of activity
adultery: usually understood as voluntary sexual intercourse between a married person and someone other than the spouse
lucrative: profitable
bear false witness: tell a lie
let the lie: that is, do not *bear* false witness in the sense of carrying it: let it carry itself
covet: desire what belongs to another
competition: the cut-throat competition of capitalism
love thy neighbor: Leviticus 19:18 and Matthew 5:43

JULIA WARD HOWE, *"The Battle Hymn of the Republic"* (page 182)

Mine eyes: "mine" instead of "my" before a vowel, like "an" instead of "a," is an archaic practice much used in the Bible, as in Psalm 121: "I will lift up mine eyes unto the hills, from whence cometh my help."

glory of the Lord: in many places in the Bible: Exodus 16:7, Isaiah 35:2, Ezekiel 10:4, Luke 2:9

trampling out the vintage: images probably derived from Isaiah 63:3: "I have trodden the winepress alone; and of the people there was none with me: for I will tread them in mine anger, and trample them in my fury; and their blood shall be sprinkled upon my garments, and I will stain all my raiment."

terrible: inspiring terror

writ: written

burnished: polished

contemners: scorners, condemners (as in Psalms 10:3 and 107:11)

crush the serpent: in Genesis 3:15, God says to the tempting serpent: "And I will put enmity between thee and the woman, and between thy seed and her seed; it shall bruise thy head, and thou shalt bruise his heel."

retreat: a bugle or trumpet passage signaling a force to retreat

MATTHEW ARNOLD, *"Dover Beach"* (page 185)

The tide is full, the moon lies fair: High tide and low tide occur twice each day through about a six-hour cycle. Since tides are caused by the gravitational attraction of the sun and moon, the greatest influence comes when sun and moon are in line, as they are when the moon is full. The full moon rises at sunset and sets at sunrise. A hurricane that hits a coast at high tide with a full moon is called a "triple whammy," with trouble from (1) the storm itself, (2) the high tide bringing water in, and (3) the full moon drawing the tide to its greatest height.

tremulous: quivering

cadence: both "rhythm" and "a falling sound"

Sophocles: fifth-century B.C. Greek tragedian

Aegean: sea between Greece and Turkey; also the nearest major body of water to Athens. It does not have tides.

turbid: confused, obscure

girdle: a sash, belt, or cord (not a corset)

drear: dreary

shingles: loose pebbles worn smooth by water

darkling: in the dark or becoming dark. The same powerful word occurs in Hardy's "The Darkling Thrush" and Keats's "Ode to a Nightingale."

ignorant armies: not specific, but maybe an allusion to European armies in the disturbances of the late 1840s and later; also maybe a night battle described by the Greek historian Thucydides (*History of the Peloponnesian War*, Book VII).

EMILY DICKINSON, *"Because I Could Not Stop for Death"* (page 188)

The Carriage: a hearse but also a more otherworldly vehicle
no haste: funerals move slowly
For his civility: in exchange for
in the Ring: could apply to boxing, wrestling, or marbles
Gazing Grain: a most original way of seeing a field of grain as something with a gaze
The Dews drew: became
Gossamer: thin, filmy fabric
Tippet—only Tulle: the hanging part of a hood or cape, made of fine silk netting
Cornice: a part of the top of a building
Ground . . . Ground: instead of rhyming "ground" with a word like "mound," the poet repeats "ground," as though to stress the monotony of the experience

EMILY DICKINSON, *"I Heard a Fly Buzz—When I Died"* (page 190)

when I died: the same words appear in Jarrell's "The Death of the Ball Turret Gunner," another American poem supposedly spoken by one already dead
wrung them dry: that is, wept themselves dry
the King: primarily death, secondarily God
keepsakes: mementos, small personal treasures
interposed: that is, the fly put itself between the speaker and the light. Note the striking formality of word choice, like the appearance of "liquefaction" in Herrick's "Upon Julia's Clothes" or "diurnal" in Wordsworth's "She Dwelt Among the Untrodden Ways."
failed: faded from sight

EMILY DICKINSON, *"A Narrow Fellow in the Grass"* (page 191)

rides: moves smoothly
notice: look, the way he looks at you
transport: strong emotion (which includes "motion," as when we say we are moved or carried away by an experience)
cordiality: warm friendship
Zero: extreme cold

LEWIS CARROLL, *"Jabberwocky"* (page 194)

These are some of Humpty Dumpty's explanations:

brillig: four o'clock in the afternoon—the time when you begin *broiling* things for dinner

slithy: slimy + lithe

toves: something like badgers . . . something like corkscrews

gyre and gimble: to go round and round like a gyroscope and to make holes like a gimlet

wabe: the grass plot around a sundial

mimsy: flimsy + miserable

borogrove: a thin shabby-looking bird with its feathers sticking out all round—something like a live mop

mome: possibly from home

rath: a sort of green pig (note that "rathe" means "early or premature"—now only in the comparative "rather"; also sounds like "wraith")

outgrabe: something between whistle and bellow (with overtones from German *Grabe*, grave, so that homeless wraiths outgrave)

THOMAS HARDY, *"The Darkling Thrush"* (page 198)

Darkling: in the dark; also used in Keats's "Ode to a Nightingale" and Arnold's "Dover Beach"

coppice: copse: a stand of hardwood trees that are cut off close to the ground to cause new growth from the stumps, fenced and gated to keep cattle out. Typically, a copse is a place of tangled vegetation favored by certain song-birds.

specter: ghost

dregs: residue, usually bitter: the least desirable part

eye of day: the sun, obscured by clouds and mists; phrase also used in Milton's first sonnet ("O Nightingale")

bine-stems: woodbine stems, rather like honeysuckle

lyre: musical instrument like a small harp

haunted nigh: lived nearby

germ: the cause of germination, growth, new life

fervorless: lacking emotion

evensong: evening song; specifically vespers. Also an afternoon or evening service in the Anglican church.

illimited: unlimited, unrestrained (a typical usage for Hardy, who was fond of coining new words or reviving old or dialect forms)

terrestrial: earthly

good-night air: a melody ("air" as in "aria")

Gerard Manley Hopkins, *"Pied Beauty"* (page 201)

Pied: originally black and white (like a magpie); later any combination of different colors

brinded: variant of "brindled," meaning "tawny with streaks and spots." Considering that this poem is titled "Pied Beauty," it is amusing that there is a European geometrid moth called "Brindled Beauty."

stipple: painting or drawing that uses dots, spots, and flecks instead of lines

chestnut-falls: fallen chestnuts, sometimes a bright orange

fold: an enclosure for livestock

fallow: left uncultivated after being ploughed and harrowed; also (an entirely different word but maybe relevant) of a reddish-yellow color—the summer coat of the fallow deer is dappled

plough: There are three sorts of rural land pieced together in this picture: folds for livestock, fallow land which has not been planted, and plough-land which has been planted.

gear and tackle and trim: All three words mean "equipment" in various senses.

counter: contrary, opposite

spare: with many senses: here probably "thin," "left over," and "kept in reserve."

adazzle: dazzling

Gerard Manley Hopkins, *"Spring and Fall"* (page 203)

Goldengrove: a grove of hardwood trees yellow with autumn. Apparently not related to the place in Wales called Golden Grove.

unleaving: losing leaves (also not leaving)

nor spare: and not spare

worlds of wanwood leafmeal lie: the coinage "wanwood" suggests a pale or stricken forest; "leafmeal" suggests both leaf by leaf (as with "piecemeal") and the mealy substance into which dry leaves are ground underfoot

ghost: one's own inner spirit (as in the interchangeable use of Holy Ghost and Holy Spirit)

Gerard Manley Hopkins, *"The Windhover"* (page 204)

windhover: local name for the small falcon usually called kestrel. A bird in flight presents a distinctly cross-shaped appearance that would be meaningful for a symbol-minded Catholic priest.

minion: favorite

dauphin: son of a king; title of the eldest son of the king of France from the Middle Ages until 1830 *dapple-dawn-drawn:* the dappled dawn (an effect also praised in Hopkins's "Pied Beauty") here has drawn the bird; "drawn" means both "pulled" and "outlined"

wimpling: bending, like the graceful wimples that are part of the habits of certain nuns

ecstasy: literally, movement in space (opposite of stasis)

Buckle: come together and fall apart; the verb is both indicative and imperative: it describes what the beauty, valor, and so forth are doing and simultaneously tells them to do it.

from thee: that is, from Christ, the speaker's chevalier, or knight in shining armor

billion: British usage in Hopkins's day gave this word the meaning "a million million": ten to the twelfth power. Modern American usage defines "billion" as "a thousand million" (ten to the ninth).

dangerous: the word is derived from Latin *dominus,* "master"

chevalier: a knightly rider; the word is related to "cavalier" and in British pronunciation ends like "cavalier," so that it rhymes with "sheer" and "dear."

sillion: ridge between furrows, worn smooth by plodding feet

Fall, gall . . . gash: The images and colors here suggest both the Crucifixion and the Eucharist.

WILLIAM BUTLER YEATS, *"The Second Coming"* (page 207)

gyre: a spiral, like the shape of a trained falcon's flight as it follows the directions of a falconer but then gets too far away to be controlled

anarchy: absence of government, as happened in many places after the First World War

blood-dimmed tide: an image of war as a great flood

Spiritus Mundi: spirit of the world: as though the phrase conjures up images from a storehouse in our collective unconscious, source of many myths, dreams, and visions

twenty centuries: that is, the time since the death of Christ

Bethlehem: Christ's birthplace, still a small town on the West Bank of the Jordan, south of Jerusalem

WILLIAM BUTLER YEATS, *"The Lake Isle of Innisfree"* (page 209)

Innisfree: sometimes pronounced Innishfree (as in the movie *The Quiet Man*); literally "Heather Island"

wattles: simple building materials made of twigs, sticks, and branches interlaced somewhat like wicker

midnight's all a glimmer, and noon a purple glow: the usual operation of day and night seems arrested, so that midnight is not so dark and noon is not so bright. The effect of glimmering midnight resembles the midnight sun in the northern latitudes during the summer. Innisfree lies at about 54° north latitude.

linnet: a small songbird. Wordsworth wrote a poem called "The Green Linnet" that marks the bird's joy of voice and pinion and like Yeats's poem includes glimmerings.

lapping: "moving with a splashing sound"; also "enfolding, caressing"

WILLIAM BUTLER YEATS, *"Leda and the Swan"* (page 210)

The broken wall: details from the destruction of Troy by the invading Greeks. Troy's steep walls and tall towers were legendary. This passage repeats, detail for detail, material from Marlowe's *Doctor Faustus*, which also asks a question concerning Helen: "Was this the face that launched a thousand ships / And burnt the topless towers of Ilium?"

Agamemnon: brother of Helen's husband Menelaus and husband of Clytemnestra. When he got home to Mycenae after the Trojan War ended, he was murdered by his wife.

indifferent: having no care for

WILLIAM BUTLER YEATS, *"Sailing to Byzantium"* (page 212)

Byzantium: founded in 660 B.C., called Byzantium until A.D. 330, when its name became Constantinople; thus until 1930, when its name became Istanbul. Now the largest city in Turkey.

paltry: unimportant

tattered coat: like that of a scarecrow (there is a scarecrow image also in Yeats's "Among School Children")

but studying: that is, studying is the only singing school

sages: wise men

gold mosaic: The Byzantine style of mosaic work, unlike the Italian, uses gold leaf as well as marble. The figures in such mosaics are often icons: stylized images of saints and other religious persons.

perne in a gyre: a favorite pattern in Yeats: spin or whirl in a spiral shape

artifice of eternity: an obscure phrase, since the idea of the artificial calls for human work to create a mortal object, whereas eternity is beyond mortality; the phrase could mean something artificial—such as a mosaic design—devoted to the eternal

Emperor: Yeats wrote, "I have read somewhere that in the Emperor's palace at Byzantium was a tree made of gold and silver, and artificial birds that sang."

ERNEST DOWSON, *"Non Sum Qualis Eram Bonae Sub Regno Cynarae"* (page 214)

yesternight: last night

betwixt: between

desolate: deeply sad and lonely

thy shadow . . . thy breath: that is, the memory of Cynara

bought: she is a prostitute

roses . . . lilies: A. C. Swinburne's "Dolores" (1866) contrasts "the lilies and languors of virtue" with "the raptures and roses of vice"

madder: less inhibited

EDWIN ARLINGTON ROBINSON, *"Miniver Cheevy"* (page 218)

Miniver Cheevy: Both names are suggestive. "Miniver" is the name of a fur, and the first element is related to "menu" and "miniature." Such fur also has significance in heraldry and royal costume. "Cheevy" combines hints of "cheap," "cheesy," and "peevish."

assailed: assaulted, attacked in word or deed

Albeit: elegant substitute for "although"

rested from his labors: a biblical-sounding way of hinting that Miniver Cheevy gave up working and started loafing

Thebes: Two cities so named were celebrated in antiquity, one in Upper Egypt and one in Greece northwest of Athens.

Camelot: legendary home of King Arthur

Priam's neighbors: Priam was the king of Troy at the time of the Trojan war.

Medici: illustrious Italian family that flourished in Florence and elsewhere in the fourteenth and fifteenth centuries; included three popes and two queens of France

khaki: light dust-colored fabric used for military uniforms, at first in warm climates in Asia and Africa. The word has been in use only since the nineteenth century.

iron clothing: armor

EDWIN ARLINGTON ROBINSON, *"Mr. Flood's Party"* (page 220)

Eben: A Hebrew name from a word meaning "stone." Possibly a shortened form of "Ebenezer," which means "stone of the help": a monument set up to honor God in the Old Testament. Also recalls Ebenezer Scrooge in Dickens's *A Christmas Carol*, another lonely old man.

hermitage: originally, where a hermit or monk lives. Here the word means an isolated dwelling.

harvest moon: the full moon nearest the autumnal equinox in September, typically on a night between September 7 and October 4. Like any full moon, it would rise at sunset and be overhead at midnight.

the poet says: Stanza 7 of Edward FitzGerald's version of "The Rubáiyát of Omar Khayyám of Naishápúr," also a poem about drinking:

> Come, fill the Cup, and in the fire of Spring
> Your winter garment of Repentance fling:
> The Bird of Time has but a little way
> To flutter—and the Bird is on the Wing.

Roland's ghost: Charlemagne's noblest knight guarded the pass at Roncevaux, refusing to blow his horn for help until it was too late.

acquiescent quaver: a tremor that sounds resigned, giving in to fate

auld lang syne: refrain of Robert Burns's famous drinking song "Auld Lang Syne," traditionally sung on New Year's Eve. The days of auld lang syne are those of old long since; that is, one drinks a cup of kindness to the old days.

two moons: This condition is called the "multiplying eye" in Thomas Hardy's novel *Far from the Madding Crowd*.

WALTER DE LA MARE, *"The Listeners"* (page 225)

turret: a small tower on top of another structure
smote upon: struck
That goes down to the empty hall: The present tense here is odd, suggesting that the house still exists.
Hearkening: listening, paying careful attention
cropping: eating, biting off the top part of grass
spake: archaic or biblical form of "spoke"
iron on stone: that is, iron horseshoes on stone pavement or cobbles

ROBERT FROST, *"Mending Wall"* (page 230)

Something there is that doesn't love a wall: among such things is frost: the poet liked to make jokes on his own name
offense: with a pun on a "fence"
old-stone: the Old Stone Age or Paleolithic Age that ended about 15,000 years ago, a time of stone tools and weapons.

T. S. ELIOT, *"The Love Song of J. Alfred Prufrock"* (page 233)

Prufrock: There were people named Prufrock living in Eliot's native St. Louis until just a few years ago. The name may be related to German *Prüfstein,* "touchstone" (and there is a clown named Touchstone in Shakespeare's *As You Like It*). In Eliot's boyhood, Prufrock's was a major furniture store in St. Louis.

S'io credessi: These words, from Dante, *Inferno*, canto XXVII (far down in hell), are spoken by the deceptive Guido da Montefeltro: "If I could believe that my response were being made to a person who might return to the world above, this flame would be still without further movement; but, since no one has ever gone back alive from this depth—if I hear the truth—I shall respond to you without fear of infamy." Since he is responding to a question from Dante, who is here reporting his words, Montefeltro is mistaken in thinking that no one will find out about his deceptions. Prufrock may be speaking with the same notion of protection, which would apply only to confessions made to oneself.

etherised: anesthetized

table: operating table

retreats: places of shelter and refuge

Streets that follow: like the charter'd streets in Blake's London, these streets are laid out like a tiresome logical case (argument)

insidious intent: meant to be threatening or harmful; "insidious" means treacherous.

Michelangelo: Michelangelo Buonarroti (1475–1564), known by his first name as a sign of respect (as is the case with Dante, Raphael, Leonardo, and Galileo), one of the greatest of Renaissance Italian artists. He was a poet and architect but is best known for painting and sculpture, particularly representing powerful heroic figures such as Moses and David, utterly unlike Prufrock.

The yellow fog: This sustained comparison of fog to a cat is the first appearance of cat images that turn up in many of Eliot's writings, where we find tigers, jaguars, and leopards as well as so-called practical cats that have generated a billion dollars' worth of posthumous success in the musical theater.

works and days: the title of Hesiod's poetic description (eighth century B.C.) of rural life in ancient Greece. Ironically, Eliot is referring to urban leisure.

time for you: Chapter 3 of Ecclesiastes begins, "To every thing there is a season, and a time to every purpose under heaven." The meaning of time was to absorb Eliot's attention for the rest of his career. "Burnt Norton" (1935), first of Eliot's *Four Quartets*, begins "Time present and time past / Are both perhaps present in time future."

the taking of a toast and tea: Maybe just teatime with slices of toast, but possibly the taking of toast softened in tea (a dish for invalids), like a similar preparation called toast-and-water. This unchallenging dish also resembles

an American preparation known as milktoast, which was so closely associ-
ated with the sickroom that H. T. Webster in 1924 invented a comic strip
called "The Timid Soul" about a very Prufrock-like character named Caspar
Milquetoast.

morning coat: a tailed coat, of solid dark color, worn with striped trousers,
associated with diplomats, undertakers, and bridegrooms

dying fall: a musical term for a phrase that ends with a faintly falling note; also
at the beginning of Shakespeare's *Twelfth Night*: "That strain again! It had
a dying fall."

pinned and wriggling: like a beetle or butterfly made into a specimen

ragged claws: a crab or other such undersea creature, mostly scavengers

malingers: pretends to be ill

ices: water-ices: the confection now known as sorbet

upon a platter: like the head of John the Baptist (Matthew 14, Mark 6); also in
Oscar Wilde's play *Salome* (1893), which Richard Strauss had made into an
opera in 1905, not long before Eliot began writing "The Love Song of J.
Alfred Prufrock"

Footman: a lower servant

some talk of you and me: the line "Some little Talk awhile of ME and THEE" is
in stanza XXXII of Edward FitzGerald's version of "The Rubáiyát of Omar
Khayyám of Naishápúr"

into a ball: See also Marvell's "To His Coy Mistress": "Let us roll all our
strength and all / Our sweetness up into one ball."

Lazarus: The raising of Lazarus from the dead is related in John, 11:1–44. Also
the subject of Robert Browning's "An Epistle Containing the Strange
Medical Experience of Karshish, the Arab Physician."

dooryards: American term for yards or gardens in front of a house

sprinkled streets: unpaved streets were sprinkled to keep down the dust

magic lantern: a contrivance like the modern slide projector. Again,
FitzGerald's "Rubáiyát" is relevant:

> We are no other than a moving row
> Of Magic Shadow-shapes that come and go
> Round with this Sun-illumined Lantern held
> In Midnight by the Master of the Show . . . (LXVIII)

Prince Hamlet: heroic but indecisive tragic character. Prufrock likens himself
to a minor character, like those presented in Tom Stoppard's *Rosencrantz
and Guildenstern Are Dead.*

to swell a progress: to enlarge a procession

Deferential: giving way to others

Politic: diplomatic

meticulous: careful about details

Full of high sentence: lofty sentiments. This part of Prufrock's character sounds like Polonius in *Hamlet*, but the phrase "ful of hy sentence" comes from Chaucer's sketch of the Clerk of Oxenford in *The Canterbury Tales* ("General Prologue," line 306)

obtuse: thick-headed, slow-witted

the Fool: the clown, jester

Shall I part my hair behind?: If he is balding, he may be tempted to part his hair horizontally near his neckline and bring it forward to cover his bald spot.

a peach: peaches were thought to be stimulating

mermaids singing: as in Donne's "Go and Catch a Falling Star"; these may also be young women at a beach

Till human voices wake us and we drown: We have been in a dream state and when we wake we will drown in reality.

WILFRED OWEN, *"Strange Meeting"* (page 240)

Strange Meeting: The phrase also occurs in Shelley's *The Revolt of Islam*.

profound: deep

titanic: gigantic; a reference to a race of mythological giants called Titans and here probably also a reminder of the vanity of the luxury ship named *Titanic*, which sank in 1912

encumbered: burdened

Too fast: too much confined, fixed, as in stuck fast

fixed: immobile

flues: ducts, chimneys

glee: both extreme delight and a musical entertainment (a gleeman was a minstrel)

truths that lie too deep: Wordsworth's "Ode: Intimations of Immortality from Recollections of Early Childhood" ends with the line "Thoughts that do often lie too deep for tears"

taint: corruption

cess: as part of words like "cesspit" and "cesspool," the word means "sewage." Another word, maybe derived from "success," occurs in the phrase "bad cess," meaning "bad luck."

parried: tried to ward off the attack

loath: unwilling

W. H. AUDEN, *"Musée des Beaux Arts"* (page 243)

Musée des Beaux Arts: Museum of Fine Arts. One section of the Musées Royaux des Beaux Arts in Brussels, Belgium, houses many paintings by

Brueghel.

Old Masters: Either painters or paintings from the distinguished period in
European art from about 1400 to 1700.

Anyhow: at random

Brueghel: Pieter Brueghel the Elder, about 1525–1569. Two versions of the
painting survive.

Icarus: The brilliant inventor Daedalus made wings for himself and his son
Icarus to escape prison on the island of Crete. Icarus, against his father's
advice, flew too high, and the sun's heat melted the wax that held the
wings together. He fell into the sea and perished. In ancient times the
southern part of the Aegean Sea was called the Icarian Sea, and there is an
island in that region called Ikaria or Icaria. Icarus is also the name of an
asteroid with an eccentric orbit that sometimes brings it within 20 million
miles of the sun.

shone / on: These words rhyme in certain British dialects.

THEODORE ROETHKE, *"My Papa's Waltz"* (page 246)

countenance: face

RANDALL JARRELL, *"The Death of the Ball Turret Gunner"*
(page 249)

the State: the national state to which citizens belong, but also the mortal
human condition into which we fall at birth

fur: his outfit would have had fur lining and trim for high-altitude flight

flak: explosive anti-aircraft shells fired from guns on the ground; a German
abbreviation (from *Fliegerabwehrkanone,* flyer-defense-gun) imported into
English during World War II

fighters: aircraft designed to attack and pursue other aircraft: fighters are
smaller, lighter, faster, and more maneuverable than bombers. Jarrell noted
that such fighters were armed with cannon firing explosive shells.

hose: according to Jarrell, a steam hose

DYLAN THOMAS, *"Do Not Go Gentle into That Good Night"* (page 251)

good night: both the conventional good night (as in "The Darkling Thrush")
and the unconventional good night of death

the last wave by: that is, the last wave having gone by

green bay: Although this is the bay that means body of water, which could nat-
urally be green, some readers may hear an echo of the green bay tree in
Psalms 37:35: "I have seen the wicked in great power, and spreading him-

self like a green bay tree."

Grave men: The adjective grave that means serious comes from the Latin *gravis,* "heavy"; the noun "grave" that means place of burial comes from German *graben,* "dig." Both words, however different their derivations, are involved here.

Curse, bless: a paradox typical of extreme situations, in which opposites like day and night, love and hate, cursing and blessing, become confused.

DYLAN THOMAS, *"Fern Hill"* (page 252)

easy: at ease
dingle: a hollow between hills
heydays: times of full flourishing, here also with a pun on hay
windfall: literally a fruit that has fallen because of wind, without human labor; figuratively, a piece of luck, something you don't have to work for. The word here keeps up the apple imagery.
horn air: maybe a hunting horn
air: the element of air, but also "air" as a song (*aria*)
nightjars: a nocturnal bird; also called "fern-owl"
ricks: a haystack, sometimes with a thatched top
Adam and maiden: that is, the situation was the Garden of Eden all over again
birth of the simple light: when God said, "Let there be light"
morning songs: with the common English pun on "mourning"
like the sea: the sea, although constrained (chained), continues to move and sing

DYLAN THOMAS, *"A Refusal to Mourn the Death, by Fire, of a Child in London"* (page 255)

Bird beast and flower: D. H. Lawrence published a book of poems called *Birds, Beasts and Flowers* in 1923.
still hour: paradoxically, a time of time standing still; "still" also means without life
is come: biblical-sounding variation of "has come." Chapter 60 of Isaiah begins: "Arise, shine; for thy light is come, and the glory of the Lord is risen upon thee."
sea tumbling in harness: one of many apocalyptic images like those in Donne's "At the Round Earth's Imagined Corners." Chapter 21 of Revelation begins: "And I saw a new heaven and a new earth: for the first heaven and the first earth were passed away; and there was no more sea."
Zion: a sacred city. The water bead symbolizes the water cycle (evaporation and condensation) that is symbolic of other cycles, like those of the day

and the year and a life.

synagogue: place of worship

corn: not necessarily maize but any cereal grain; in England probably wheat

salt seed: tears, with also a suggestion of semen

sackcloth: rough cloth used for making sacks (like burlap) and garments suitable for mourning. The phrase "sackcloth and ashes" occurs more than once in the Bible (Esther 4:1, Daniel 9:3, Matthew 11:21). Revelation 6:12 is relevant: "And I beheld when he had opened the sixth seal, and, lo, there was a great earthquake; and the sun became black as sackcloth of hair, and the moon became as blood."

stations: stopping places in general but also the Stations of the Cross

dark veins: literal blood vessels of the mother but also the dark veins of coal under the earth, particularly in Wales

After the first death: Hardy's "In Tenebris: I" includes the line "Twice no one dies."

GLOSSARY OF TECHNICAL TERMS

Allegory: An allegory is a symbolic story that signifies meaning beyond the surface of actual events. An allegory can be historical, political, or moral. It is similar to fables, parables, and metaphors, though it differs from them in length and intricacy. Gerard Manley Hopkins's "The Windhover" can be read as an allegory of Christ's crucifixion. Robert Frost's "Mending Wall" has been interpreted as an allegory for personal conduct and even for foreign policy.

Allegorical: See *allegory*.

Alliteration: The close repetition of initial consonants in poetry or prose. A powerful example of alliteration can be found in line 9 of Gerard Manley Hopkins's "Pied Beauty": "With swift, slow; sweet, sour; adazzle, dim."

Allusion: Indirect reference to someone or something outside the present text, as in T. S. Eliot's "The Love Song of J. Alfred Prufrock" when the speaker says, "I have heard the mermaids singing," which may be an allusion to John Donne's "Go and Catch a Falling Star."

Anapest: A foot of three syllables, the first two unaccented, the third accented, as in this line from Alfred, Lord Tennyson's "Break, Break, Break": "And the sound of a voice that is still."

Anthropomorphism: When nonhuman things are given human characteristics (from the Greek *anthropos* [man] and *morphos* [form]). When Edmund Waller addresses a rose in "Go, Lovely Rose" as a messenger, he is anthropomorphising it.

Apostrophe: A figure of speech in which a person, a thing, or an abstraction is addressed directly as "you." Sir Philip Sidney's "With How Sad Steps, O Moon" and John Donne's "Death, Be Not Proud" are two among the many examples in these hundred poems.

Assonance: The repetition of vowel sounds, without repetition of consonants. This very common feature of poetry can be heard in Edgar Allan Poe's "To Helen": "The agate lamp within thy hand."

Aubade: A lyric about the morning, particularly about lovers leaving each other in the morning. John Donne's "The Good Morrow" is a variation on the form.

Ballad: In literature, a short, narrative form, usually of four-line stanzas, and usually relating a single, dramatic event in progress. It has changed from an oral form (the folk, traditional, or popular ballad) to a more complex written version. Examples include "Sir Patrick Spens" and John Keats's "La Belle Dame sans Merci."

Ballad measure: Stanzas of four lines, typically rhyming *abcb,* with four feet in the first and third lines, and with three feet in the second and fourth lines. "The Ballad of Sir Patrick Spens" uses ballad measure:

> The king sits in Dunfermline town
> Drinking the blude-red wine;
> "O whare will I get a skeely skipper
> To sail this new ship o' mine?"

Blank verse: Verse characterized by unrhymed lines of iambic pentameter. This flexible form became the standard for Shakespeare and other Elizabethan dramatists. Alfred, Lord Tennyson uses blank verse in his poem "Ulysses":

> It little profits that an idle king
> By this still hearth, among these barren crags,
> Matched with an aged wife, I mete and dole
> Unequal laws unto a savage race
> That hoard, and sleep, and feed, and know not me.

Blason: See blazon.

Blazon: A poem listing the elements of physical attraction. Andrew Marvell's "To His Coy Mistress," Thomas Carew's "Ask Me No More Where Jove Bestows," and Lord Byron's "She Walks in Beauty" are examples of blazons.

Cadence: The term has two meanings: the narrower meaning is that of a "fall" at the end of a sentence or poetic unit; the broader meaning is of a freer method of conveying rhythm than meter, used primarily in free verse. In this sense, cadence emphasizes the stress and balance of poetic phrases, rather than strict patterns of rhyme and rhythm.

Canto: A part of a long poem.

Caricature: In poetry as in drawing, the exaggeration of features of someone or something for effect, generally amusing. The main characters in Edward Arlington Robinson's "Miniver Cheevy" and "Mr. Flood's Party" are caricatures.

Carpe diem: An exhortation to live for the moment. It is a Latin phrase meaning "seize the day" that was first used by Horace. *Carpe diem* was a popular theme with the Cavalier Poets, as in Robert Herrick's "To the Virgins, to Make Much of Time."

Cavalier poets: Poets connected with the court of Charles I (1625–1649), such as Thomas Carew, Richard Lovelace, and Sir John Suckling, who wrote elegant, often witty lyrics. Robert Herrick, a parson, wrote poetry at the same time and of the same sort, and is therefore often considered a Cavalier poet.

Classical (of literature): Pertaining to the literature of ancient Greece and Rome.

Common measure: See *common meter.*

Common meter: A quatrain rhyming *abab* or *abcb,* of which the first and third lines are iambic tetrameters and whose second and fourth lines are iambic trimeters. An example is Emily Dickinson's "Because I Could Not Stop for Death":

> Because I could not stop for Death—
> He kindly stopped for me—
> The Carriage held but just ourselves—
> And Immortality.

Complaint: A lyric that is usually a monologue and, as its name implies, relays the speaker's misery. It can be lighthearted or serious. Alfred, Lord Tennyson's "Break, Break, Break" is an example of a complaint.

Conceit: An ingenious metaphor. It draws together unrelated words and concepts to elucidate a complicated and subtle thought or emotion. It was first developed by Petrarch and spread to sixteenth-century England. Conceits were used by the Metaphysical poets, who drew them from the fields of science, religion, learning, and practical life. Their aim was to startle a reader into an emotional or intellectual revelation on discovering the connection of the metaphor's components. John Donne's conceit of a compass in "A Valediction: Forbidding Mourning" is a famous example. A startling conceit in the modern period was used by T. S. Eliot in "The Love Song of J. Alfred Prufrock":

> When the evening is spread out against the sky
> Like a patient etherised upon a table.

Couplet: Two lines of verse grouped together as a stanza, or because they share a common rhyme scheme or metrical form. The lines of a couplet usually form a complete thought. An example of a couplet is found in Robert Herrick's poem "Delight in Disorder":

> A sweet disorder in the dress
> Kindles in clothes a wantonness.

Curtal sonnet: Gerard Manley Hopkins coined this term for his type of "curtailed" sonnet. It has ten and a half lines, consisting of a sestet rhyming *abcabc,* a quatrain rhyming *dbcd* or *dcbd,* and a half line rhyming *c.* "Pied Beauty" is an example.

Decadent: In literature, a term loosely applied to fin-de-siècle nineteenth-century European artists, originating in France, who believed in art for art's sake—independent of social and moral concerns. They indulged in the most flamboyant, macabre, and morbid expressions of human emotion, emphasized the artist's necessary hostility to middle-class values, and searched for sensual experience. Decadent writers in England included Ernest Dowson, Oscar Wilde, and Aubrey Beardsley.

Dialect: A variety (particularly regional) of a language. The poem "Sir Patrick Spens" is in a Scottish dialect of English.

Dimeter: Line of poetry with two feet, as in the last line of John Keats's "La Belle Dame sans Merci": "And no birds sing."

Dramatic monologue: The speech of a person talking to another person who is silent in a situation that is clearly dramatic. Robert Browning's "My Last Duchess" is a classic example.

Elegy: In English poetry since the sixteenth century, elegies have been reflective poems lamenting the death of someone, in no set metrical form. An elegy can mourn one person, as in Ben Jonson's "On My First Son," or many people, as in Thomas Gray's "Elegy Written in a Country Churchyard."

Elizabethan: Sometimes used for the whole period between 1550 and about 1620, at other times restricted to the years when Queen Elizabeth I was on the throne (1558–1603).

Encomium: Poem that praises God, a lover, or a hero. Edgar Allan Poe's "To Helen" and Lord Byron's "She Walks in Beauty" are examples.

End-stopped line: A line whose literal end coincides with the ending of its sense and grammar, as in the first line of William Butler Yeats's "The Lake Isle of Innisfree": "I will arise and go now and go to Innisfree." Many lines in many of the poems in this collection are end-stopped. "Enjambment" is the opposite of end-stopping lines.

English (or Shakespearean) sonnet: Sonnet with three quatrains rhyming *abab cdcd efef,* followed by a couplet rhyming *gg.* William Shakespeare's "When to the Sessions of Sweet Silent Thought" is an example.

Enjambment: The flow of sense, as in ordinary prose, between the end of one line of poetry and the beginning of the next. The second and third of the following lines from Robert Browning's "My Last Duchess" illustrate enjambment:

> That's my last duchess painted on the wall,
> Looking as if she were alive. I call
> That piece a wonder now: Fra Pandolf's hands
> Worked busily a day, and there she stands.

Enlightenment: The Enlightenment was an eighteenth-century movement that applied reason to philosophical matters and sought to find and establish a logical basis for human conduct and government.

Epic: A long, narrative poem that focuses on a large, serious subject and depicts a heroic figure who may embody national, cultural, or religious ideals. The actions of the hero usually determine the fate of his people, history, or eternal human problems. Homer's *Iliad* and *Odyssey,* Virgil's *Aeneid,* and Milton's *Paradise Lost* are epics.

Epigram: A short, profound, and/or witty statement that often has a satiric or paradoxical twist at the end. For example, Oscar Wilde's statement "I can resist everything except temptation" is an epigram. The epigram flourished in the writings of such English poets as John Donne, Robert Herrick, Ben Jonson, Lord Byron, and Samuel Taylor Coleridge. More recent poets who used epigrams include William Butler Yeats and Ezra Pound. William Blake's "Auguries of Innocence" is a poem composed almost entirely of epigrams.

Epitaph: Statement used to commemorate the dead. It is usually short and can sometimes be humorous. Ben Jonson was considered a master of the epitaph. His own epitaph "O rare Ben Jonson" puns on the Latin *orare,* "pray."

Epithalamium: Poem that celebrates a marriage. John Donne, Alfred, Lord Tennyson, Ben Jonson, Robert Herrick, Percy Bysshe Shelley, and W. H. Auden all wrote epithalamiums.

Fable: Story, often about animals, with a moral at the end. An example is Thomas Gray's "Ode on the Death of a Favorite Cat, Drowned in a Tub of Gold Fishes."

Feminine rhyme: Rhyme with one or more unstressed syllables following a stressed rhyming syllable, as at the end of the second and fourth lines of the following stanza from Edward Arlington Robinson's "Miniver Cheevy":

> Miniver Cheevy, child of scorn,
> > Grew lean while he assailed the seasons;
> He wept that he was ever born,
> > And he had reasons.

Folk ballad: Anonymous ballad that has attained currency orally. An example is "Edwin, Edwin."

Foot: In poetry, the unit of meter in a line of verse. In modern English verse, a foot is a pattern of stressed and unstressed syllables, with the lamb (unstressed followed by stressed, as in "about") being by far the most common. The following is a division of the first line of Thomas Gray's "Elegy Written in a Country Churchyard" into five feet:

> The cur / few tolls / the knell / of par / ting day.

In this case, the feet are iambs, so the poem is written in iambic pentameter.

Free verse: Generally unrhymed verse free from metrical structures.

Genre: In poetry, the form of a poem, in particular relation to its content. In this collection, the term encompasses not only pastoral and lyric, which are conventional genres, but also apostrophe, dramatic monologue, nocturne, and so on. In contrast, "metrical form" is the term used in this collection for such forms as sonnet, ballad, and villanelle.

Headless line: A line starting with a stress, when an unstressed syllable was expected. An example is the first line of William Blake's "The Tyger": "Tyger! Tyger! burning bright."

Heptameter: Poetic line of seven feet. An example is the last line of Randall

Jarrell's "The Death of the Ball Turret Gunner": "When I died they washed me out of the turret with a hose."

Heroic couplet: Two rhymed lines in iambic pentameter. Robert Browning uses heroic couplets throughout "My Last Duchess," and the English sonnet ends with a heroic couplet:

> If this be error and upon me proved,
> I never writ, nor no man ever loved.

Heroic quatrain: Quatrain of iambic pentameters, rhyming *abab*. Thomas Gray's "Elegy Written in a Country Churchyard" employs the form:

> The curfew tolls the knell of parting day,
> The lowing herd wind slowly o'er the lea,
> The plowman homeward plods his weary way,
> And leaves the world to darkness and to me.

Hexameter: Poetic line of six feet, as in the last lines of the stanzas in John Donne's "The Good Morrow:" "Love so alike, that none can slacken, none can die."

Hymn: Poem of praise, but especially a religious poem of praise. Most hymns are written to be sung by a chorus. A stirring example is Julia Ward Howe's "Battle Hymn of the Republic."

Hyperbole: Exceptional exaggeration for comic or dramatic effect. Andrew Marvell uses hyperbole in "To His Coy Mistress":

> An hundred years should go to praise
> Thine eyes, and on thy forehead gaze,
> Two hundred to adore each breast,
> But thirty thousand to the rest.

Iamb: Metrical unit or foot in which the first syllable is unstressed and the second is stressed. "The sea is calm tonight" in Matthew Arnold's "Dover Beach" consists of three consecutive iambs. The most popular metrical foot in English verse, the iamb is considered the closest to the patterns of ordinary speech.

Iambic Pentameter: Line of poetry with five iambs, a common metrical form in English verse. It is the typical line used in blank verse, heroic couplets, and sonnets. The lines in William Butler Yeats's "Sailing to Byzantium" are iambic pentameters:

> Or set upon a golden bough to sing
> To lords and ladies of Byzantium
> Of what is past, or passing, or to come.

Icon: Image or representation that often has religious connotations.

Image: In poetry, the expression of an idea, object, or action by creating an actual or symbolic sensation. William Blake uses the image of the tiger in his poem "The Tyger" to depict the destructive and creative potential in the world of experience.

Irony: Figure of speech in which what is stated is not what is meant. In the simplest form of irony, the two are opposites. Edwin Arlington Robinson uses irony in a title: "Mr. Flood's Party" (Eben Flood, it turns out, is alone).

Italian (or Petrarchan) sonnet: Strictly, a sonnet with octave rhyming *abbaabba,* followed by a sestet rhyming *cdecde.* There are many modifications of this rhyme scheme, especially in the sestet.

Jacobean: Referring to the reign of King James I, who was on the throne from 1603 to 1625.

Lament: Poem that expresses sorrow in a non-narrative form. Shakespeare's "When to the Sessions of Sweet Silent Thought" and Blake's "London" are examples of laments.

Long measure: Quatrain of iambic tetrameters rhyming *abab* or *abcb.* An example is William Blake's "And Did Those Feet":

> And did those feet in ancient time
> Walk upon England's mountains green?
> And was the holy Lamb of God
> On England's pleasant pastures seen?

Lyric: In ancient Greece, lyric poetry was accompanied by a musical instrument, usually a lyre—hence the name "lyric." Today, "lyric" usually refers to any short poem that expresses a personal emotion. In the Middle Ages, the lyric form was common in Christian hymns and folk songs. In the Renaissance and later, lyric poetry achieved its most finished form in the sonnets of Shakespeare and the short poems of Jonson, Donne, and Herrick. The Romantic poets emphasized the expression of personal emotion and wrote innumerable lyrics. Among the best are those of Wordsworth, Shelley, and Keats.

Masculine rhyme: Rhyme on the last stressed word or syllable of a word, as at the end of the first and third lines of the following stanza from Edward Arlington Robinson's "Miniver Cheevy":

> Miniver Cheevy, child of scorn,
> > Grew lean while he assailed the seasons;
> He wept that he was ever born,
> > And he had reasons.

Metaphor: Figure of speech that substitutes one object for another. Whereas a simile states that A is like B, a metaphor says A is B. William Blake uses a vivid metaphor in "London" when he writes that the sigh of a hapless soldier "runs in blood down palace walls."

Metaphysical poets: Group of English lyric poets of the seventeenth century whose important members included John Donne, George Herbert, Henry Vaughan, Abraham Cowley, Richard Crashaw, and Andrew Marvell.

They were not a school or formal movement, but typically used conceits in their poetry which Samuel Johnson, in *The Lives of the Poets,* described as a kind of "discordia concors" (discordant harmony) in which "the most heterogeneous ideas are yoked by violence together."

The Metaphysical poets achieved a freshness and originality of style by means of wit, irony, and intellectual argument. In the twentieth century, T. S. Eliot renewed interest in the Metaphysical poets.

Meter: In poetry, a system for measuring the number of feet of a certain rhythm and organizing them into lines. For example, monometer is a meter of one foot while pentameter is a meter of five feet.

In a phrase like "iambic pentameter," "iambic" refers to rhythm and "pentameter" refers to meter.

Modernism: In the arts, and especially in literature, a broad movement generally thought to have begun in the 1890s and to have lasted through the 1950s. However, its influence can still be seen in much contemporary literature and its origins have been traced back as far as the mid-nineteenth-century American poets Walt Whitman and Emily Dickinson. Modernist literature is marked by innovation in style as well as in theme. In his critical essays, the American poet and critic Ezra Pound formulated many of the ideas associated with modernism and demonstrated them in his poetry through his experimental approach to meter and the inclusion of visual effects like Chinese characters. Two other key figures in the modernist movement were T. S. Eliot, who kept in close contact with Pound, and James Joyce, who wrote poetry but is most renowned for his novels. Modernist writing is frequently difficult and demands considerable explication. Eliot, for example, appended extensive footnotes to his poem *The Waste Land* to explain his wide-ranging literary allusions. Most literary historians regard 1922 as the pinnacle of "high modernism" because that is when two of modernism's most important works were published: Eliot's poem *The Waste Land*, and Joyce's novel *Ulysses*.

Monologue: Speech by one person when others may be present but are silent. An example is Matthew Arnold's "Dover Beach."

Nocturne: Romantic or lyrical poem inspired by evening moods. An example is Thomas Gray's "Elegy Written in a Country Churchyard."

Nursery rhymes: Poems for children, often anonymous, with jingly rhythms and obvious rhymes. Blake's "The Lamb" comes close to the style of the nursery rhyme.

Octameter: Poetic line of eight feet, as in Tennyson's "Locksley Hall": "In the Spring a young man's fancy lightly turns to thoughts of love." No poem in this collection uses this meter.

Octave: Stanza or subdivision of eight lines.

Ode: Elaborate lyric poem of extended length. It originated in ancient Greek choral songs. There were two varieties of classical ode: Pindar's formal ode of praise or glorification, and Horace's simpler, more personal version. Seventeenth-century poets Ben Jonson, Robert Herrick, and Andrew Marvell were inspired by the freer Horatian ode. The form achieved its height with the nineteenth-century Romantic poets, Wordsworth,

Coleridge, Shelley, and Keats. Examples are Keats's "Ode to a Nightingale" and Percy Bysshe Shelley's "Ode to the West Wind."

Ottava rima: Eight-line stanza of iambic pentameter rhyming *abababcc.* An example is William Butler Yeats's "Sailing to Byzantium":

> That is no country for old men. The young
> In one another's arms, birds in the trees
> —Those dying generations—at their song,
> The salmon-falls, the mackerel-crowded seas,
> Fish, flesh, or fowl, commend all summer long
> Whatever is begotten, born, and dies.
> Caught in that sensual music all neglect
> Monuments of unageing intellect.

Oxymoron: Self-contradiction in words, as when an adjective does not go with a noun. "Brute beauty" in Hopkins's "The Windhover" is an example.

Paean: Poem of praise, appreciation, or joy. Examples of paeans include Gerard Manley Hopkins's "Pied Beauty," Percy Bysshe Shelley's "Ode to the West Wind," and William Wordsworth's "Composed upon Westminster Bridge."

Paradox: Paradox is a statement that appears self-contradictory but actually has a basis in truth. Richard Lovelace uses paradox in "To Althea, From Prison" to express the unconfinable freedom of the heart, mind, and soul:

> Stone walls do not a prison make,
> Nor iron bars a cage.

Donne's "Go and Catch a Falling Star" is a series of paradoxes.

Parody: Parody is the mocking imitation in verse or prose of a literary work. It is an ancient device that has been used for both comic effect and serious criticism. Lewis Carroll's "Jabberwocky" began as a parody of medieval poetry.

Pastoral: Convention in literature which contrasts the purity and simplicity of a shepherd's, or country, life with the corruption of the court or city. It is found in poetry, drama, and fiction. Pastoral dates back to the Greek poet Theocritus in the third century B.C. Examples of pastoral poems include Christopher Marlowe's "The Passionate Shepherd to His Love" and John Milton's "Lycidas."

Pastoral elegy: Elegy in the pastoral mode, used especially by poets mourning the death of other poets. See the commentary on John Milton's "Lycidas."

Pentameter: Line of poetry with five metrical units or feet. Keats uses pentameter in "Ode to a Nightingale":

> My heart / aches, and / a drow / sy numb / ness pains.

Persona: In poetry, a speaking presence in a poem. The term is typically used to distinguish this presence from the poet himself or herself. The "I" in John Keats's "Ode to a Nightingale" is a persona created by Keats. That is, readers need not necessarily assume that Keats was contemplating suicide as he wrote it.

Personification: Treating nonhuman things as if they are human. An example
is George Herbert's depiction of love as a person in "Love III":

> Love bade me welcome; yet my soul drew back,
>> Guilty of lust and sin.
> But quick-eyed Love, observing me grow slack
>> From my first entrance in,
> Drew nearer to me, sweetly questioning
>> If I lacked anything.

Petrarchan sonnet: see *Italian sonnet.*

Pun: Play on words, typically on words that sound the same but are different.
John Donne punned on his own name when he wrote "John Donne, Anne
Donne, Undone." Frost's "Mending Wall" includes play on "a fence" and
"offense."

Quatrain: Stanza of four lines. The lines may or may not be rhymed. The
quatrain is a very common stanza in English.

Refrain: In poetry, a stanza, line, or phrase that is repeated regularly or irreg-
ularly throughout a work. It can be used to emphasize thematic, rhythmic,
or stylistic qualities. In George Herbert's "Virtue" the last lines of the first
three stanzas ("For thou must die," "And thou must die," and "And all must
die") amount to a refrain, and leading up to the effective last line of the
poem: "Then chiefly lives."

Renaissance: French word meaning "rebirth." The Renaissance in European
history is the period, beginning in the fourteenth century Italy and lasting
through the seventeenth century, that marked the transition from medieval
to modern times. One of its central tenets is traceable to the twelfth-centu-
ry revival of the influence of Greek and Roman arts and literature. This
subsequently led to fourteenth-century humanism (founded by the Italian
poet Petrarch and central to the Renaissance), which emphasized the sig-
nificance of the individual in society. Renaissance values include sincerity,
honesty, and self-discipline. Some of the greatest Renaissance writers are
the Italian poet Dante Alighieri, William Shakespeare, Christopher
Marlowe, Ben Jonson, John Donne, and John Milton.

Rhetorical question: Something in the form of a question that really makes a
statement, usually negative. Tone of voice is a tip-off. Said in one way,
"Who cares" may be a genuine question from someone who wants to
know who is concerned. In the usual sounding, however, "Who cares?"
amounts to "Nobody cares."

The first two-thirds of Suckling's "Why So Pale and Wan, Fond Lover?"
consists of a series of rhetorical questions.

Rhyme: Rhyme is the recurrence of identical or similar sounds which, in poet-
ry, can occur at the end, beginning, or middle of a line; end rhyme is the
most common in poetry. Certain types of poems have formal end-rhyming

patterns. For instance, a Shakespearean sonnet rhymes *abab cdcd efef gg*. The following stanza from Sir John Suckling's "Why So Pale and Wan, Fond Lover?" is rhymed *ababb*:

> Why so pale and wan, fond lover?
>> Prithee, why so pale?
> Will, when looking well can't move her,
>> Looking ill prevail?
>> Prithee, why so pale?

Rhyme royal: Stanza of seven lines of iambic pentameter, rhyming *ababbcc,* as in Sir Thomas Wyatt's "They Flee From Me That Sometime Did Me Seek":

> They flee from me that sometime did me seek
> With naked foot stalking in my chamber.
> I have seen them gentle, tame, and meek
> That now are wild and do not remember
> That sometime they put themselves in danger
> To take bread at my hand; and now they range
> Busily seeking with a continual change.

Rhythm: The sense of movement caused by patterning of stressed and unstressed syllables. No feature of poetry is more expressive. William Blake's "The Tyger" uses a very powerful rhythm:

> Tyger! Tyger! burning bright,
> In the forests of the night;
> What immortal hand or eye,
> Could frame thy fearful symmetry?

Riddle: One of the oldest poetic forms. It provides a type of puzzle by describing something without actually naming it. Emily Dickinson's "A Narrow Fellow in the Grass" is a riddle.

Romanticism: Loosely, European literary and artistic movements of the eighteenth and nineteenth centuries which revolted against the rigid rules of classical literature. Formed by the ideals of liberty and equality which inspired the French and American revolutions, Romanticism sought a return to nature and the goodness of man, the rediscovery of the artist as the supremely individual creator, the development of nationalistic pride, and the exaltation of the senses and emotion over reason and the intellect. The 1798 publication of William Wordsworth's and Samuel Taylor Coleridge's *Lyrical Ballads,* marks the beginning of the English Romantic movement. Other Romantic poets include William Blake, Lord Byron, Percy Bysshe Shelley, and John Keats.

Satire: Any literary or artistic work whose purpose is to ridicule in order to effect change. From ancient times satirists have shared a common aim: to expose foolishness, vanity, hypocrisy, idolatry, bigotry, and sentimentality. Pope and Byron wrote poetic satires. An example is Clough's "The Latest

Decalogue."

Sestet: Stanza or subdivision of six lines, usually referring to the last six lines of an Italian sonnet, typically rhyming *cdecde* or *cdcdcd.* An example is the ending of William Wordsworth's sonnet "Composed upon Westminster Bridge, September 3, 1802":

> Never did sun more beautifully steep
> In his first splendor, valley, rock, or hill;
> Ne'er saw I, never felt, a calm so deep!
> The river glideth at his own sweet will:
> Dear God! The very houses seem asleep;
> And all that mighty heart is lying still!

Shakespearean sonnet: See *English sonnet.*

Short measure: Quatrain rhyming *abab* or *abcb,* with the first, second, and fourth lines in iambic trimeter, and the third in iambic tetrameter. The stanza form is often used in hymns. No poem in this collection is in short measure, but Emily Dickinson and Thomas Hardy used the form. Here is an example from Dickinson:

> A Bird came down the Walk—
> He did not know I saw—
> He bit an Angleworm in halves
> And ate the fellow, raw.

Simile: Figure of speech that compares two objects by using the words "as," "as if" or "like." Unlike a metaphor, it does not substitute objects. George Herbert uses a simile in "Virtue":

> Only a sweet and virtuous soul,
> Like seasoned timber, never gives.

Presumably, an overt gesture of comparison, as in Shakespeare's "Shall I Compare Thee to a Summer's Day?" is also a simile.

Soliloquy: Speech by a character, usually in a play, that is delivered when the speaker is alone, and is sometimes addressed to the audience. T. S. Eliot's "The Love Song of J. Alfred Prufrock" may be a soliloquy.

Song: Poem that can be sung, or a short simple lyrical poem. An example is Ben Jonson's "Song: To Celia."

Sonnet: Poem of fourteen lines, usually in iambic pentameter, that is restricted to a definite rhyme scheme. There are two prominent types: the Italian, or Petrarchan, sonnet, composed of an octave and a sestet (most often rhyming *abbaabba cdecde*), and the English, or Shakespearean, sonnet, consisting of three quatrains and a couplet (rhyming *abab cdcd efef gg*). Shakespeare, Milton, Wordsworth, and Keats all wrote great sonnets.

Stanza: In poetry, a regular, rhymed, recurrent pattern of lines. The counterpart of a paragraph in prose, except that it is regulated by form (numbers of lines, rhyme scheme, meter, and so on), and customarily divided from other stanzas by spaces.

Tercet: Stanza with three lines that may or may not be rhymed. Robert
   Herrick's "Upon Julia's Clothes" is made of two tercets:
   > Whenas in silks my Julia goes,
   > Then, then, methinks how sweetly flows
   > That liquefaction of her clothes.

   > Next, when I cast mine eyes and see
   > That brave vibration, each way free,
   > O how that glittering taketh me!

Terza rima: System of three-lined stanzas rhyming *aba bcb cdc ede fef*, and so
   on. An example is Percy Bysshe Shelley's "Ode to the West Wind":
   > O wild West Wind, thou breath of Autumn's being,
   > Thou, from whose unseen presence the leaves dead
   > Are driven, like ghosts from an enchanter fleeing,

   > Yellow, and pale, and hectic red,
   > Pestilence-sticken multitudes: O thou,
   > Who chariotest to their dark wintry bed. . . .

Tetrameter: Poetic line of four feet such as iambs. The iambic tetrameter is
   one of the most widely used measures in English poetry. Andrew Marvell
   uses the iambic tetrameter arranged in a couplet form throughout "To His
   Coy Mistress":
   > Had we / but world / enough / and time,
   > This coy/ness, la/dy, were / no crime. . . .

Trimeter: Poetic line of three feet, as in the last line of George Herbert's
   "Love III": "So I did sit and eat."

Triplet: Three consecutive lines joined by rhyme or another device, not as a
   stanza (which is the definition of "tercet") but as a variation from the pre-
   vailing couplet. Owen's "Strange Meeting," for example, consists of cou-
   plets joined by a rhymelike combination of alliteration and consonance (as
   with "years" and "yours"), but one three-line passage (lines 19–21) presents
   the terminations "hair," "hour," and "here."

Victorian: In English culture, the period named after the reign of Queen
   Victoria (1837–1901). The period is generally divided into two phases, each
   of roughly thirty years. The first marked a prosperous time in England
   with moderate political reforms, rapid industrial growth that heralded the
   rise of an industrial middle class suddenly in conflict with the working
   class and the aristocracy, and a sharp population increase. The second
   phase was more bleak with rising unemployment, a drop in the birth rate,
   and the subversion of traditional religious values by science, as in Charles
   Darwin's treatise on evolution, *The Origin of Species* (1859). Victorian litera-
   ture reflected the conflicts of the time by focusing on class struggles and
   morality. Charles Dickens's famous novel of poverty and crime, *Oliver
   Twist*, was written during the Victorian period. The period also spawned a

wave of moral reformers who emphasized etiquette and formality and cele-
brated the supremacy of England over her allegedly barbaric colonies.
Victorian poets include Matthew Arnold, Alfred, Lord Tennyson, Robert
Browning, and Thomas Hardy.

Villanelle: A French verse form derived from a folk song pattern used in the
Italian Renaissance. It is generally made of nineteen lines arranged in six
stanzas; the first five stanzas are three-lined tercets and the final is a four-
lined quatrain. The first and third lines of the initial stanza make up the
poem's refrain; these lines are alternately repeated in the third line of the
middle stanzas and comprise the last two lines of the final stanza. A vil-
lanelle has a fixed rhyme scheme. Dylan Thomas's "Do Not Go Gentle
into That Good Night" is an example.

Further Reading

Anonymous, *"Sir Patrick Spens"* (page 1)

Battersby, James L. " 'The Character of 'Sir Patrick Spens'. " *Hypotheses: Neo-Aristotelian Analysis* 9 (Spring 1994): 10–13.

Maclaine, Allan H. " 'Haf Owre to Aberdour': A Note on 'Sir Patrick Spens'." In Betsy F. Colquitt, *Studies in Medieval, Renaissance and American Literature*. Fort Worth, Tx.: Christian University Press, 1971, 57–61.

Ryan, William M. "Formula and Tragic Irony in 'Sir Patrick Spens'." *Southern Folklore Quarterly* 44 (1980): 73–83.

Anonymous, *"Edward, Edward"* (page 5)

Blum, Margaret Morton. " 'Edward' and the Folk Tradition." *Southern Folklore Quarterly* 21 (3) (September 1957): 131–42.

Bronson, Bertrand H. " 'Edward, Edward': A Scottish Ballad." *Southern Folklore Quarterly* 4 (1) (March 1940): 1–13.

Coffin, Tristram P. "The Murder Motive in 'Edward.' " *Western Folklore* 8 (1949): 314–19.

Anonymous, *"Western Wind"* (page 8)

Frey, Charles. "Interpreting 'Western Wind'." *Journal of English Literary History* 43 (1976): 259–78.

Frey, Charles. "Transcribing and Editing 'Western Wind'." *Manuscripta* 23 (1979): 108–11.

Jungman, Robert E. " 'Western Wind' and 'Tibullus I.45–48.' " *English Language Notes* 27 (2) (December 1989): 19–26.

Sir Thomas Wyatt, *"They Flee from Me That Sometime Did Me Seek"* (page 10)

Cary, Cecile Williamson. "Sexual Identity in 'They Flee from Me' and Other

Poems by Sir Thomas Wyatt." *Assays: Critical Approaches to Medieval and Renaissance Texts* 4 (1987): 85–96.

Estrin, Barbara L. "Wyatt's Unlikely Likenesses: Or, Has the Lady Read Petrarch?" In Peter C. Herman, ed., *Rethinking the Henrician Era: Essays on Early Tudor Texts and Contexts*. Urbana: University of Illinois Press, 1994, 219–39.

Winser, Leigh. "The Question of Love Tradition in Wyatt's 'They Flee from Me'." *Essays in Literature* 2 (1975): 3–9.

SIR WALTER RALEGH, *"The Nymph's Reply to the Shepherd"* (page 13)

Gadomski, Kenneth E. "Williams' 'Ralegh Was Right'." *The Explicator* 43 (3) (Spring 1985): 31–34.

Lacey, Robert. *Sir Walter Ralegh*. New York: Atheneum, 1974, 117.

Oakeshott, Walter. *The Queen and the Poet*. London: Faber and Faber, 1960, 34–35.

SIR PHILIP SIDNEY, *"With How Sad Steps, O Moon"* (page 16)

Allan, M. J. B., Dominic Baker-Smith, Arthur F. Kinney, and Margaret Sullivan, eds. *Sir Philip Sydney's Achievements*. New York: AMS Press, 1990.

Kay, Dennis, ed. *Sir Philip Sidney: An Anthology of Modern Criticism*. Oxford: The Clarendon Press, 1987.

Kinney, Arthur F., ed. *Essential Articles for the Study of Sir Philip Sidney*. Hamden, Conn.: Archon, 1986.

CHRISTOPHER MARLOWE, *"The Passionate Shepherd to His Love"* (page 19)

Bruster, Douglas. "Come to the Tent Again: 'The Passionate Shepherd'." *Criticism: A Quarterly for Literature and the Arts* 33 (1) (Winter 1991): 49–72.

Chan, Mary Joiner and Frederick W. Stemfield, eds. "Come Live With Me and Be My Love." *Comparative Literature* 22 (Spring 1970): 173–87.

Leiter, Louis H. "Deification through Love: Marlowe's 'The Passionate Shepherd to His Love'." *College English* 27 (1966): 444–49.

WILLIAM SHAKESPEARE, *"Fear No More the Heat o' the Sun"* (page 23)

Albright, Daniel. *Lyricality in English Literature*. Lincoln and London: University of Nebraska Press, 1985, 33.

Bloom, Edward A., Charles H. Philbrick, and Elmer M. Blistein. *The Order of Poetry: An Introduction*. New York: The Odyssey Press, 1961, 6–7, 54.

Stein, Arnold. *The House of Death: Messages from the English Renaissance*. Baltimore and London: Johns Hopkins University Press, 1986, 277–79.

WILLIAM SHAKESPEARE, *"When to the Sessions of Sweet Silent Thought"* (page 25)

Hall, Donald. *The Pleasures of Poetry*. New York: Harper and Row, 1971, 25–26.

Muir, Kenneth *Shakespeare's Sonnets*. London: George Allen & Unwin, 1979, 57–58.

Vendler, Helen. *The Art of Shakespeare's Sonnets*. Cambridge, MA: Harvard University Press, 1997.

WILLIAM SHAKESPEARE, *"Let Me Not to the Marriage of True Minds"* (page 26)

Booth, Stephen. *Commentary to Shakespeare's Sonnets*. New Haven: Yale University Press, 1977, 384–92.

Toliver, Harold. *Lyric Provinces in the English Renaissance*. Columbus: Ohio State University Press, 1985, 24–26.

Vendler, Helen. *The Art of Shakespeare's Sonnets*. Cambridge, MA: Harvard University Press, 1997.

WILLIAM SHAKESPEARE, *"Shall I Compare Thee to a Summer's Day?"* (page 27)

Ferry, Anne. *The Art of Naming*. Chicago: University of Chicago Press, 1988, 134–35, 137.

Vendler, Helen. *The Art of Shakespeare's Sonnets*. Cambridge, MA: Harvard University Press, 1997.

Weiser, David K. *Mind in Character: Shakespeare's Speaker in the Sonnets*. Columbia: University of Missouri Press, 1987, 128–38.

WILLIAM SHAKESPEARE, *"The Expense of Spirit in a Waste of Shame"* (page 28)

Booth, Stephen. *Commentary to Shakespeare's Sonnets*. New Haven: Yale University Press, 1977, 441–52.

Pequigney, Joseph. *Such Is My Love: A Study of Shakespeare's Sonnets*. Chicago: University of Chicago Press, 1985, 157–65.

Vendler, Helen. *The Art of Shakespeare's Sonnets*. Cambridge, MA: Harvard University Press, 1997.

WILLIAM SHAKESPEARE, *"That Time of Year Thou Mayst in Me Behold"* (page 29)

Fetrow, Fred M. "Strata and Structure: A Reading of Shakespeare's Sonnet 73." *Concerning Poetry* (Fall 1976): 23–25.
Hedley, Jane. *Power in Verse: Metaphor and Metonymy in the Renaissance Lyric.* University Park: Pennsylvania State University Press, 1988, 77–78.
Vendler, Helen. *The Art of Shakespeare's Sonnets.* Cambridge, MA: Harvard University Press, 1997.

WILLIAM SHAKESPEARE, *"When Icicles Hang by the Wall"* (page 30)

Bronson, Bertrand H. "Daisies Pied and Icicles." *Modern Language Notes* 63 (January 1948): 35–38.
Daniels, Earl. *The Art of Reading Poetry.* New York: Farrar and Rinehart, 1941, 50–51.
Perrine, Laurence. *Sound and Sense: An Introduction to Poetry.* New York: Harcourt, Brace, 1963, 7–8.

JOHN DONNE, *"Death, Be Not Proud"* (page 32)

Carey, John. *John Donne: Life, Mind and Art.* New York: Oxford University Press, 1981, 198–200.
Rostan, Murray. *The Soul of Wit.* London: Oxford University Press, 1974, 189–91.
Stachniewski, John, "John Donne: the Despair of the 'Holy Sonnets'." *English Literary History* 48 (1981): 677–705.

JOHN DONNE, *"Batter My Heart, Three-Personed God"* (page 33)

Cayward, Margaret, "Donne's 'Batter My Heart, Three-Personed God'." *The Explicator* 38 (3) (1980).
Kerrigan, William. "The Fearful Accommodations of John Donne." *English Literary Renaissance* 4 (1972): 337–63.
Stachniewski, John. "John Donne: The Despair of the 'Holy Sonnets'." *English Literary History* 48 (1981): 677–705.

JOHN DONNE, *"At the Round Earth's Imagined Corners"* (page 34)

Skelton, Robin. *Poetic Truth.* London: Heinemann, New York: Barnes & Noble, Agincourt: The Book Society of Canada, 1978, 67–68.
Stachniewski, John. "John Donne: The Despair of the 'Holy Sonnets'." *English Literary History* 48 (1981): 677–705.

White, Gertrude M. and Joan G. Rosen, eds. *A Moment's Monument: The Development of the Sonnet*. New York: Charles Scribner's Sons, 1972, 51–55.

JOHN DONNE, *"The Good Morrow"* (page 35)

Payne, F. W. *John Donne and His Poetry*. Folcroft, Pa.: The Folcroft Press, 1969, 41–43.
Pinka, Patricia Garland. *The Dialogue of One: The "Songs and Sonnets" of John Donne*. Montgomery: University of Alabama Press, 1982, 108–13.
Stamper, Judah. *John Donne and the Metaphysical Gesture*. New York: Funk & Wagnalls, 1970, 141–51.

JOHN DONNE, *"The Sun Rising"* (page 37)

Pinka, Patricia Garland. *The Dialogue of One: The "Songs and Sonnets" of John Donne*. Montgomery: University of Alabama Press, 1982, 113–17.
Roston, Murray. *The Soul of Wit*. Oxford: Clarendon, 1974, 13–18.
Stamper, Judah. *John Donne and the Metaphysical Gesture*. New York: Funk & Wagnalls, 1970, 146–55.

JOHN DONNE, *"A Valediction: Forbidding Mourning"* (page 39)

Chambers, A. B. "Glorified Bodies and the 'Valediction Forbidding Mourning'." *John Donne Journal* 1 (1–2) (1982): 1–20.
Jahn, J. D. "Donne's 'A Valediction Forbidding Mourning'." *College Literature* 5 (1978): 34–47.
Linden, Stanton J. "Compasses and Cartography." *John Donne Journal* 3 (1) (1984): 23–34.

JOHN DONNE, *"Go and Catch a Falling Star"* (page 41)

Clark, John R. and Anna Motto, eds. *Satire–That Blasted Art*. New York: G. P. Putnam's Sons and Capricorn Books, 1969, 1–23.
Pinka, Patricia Garland. *The Dialogue of One: The "Songs and Sonnets" of John Donne*. Montgomery: University of Alabama Press, 1982, 78–81.
Stamper, Judah. *John Donne and the Metaphysical Gesture*. New York: Funk & Wagnalls, 1970, 65–79.

BEN JONSON, *"On My First Son"* (page 44)

Cain, William E. "Self and Others," *Studies in Philology* 80 (2) (Spring 1983): 163–82.
Miller, David Lee. "Writing the Specular Son." In Valeria Finucci, ed., *Desire in the Renaissance*. Princeton: Princeton University Press, 1994, 233–60.

Silberman, Lauren. "To Write Sorrow in Jonson's 'On My First Sonne'." *John Donne Journal* 9 (2) (1990): 149–55.

BEN JONSON, *"Song: To Celia"* (page 45)

Nichols, J. G. *The Poetry of Ben Jonson*. New York: Barnes & Noble, Inc., 1969, 22–30.
Smith, Barbara. *The Women of Ben Jonson's Poetry*. Cambridge: Scolar Press, 1995, 12–13, 21.
Wittenberg, Robert. *Ben Jonson and Self-Love, The Subtlest Maze of All*. Columbia: University of Missouri Press, 1990, 111–12.

BEN JONSON, *"Still to Be Neat"* (page 46)

Peterson, Richard S. *Imitation and Praise in the Poems of Ben Jonson*. New Haven: Yale University Press, 1981.
Smith, Barbara. *The Women of Ben Jonson's Poetry*. Cambridge: Scolar Press, 1995, 13.
Trimpi, Wesley. *Ben Jonson's Poems: A Study of the Plain Style*. Stanford: Stanford University Press, 1962.

ROBERT HERRICK, *"To the Virgins, to Make Much of Time"* (page 48)

Mollenkott, Virginia R. " 'Gather Ye Rosebuds': An Expanded Interpretation." *Christianity and Literature* 23 (Spring 1974): 47–48.
Rollin, Roger B. *Robert Herrick*. New York: Twayne, 1992, 34, 82, 83–84, 90, 194.
Rollin, Roger B. and J. Max Patrick, eds. *"Trust to Good Verses": Herrick Tercentenary Essays*. Pittsburgh: University of Pittsburgh Press, 1978, 65, 67, 68, 70, 132–34, 193.

ROBERT HERRICK, *"Upon Julia's Clothes"* (page 49)

Coiro, Ann Baynes. "Herrick's 'Julia' Poems." *John Donne Journal: Studies in the Age of Donne* 6 (1) (1987): 67–89.
Montague, Gene. "Herrick's 'Upon Julia's Clothes'." *The Explicator* 36 (3) (Spring 1978): 21–22.
Preston, Michael. "Herrick's 'Upon Julia's Clothes'." *The Explicator* 30 (1972): Item 82.

ROBERT HERRICK, *"Delight in Disorder"* (page 50)

Schanfield, Lillian. "Tickled with Desire." *Literature and Psychology* 39 (1–2) (1993): 63–83.
Shadoian, Jack. "Herrick's 'Delight in Disorder'." In Grayburn, et. al., eds.,

Studies in the Humanities. Bloomington: Indiana University Press, 1971, 23–25.

Spitzer, Leo. "Herrick's 'Delight in Disorder'." In Anna Hatcher, ed., *Essays on English and American Literature by Leo Spitzer*. New York: Gordian Press, 1984.

GEORGE HERBERT, *"Love III"* (page 52)

Martin, Anthony. "Herbert's 'Love' Sonnets and Love Poetry." *George Herbert Journal* 17 (2) (Spring 1994): 37–49.

Strier, Richard. *Love Known: Theology and Experience in George Herbert's Poetry*. Chicago: University of Chicago Press, 1983, 6, 17, 73–83, 94, 117, 120, 139.

Toliver, Harold. *George Herbert's Christian Narrative*. University Park: Pennsylvania State University Press, 1993, 240–49.

GEORGE HERBERT, *"The Pulley"* (page 54)

Guerin, Wilfred L. "Herbert's 'The Pulley'." *The Explicator* 53 (2) (Winter 1995): 70–72.

Routh, Michael. "A Crux of 'The Pulley'." *Seventeenth Century News* 48 (3) (Fall 1982): 44–45.

Waddington, Raymond B. "The Title Image of Herbert's 'The Pulley'." *George Herbert Journal* 9 (2) (Spring 1986): 49–53.

GEORGE HERBERT, *"Virtue"* (page 55)

McDonald, Suzanne. "George Herbert's 'Vertue': An Easter Poem?" *George Herbert Journal* 17 (1) (Fall 1993): 61–69.

Stein, Arnold. *George Herbert's Lyrics*. Baltimore: Johns Hopkins University Press, 1968, 178–82, 187–91 note.

White, James Boyd. *"This Book of Starres": Learning to Read George Herbert*. Ann Arbor: University of Michigan Press, 1994, 4–10.

THOMAS CAREW, *"Ask Me No More Where Jove Bestows"* (page 57)

Martz, Louis. *The Wit of Love*. Notre Dame, Ind.: University of Notre Dame Press, 1969, 107–10.

Miner, Earl Roy. *The Cavalier Mode From Jonson to Cotton*. Princeton: Princeton University Press, 1971, 85–86, 135–37.

Sadler, Lynn. *Thomas Carew*. Boston: Twayne, 1979, 55–56, 143, 145.

EDMUND WALLER, *"Go, Lovely Rose"* (page 60)

Allison, A. W. *Toward an Augustan Poetic*. Oxford: Oxford University Press, 1962.

Chernaik, Warren L. *The Poetry of Limitation: A Study of Edmund Waller*. New Haven: Yale University Press, 1968, 80, 99, 107–10.

Gilbert, Jack Glenn. *Edmund Waller*. Boston: Twayne, 1979, 20, 53–54.

JOHN MILTON, *"Lycidas"* (page 64)

McLoone, George H. " 'Lycidas': Hurled Bones and the Noble Mind of Reformed Congregations." *Milton Studies* 26 (1991): 59–80.

Patrides, C. A., ed. *Milton's "Lycidas": The Tradition and the Poem*. Columbia: University of Missouri Press, 1983.

Silver, Victoria. " 'Lycidas' and the Grammar of Revelation." *English Literary History* 58 (4) (Winter 1991): 779–808.

SIR JOHN SUCKLING, *"Why So Pale and Wan, Fond Lover?"* (page 72)

Anselment, Raymond A. "Men Most of All Enjoy, When Least They Do: The Love Poetry of Sir John Suckling." *University of Texas Studies in Literature and Language* 14 (1972): 17–32.

Beaurline, L. A. " 'Why So Pale and Wan': An Essay in Critical Method." *Texas Studies in Literature and Language* 4 (1962): 553–63.

Squier, Charles L. *Sir John Suckling*. Boston: Twayne, 1978.

RICHARD LOVELACE, *"To Lucasta, Going to the Wars"* (page 75)

Hartmann, Cyril H. *The Cavalier Spirit and Its Influence on the Life and Work of Richard Lovelace*. Folcroft, Pa.: Folcroft Press, 1970, 53–81.

Jones, G. F. "Lov'd I Not Honour More: The Durability of A Literary Motif." *Comparative Literature* 11 (1959): 131–43.

Nassaar, Christopher S. " 'To Lucasta Going to the Wars'." *The Explicator* 39 (3) (Spring 1981): 44–45.

RICHARD LOVELACE, *"To Althea, from Prison"* (page 76)

Clayton, Thomas. "Some Versions, Texts, and Readings of 'To Althea, from Prison'." *Papers of the Bibliographical Society of America* 68 (1974): 225–35.

Hartmann, Cyril H. *The Cavalier Spirit and Its Influence on the Life and Work of Richard Lovelace*. Folcroft, Pa: The Folcroft Press, 1970, 45, 46, 51, 76 note, 121.

Hastings, A. Waller. "Stone Walls, Iron Bars, and Liberal Political Theory." In Jay Ruud, ed., *Proceedings of the First South Dakotas Conference on Earlier British Literature*. Aberdeen: Northern State University Press, 1993, 74–85.

ANDREW MARVELL, *"To His Coy Mistress"* (page 79)

Brody, Jules. "The Resurrection of the Body." *English Literary History* 56 (1) (Spring 1989): 53–79.

Fogle, French. "Marvell's 'Tough Reasonableness' and the Coy Mistress." In Kenneth Friedenreich, ed., *Tercentenary Essays in Honor of Andrew Marvell.* Hamden, Conn.: Archon, 1977, 140–52.

Taylor, Mark. "Marvell's 'To His Coy Mistress'." *The Explicator* 53 (1) (Fall 1994): 15–16.

ANDREW MARVELL, *"The Garden"* (page 81)

Brooks, Cleanth. "Andrew Marvell: Puritan Austerity with Classical Grace." In George de Forest and Maynard Mack, eds., *Poetic Traditions of the English Renaissance.* New Haven: Yale University Press, 1982, 219–28.

Crewe, Jonathan. "The Garden State: Marvell's Poetics of Enclosure." In John Michael Archer and Richard Burt, eds., *Enclosure Acts.* Ithaca: Cornell University Press, 1994, 270–89.

Hartwig, Joan. "Tears as a Way of Seeing." In Ted-Larry Pebworth and Claude J. Summers, eds., *On the Celebrated and Neglected Poems of Andrew Marvell.* Columbia: University of Missouri Press, 1992.

HENRY VAUGHAN, *"The Retreat"* (page 85)

Calhoun, Thomas O. *Henry Vaughan: The Achievement of "Silex Scintillans".* Newark: University of Delaware Press, 1981, 69, 159.

Martin, L. C. "Henry Vaughan and the Theme of Infancy." In Alan Rudrum, ed., *Essential Articles for the Study of Henry Vaughan.* Hamden, Conn.: Archon Books, 1987, 46–58.

Post, Jonathan F. S. *Henry Vaughan: The Unfolding Vision.* Princeton: Princeton University Press, 1982, 77, 79, 155, 161–62.

THOMAS GRAY, *"Elegy Written in a Country Churchyard"* (page 88)

Bloom, Harold, ed. *Thomas Gray's "Elegy Written in a Country Churchyard".* New York: Chelsea House Publishers, 1987.

Starr, Herbert, ed. *Twentieth Century Interpretations of Gray's "Elegy".* Englewood Cliffs, N.J.: Prentice-Hall, 1968.

Weinfield, Henry. *The Poet Without A Name: Gray's "Elegy" and the Problem of History.* Carbondale and Edwardsville: Southern Illinois University Press, 1991.

THOMAS GRAY, *"Ode on the Death of a Favorite Cat, Drowned in a Tub of Gold Fishes"* (page 93)

Kaul, Suvir. "Why Selima Drowns." *Publications of the Modern Language Association* 105 (2) (March 1990): 223–32.

Pattison, Robert. "Gray's 'Ode on the Death of a Favorite Cat'." *University of Toronto Quarterly* 49 (2) (Winter 1979/80): 156–65.

Tillotson, Geoffrey. "Gray's 'Ode on the Death of a Favorite Cat, Drowned in a Tub of Gold Fishes'." In *Augustan Studies*. London: Athlone, 1961, 216–23.

WILLIAM BLAKE, *"The Tyger"* (page 96)

Bloom, Harold. *Blake's Apocalypse*. New York: Doubleday, 1963, 137–39.

Erdman, David. *Blake: Prophet Against Empire*. Princeton: Princeton University Press, 1954, 178–81.

Hilton, Nelson. "Spears, Spheres, and Spiritual Tears: Blake's 'The Tyger'." *Philological Quarterly* 59 (4) (Fall 1980): 515–29.

WILLIAM BLAKE, *"London"* (page 98)

Ferber, Michael. " 'London' and Its Politics." *English Literary History* 48 (2) (Summer 1981): 310–38.

Punter, David. "Blake and the Shapes of London." *Criticism: A Quarterly for Literature and the Arts* 23 (1) (Winter 1981): 1–23.

Thompson, E. P. " 'London'." In Michael Phillips, ed., *Interpreting Blake*. Cambridge: Cambridge University Press, 1978, 5–31.

WILLIAM BLAKE, *"And Did Those Feet in Ancient Time"* (page 100)

Curran, Stuart. "The Structure of Jerusalem." In Stuart Curran and Joseph A. Wittreich, eds., *Blake's Sublime Allegory*. Madison: University of Wisconsin Press, 1973, 329–46.

Doskow, Minna. *William Blake's Jerusalem*. East Brunswick, N.J.: Associated University Presses, 1982.

Paley, Morton D. *The Continuing City: William Blake's Jerusalem*. Oxford: The Clarendon Press, 1983.

WILLIAM BLAKE, *"The Lamb"* (page 102)

Borck, Jim S. "Blake's 'The Lamb': The Punctuation of Innocence." *Tennessee Studies in Literature* 19 (1974): 163–75.

Hagstrum, Jean H. " 'The Wrath of the Lamb': A Study of William Blake's Conversions." In Hilles and Bloom, eds., *From Sensibility to Romanticism:*

Essays Presented to Frederick A. Pottle. New York: Oxford University Press, 1965, 311–30.

Williams, Harry. "The Tyger and the Lamb." *Concerning Poetry* 5 (1) (1972): 49–56.

WILLIAM BLAKE, *"Auguries of Innocence"* (page 103)

Damrosch, Leopold. *Symbol and Truth in Blake's Myth*. Princeton: Princeton University Press, 1980.

Grant, John E. "Apocalypse in Blake's 'Auguries of Innocence'." *Texas Studies in Literature and Language* 5 (1964): 489–508.

Warner, Janet. "Blake's 'Auguries of Innocence'." *Colby Literary Quarterly* 12 (1976): 126–38.

ROBERT BURNS, *"A Red, Red Rose"* (page 108)

Bentman, Raymond. *Robert Burns*. Boston: Twayne Publishers, 1987, 77, 96, 102–3, 145*n*27.

Bold, Alan. *A Burns Companion*. London: Macmillan, 1991, 341–44.

Crawford, Thomas. *Burns: A Study of the Poems and Songs*. Edinburgh, Scotland: Canongate Academic, 1994, 176*n*72, 268, 278–81, 335, 342.

WILLIAM WORDSWORTH, *"She Dwelt Among the Untrodden Ways"* (page 112)

Blank, G. Kim. *Wordsworth and Feeling*. Madison, N.J.: Associated University Presses, 1995, 149–53, 156.

Dilworth, Thomas. "Wordsworth's 'She Dwelt Among the Untrodden Ways'." *The Explicator* 42 (3) (Spring 1984): 22–23.

Jones, Mark. *The Lucy Poems: A Case Study in Literary Knowledge*. Toronto: University of Toronto Press, 1995.

WILLIAM WORDSWORTH, *"The World Is Too Much with Us"* (page 113)

Fox, Arnold, and Martin Kallich. "Wordsworth's Sentimental Naturalism." *The Wordsworth Circle* 8 (1977): 327–32.

Kroeber, Karl. "A New Reading of 'The World Is Too Much with Us'." *Studies in Romanticism* 2 (1963): 183–88.

Proffitt, Edward. " 'This Pleasant Lea'." *The Wordsworth Circle* 11 (1980): 75–77.

WILLIAM WORDSWORTH, *"The Solitary Reaper"* (page 114)

Alexander, J. H. *Reading Wordsworth*. London: Routledge and Kegan Paul,

1987, 106, 110–12, 114, 129.

Finch, Geoffrey J. "Wordsworth's Solitary Song." *Ariel* 6 (3) (1975): 91–100.

Woodring, Carl. *Wordsworth*. Cambridge: Harvard University Press, 1968, 78, 79–82.

WILLIAM WORDSWORTH, *"Composed upon Westminster Bridge, September 3, 1802"* (page 116)

Fry, Paul H. "The Diligence of Desire." *The Wordsworth Circle* 23 (3) (Summer 1992): 162–64.

Holland, Patrick. "The Two Contrasts of Wordsworth's 'Westminster' Sonnet." *The Wordsworth Circle* 8 (1977): 32–34.

Woodring, Carl. *Wordsworth*. Cambridge: Harvard University Press, 1968, 166–68.

WILLIAM WORDSWORTH, *"A Slumber Did My Spirit Seal"* (page 117)

Minot, Walter S. "Wordsworth's Use of Diurnal in 'A Slumber Did My Spirit Seal'." *Papers on Language and Literature* 9 (1973): 319–22.

Moise, Edwin. "Wordsworth's 'A Slumber Did My Spirit Seal'." *The Explicator* 53 (4) (Summer 1995): 196–97.

Nixon, David. "Wordsworth's 'A Slumber Did My Spirit Seal'." *The Explicator* 41 (2) (Fall 1982): 25–26.

SAMUEL TAYLOR COLERIDGE, *"Kubla Khan"* (page 120)

Beer, John. "The Languages of 'Kubla Khan'." In Richard Gravil et al., eds., *Coleridge's Imagination: Essays in Memory of Pete Laver*. Cambridge: Cambridge University Press, 1985, 220–62.

Lowes, John Livingston. *The Road to Xanadu*. Princeton: Princeton University Press, 1986.

Magnuson, Paul. " 'Kubla Khan': That Phantom-World So Fair." In Leonard Orr, ed., *Critical Essays on Samuel Taylor Coleridge*. New York: G. K. Hall, 1994, 71–80.

GEORGE GORDON BYRON, 6TH BARON BYRON, *"So, We'll Go No More a-Roving"* (page 125)

Calder, Angus. *Byron*. Philadelphia: Open University Press, 1988, 40–41.

Shilstone, Frederick W. *Byron and the Myth of Tradition*. Lincoln: University of Nebraska Press, 1988, 119.

Witt, Robert W. " 'So We'll Go No More a-Roving'." *University of Mississippi Studies in English* 9 (1968): 69–84.

GEORGE GORDON BYRON, 6TH BARON BYRON, *"She Walks in Beauty"* (page 126)

Ashton, Thomas L. *Byron's Hebrew Melodies*. Austin: University of Texas Press, 1972, 132–33.

Elwin, Malcolm. *Lord Byron's Wife*. New York: Harcourt, Brace, 1962, 426.

Shilstone, Frederick W. "The Lyric Collection as Genre: Byron's Hebrew Melodies." *Concerning Poetry* 12 (1) (1979): 45–52.

PERCY BYSSHE SHELLEY, *"Ode to the West Wind"* (page 129)

Chayes, Irene H. "Rhetoric as Drama: An Approach to the Romantic Ode." *Publications of the Modern Language Association of America* 79 (March 1964): 71–74.

Duffy, Edward. "Where Shelley Wrote and What He Wrote: The Example of 'Ode to the West Wind'." *Studies in Romanticism* 23 (3) (Fall 1984): 351–77.

Friedrich, Reinhard H. "The Apocalyptic Mode and Shelley's 'Ode to the West Wind'." *Renascence* 36 (3) (Spring 1984): 161–70.

PERCY BYSSHE SHELLEY, *"Ozymandias"* (page 133)

Freedman, William, "Postponement and Perspectives in Shelley's 'Ozymandias'." *Studies in Romanticism* 25 (1) (Spring 1986): 63–73.

Fruman, Norman. " 'Ozymandias' and the Reconciliation of Opposites." *Studies in the Literary Imagination* 19 (2) (Fall 1986): 71–87.

Janowitz, Anne. "Shelley's Monument to 'Ozymandias'." *Philological Quarterly* 63 (4) (Fall 1984): 477–91.

PERCY BYSSHE SHELLEY, *"To a Skylark"* (page 134)

Cervo, Nathan. "Hopkins' 'The Caged Skylark' and Shelley's 'To A Skylark'." *The Explicator* 47 (1) (Fall 1988): 16–20.

Harvey, C. J. D. "Wordsworth and the Young Romantics: An Analysis of 'To A Skylark'." In Brian Green, ed., *Generous Converse*. Oxford: Oxford University Press, 1980, 64–70.

Ulmer, William A. "Some Hidden Want: Aspiration in 'To A Skylark'." *Studies in Romanticism* 23 (2) (Summer 1984): 245–58.

JOHN KEATS, *"To Autumn"* (page 141)

Hartmann, Geoffrey H. "Poem and Ideology: A Study of Keats' 'To Autumn'." In Brady, et. al., eds., *Literary Theory and Structure: Essays in Honor of William K. Wimsatt*. New Haven: Yale University Press, 1973, 305–30.

Macksey, Richard. " 'To Autumn' and the Music of Mortality." In Reed,

Arden, eds., *Romanticism and Language*. Ithaca: Cornell University Press, 1984, 263–308.

Vendler, Helen. *The Odes of John Keats*. Cambridge: Harvard University Press, 1983, 227–88.

JOHN KEATS, *"La Belle Dame sans Merci"* (page 143)

Alwes, Karla. *Imagination Transformed*. Carbondale and Edwardsville: Southern Illinois University Press, 1993, 6–7, 103–12.

Cohen, Jane R. "Keats's Humor in 'La Belle Dame Sans Merci'." *Keats-Shelley Journal* 17 (1968): 10–13.

Moise, Edwin. "Keats's 'La Belle Dame sans Merci'." *The Explicator* 50 (2) (Winter 1992): 72–74.

JOHN KEATS, *"On First Looking into Chapman's Homer"* (page 146)

Bernhard, Frank. "Keats's 'On First Looking into Chapman's Homer'." *The Explicator* 42 (1) (Fall 1983): 20–21.

Carroll, D. Allen. "Keats's 'Chapman's Homer' and the Vagaries of Identification." In John A. Alford and Donald Schoonmaker, eds., *English Romanticism*. East Lansing, Mich.: Colleagues Press, 1993, 59–70.

Flautz, John. "On Most Recently Looking into 'On First Looking into Chapman's Homer'." *CEA Critic: An Official Journal of the College English Association* 40 (3) (1978): 24–27.

JOHN KEATS, *"Ode to a Nightingale"* (page 148)

Farrell, Jennifer. *Keats—The Progress of the Odes*. Frankfurt am Main: Peter Lang, 1989, 26–53.

Fraser, G. S. *John Keats: Odes*. London: Macmillan, 1971.

Vendler, Helen. *The Odes of John Keats*. Cambridge: Harvard University Press, 1983, 71–109.

ELIZABETH BARRETT BROWNING, *"How Do I Love Thee? Let Me Count the Ways"* (page 154)

Blank, G. Kim. *Wordsworth and Feeling*. Madison, N.J.: Associated University Presses, 1995, 149–53, 156.

Dilworth, Thomas. "Wordsworth's 'She Dwelt Among the Untrodden Ways'." *The Explicator* (42) (3) (Spring 1984): 22–23.

Jones, Mark. *The Lucy Poems: A Case Study in Literary Knowledge*. Toronto: University of Toronto Press, 1995.

EDGAR ALLAN POE, *"To Helen"* (page 156)

Davidson, Edward H. *Poe, A Critical Study*. Cambridge: Harvard University
   Press, 1957, 32–34, 36, 37, 41, 92.
Hammond, J. R. *An Edgar Allan Poe Companion*. London: Macmillan, 1981,
   9, 55, 156–57.
Hoffman, Daniel. *Poe, Poe, Poe, Poe, Poe, Poe, Poe*. New York: Fred Ungar
   Publishing Co., 1984, 37, 96–98.

EDGAR ALLAN POE, *"Annabel Lee"* (page 158)

Jones, Buford, and Kent Lungquist. "Poe, Mrs. Osgood, and 'Annabel Lee'."
   Studies in the American Renaissance 1983, 275–80.
Knapp, Bettina L. *Edgar Allan Poe*. New York: Fred Ungar Publishing Co.,
   1984, 37, 96–98.
Nagy, Deborah K. " 'Annabel Lee': Poe's Ballad." *Artes Liberales* 3 (2) (1977):
   29–34.

ALFRED, LORD TENNYSON, *"Break, Break, Break"* (page 162)

Assad, Thomas J. "Tennyson's 'Break, Break, Break'." *Tulane Studies in English*
   12 (1963): 71–80.
Ricks, Christopher. *Tennyson*. London: Macmillan, 1989, 111, 133–34, 161.
Sopher, H. "The 'Puzzling Plainness' of 'Break, Break, Break'." *Victorian Poetry*
   19 (1) (Spring 1981): 87–93.

ALFRED, LORD TENNYSON, *"The Eagle"* (page 164)

Culler, A. Dwight. *The Poetry of Tennyson*. New Haven: Yale University Press,
   1977, 242–43.
Sutherland, Raymond C. "The 'St. John Sense' Underlying 'The Eagle'."
   Studies in the Literary Imagination 1 (1) (1968): 23–35.
Tucker, Herbert F. *Tennyson and the Doom of Romanticism*. Cambridge:
   Harvard University Press, 1988.

ALFRED, LORD TENNYSON, *"Ulysses"* (page 165)

Austin, Timothy R. " 'Sadness and Stoicism': Stylistic Reflections on 'Ulysses,'
   Tennyson's Elusive Elegy." *Language and Style* 22 (4) (Fall 1989): 459–76.
Dramin, Edward. " 'Work of Noble Note': Tennyson's 'Ulysses' and Victorian
   Heroic Ideals." *Victorian Literature and Culture* 20 (1992): 117–39.
Rowlinson, Matthew. "The Ideological Moment of Tennyson's 'Ulysses'."
   Victorian Poetry 30 (3–4) (Autumn–Winter 1992): 265–76.

ROBERT BROWNING, *"My Last Duchess"* (page 170)

Adler, Joshua. "Structure and Meaning in Browning's 'My Last Duchess'."
  Victorian Poetry 15 (1977): 219–27.
Gemette, Elizabeth V. "Browning's 'My Last Duchess': An Untenable
  Position." *Studies in Browning and His Circle* 10 (1) (Spring 1982): 40–45.
Miller, L. M. " 'My Last Duchess': A Studiolo Setting?" *Victorian Poetry* 23 (2)
  (Summer 1985): 188–93.

ROBERT BROWNING, *"Meeting at Night"* (page 174)

Kroeber, Karl. "Touchstones for Browning's Victorian Complexity." *Victorian
  Poetry* 3 (2) (Spring 1965): 101–7.
McNally, James. "Suiting Sight and Sound to Sense in 'Meeting at Night' and
  'Parting at Morning'." *Victorian Poetry* 5 (1967): 219–24.
Solimine, Joseph, Jr. "Browning's 'My Last Duchess'." *The Explicator* 26
  (1967): Item 11.

ROBERT BROWNING, *"Home-Thoughts, from Abroad"* (page 176)

Gibson, Mary Ellis, ed. *Critical Essays on Robert Browning.* New York: G. K.
  Hall, 1992, 16.
Phelps, William Lyon. *Robert Browning.* Hamden, Conn.: Archon Books,
  1968, 83–84, 85, 100.
Werlich, Egon. "Robert Browning, 'Home-Thoughts, from Abroad': An
  Interpretation with Particular Emphasis on the Poem's Structural and
  Syntactical Symbolism." *Praxis: A Journal of Culture and Criticism* (1968):
  135–42.

ARTHUR HUGH CLOUGH, *"The Latest Decalogue"* (page 179)

Biswas, Robindra Kumar. *Anthony Hugh Clough: Towards a Reconsideration.*
  Oxford: The Clarendon Press, 1972, 198, 211, 372.
Houghton, Walter E. *The Poetry of Clough: An Essay in Revaluation.* New
  York: Octagon, 1979, 38, 56, 72–73.
Phelan, J. P. *Clough.* London and New York: Longman, 1995, 264–65.

JULIA WARD HOWE, *"The Battle Hymn of the Republic"* (page 182)

Clifford, Deborah Pickman. *Mine Eyes Have Seen the Glory.* Boston: Little,
  Brown, 1979, 144–48, 159, 168, 182, 186, 223, 260, 276, 277.
Snyder, Edward D. "The Biblical Background of the Battle Hymn." *New
  England Quarterly* 24 (1951): 231–38.
Wilson, Edmund. *Patriotic Gore: Studies in the Literature of the American Civil
  War.* New York: Oxford University Press, 1962, 91–96.

MATTHEW ARNOLD, *"Dover Beach"* (page 185)

Harris, Wendell V. and Norman N. Holland. "Psychological Depths and 'Dover Beach'." *Victorian Studies* (1966): 5–28, 70–82.

Honan, Park. *Matthew Arnold: A Life*. New York: McGraw-Hill, 1981, 233–37.

Ulmer, William A. "The 'Bright Girdle' of 'Dover Beach'." *English Language Notes* 22 (4) (June 1985): 54–58.

EMILY DICKINSON, *"Because I Could Not Stop for Death"* (page 188)

Browsky, Francis. "A Continuation of the Tradition of the Irony of Death." *Dickinson Studies* 54 (1984): 33–42.

Galperin, William H. "Emily Dickinson's Marriage Hearse." *Denver Quarterly* 18 (4) (Winter 1984) 62–73.

Green, John M. "Dickinson's 'Because I Could Not Stop For Death'." *The Explicator* 49 (4) (Summer 1991): 218–19.

EMILY DICKINSON, *"I Heard a Fly Buzz—When I Died"* (page 190)

Bachinger, Katrina. "Dickinson's 'I Heard A Fly Buzz'." *The Explicator* 43 (3) (Spring 1985): 12–15.

Monteiro, George. "Dickinson's 'I Heard A Fly Buzz'." *The Explicator* 43 (1) (Fall 1984): 43–45.

Rachal, John. "Probing the Final Mystery in Dickinson's 'I Heard A Fly Buzz'." *Dickinson Studies* 39 (1981): 44–46.

EMILY DICKINSON, *"A Narrow Fellow in the Grass"* (page 191)

Johnson, Greg. *Emily Dickinson: Perception and the Poet's Quest*. Montgomery: University of Alabama Press, 1985, 35–37.

Monteiro, George. "Dickinson's 'A Narrow Fellow in the Grass'." *The Explicator* 51 (1) (Fall 1992): 20–22.

Sciarra, T. "A Woman Looking Inward." *Dickinson Studies* 39 (1981): 36–40.

LEWIS CARROLL, *"Jabberwocky"* (page 194)

Clark, Beverly Lyon. "Carroll's Well-Versed Narrative: Through the Looking Glass." In Guiliano, Edward, and Kincaid, eds., *Carroll Studies No. 6: Soaring with the Dodo*. The Lewis Carroll Society of North America and The University Press of Virginia, 1982, 65–76.

Richards, Fran. "The Poetic Structure of 'Jabberwocky'." *Jabberwocky: The Journal of the Lewis Carroll Society* 8 (1) (1978–79 Winter): 16–19.

Tuckerman, Charles S. "Carroll's 'Jabberwocky'." *The Explicator* 31 (1972): Item 16.

THOMAS HARDY, *"The Darkling Thrush"* (page 198)

Burns, R. A. "Imagery in Hardy's 'The Darkling Thrush'." *Concerning Poetry*
    10 (1) (1977): 87–89.
May, Charles E. "Hardy's 'Darkling Thrush'." *Victorian Poetry* 11 (1973): 62–65.
Williams, Merry. *A Preface to Hardy*. London: Longman, 1993, 58, 150–53.

GERARD MANLEY HOPKINS, *"Pied Beauty"* (page 201)

Dunlap, Elizabeth D. "Sound and Sense in 'Pied Beauty'." *The Hopkins
    Quarterly* 3 (1) (April 1976): 35–38.
Kuhn, Joaquin. "The Completeness of 'Pied Beauty'." *Studies in English
    Literature 1500–1900* 18 (1978): 677–92.
Lowenstein, Amy. "Seeing 'Pied Beauty': A Key to Theme and Structure."
    Victorian Poetry 14 (1976): 64–66.

GERARD MANLEY HOPKINS, *"Spring and Fall"* (page 203)

Doherty, Paul C. "Hopkins' 'Spring and Fall: To a Young Child'." *Victorian
    Poetry* 5 (2) (Summer 1967): 140–43.
Gardner, W. H. *Gerard Manley Hopkins*. London: Oxford University Press,
    1966, 238–40.
Myers, John A., Jr. "Intimations of Mortality: An Analysis of Hopkins'
    'Spring and Fall'." *The English Journal* 51 (8) (November 1962): 585–87.

GERARD MANLEY HOPKINS, *"The Windhover"* (page 204)

Bump, Jerome. *Gerard Manley Hopkins*. Boston: Twayne, 1982, 88–93.
Robinson, John. *In Extremity: A Study of Gerard Manley Hopkins*. Cambridge:
    Cambridge University Press, 1978, 42–52.
Schoder, Raymond V. "What Does 'The Windhover' Mean?" In *Immortal
    Diamond: Studies in Gerard Manley Hopkins*. New York: Octagon, 1969,
    275–306.

WILLIAM BUTLER YEATS, 1865-1939 (page 206)

Poems. Richard Finneran, ed. New York: Macmillan, 1983.
Donoghue, Denis. *William Butler Yeats*. New York: Ecco Press, 1989.
Ellmann, Richard. *The Identity of Yeats*. New York: Oxford University Press,
    1964.

WILLIAM BUTLER YEATS, *"The Second Coming"* (page 207)

Cervo, Nathan. "Yeats's 'The Second Coming'." *The Explicator* 53 (3) (Spring
    1995): 161–63.

Murphy, Russell E. "The 'Rough Beast' and Historical Necessity." *Studies in the Literary Imagination* 14 (1) (Spring 1981): 101–10.

Wheeler, Richard P. "Yeats's 'Second Coming': What Rough Beast?" *American Imago* 31 (1974): 233–51.

WILLIAM BUTLER YEATS, *"The Lake Isle of Innisfree"* (page 209)

Bloom, Harold. *Yeats*. New York: Oxford University Press, 1970, 112–13, 125.

Kinahan, Frank. *Yeats, Folklore and Occultism*. Boston: Unwin, Hyman, Inc., 1988, 188–89, 209, 213 note.

Malins, Edward and John Purkis. *A Preface to Yeats*. London: Longman, 1994, 82, 174–75.

WILLIAM BUTLER YEATS, *"Leda and the Swan"* (page 210)

Fletcher, Ian. " 'Leda and the Swan' as Iconic Poem." In Richard J. Finneran, ed., *Yeats Annual* 1 (1982): 82–113.

Nitsche, Jessica and Monica I. Parry. "Yeats's View of Power in 'Leda and the Swan'." *Notes on Contemporary Literature* 22 (5) (November 1992): 9–11.

Pritchard, William H., ed. *W. B. Yeats: A Critical Anthology*. Baltimore, Md: Penguin, 1972, 111, 133–34, 218, 265–67, 343, 363.

WILLIAM BUTLER YEATS, *"Sailing to Byzantium"* (page 212)

Allen, James Lovic. "From Innisfree to Hagia Sophia: The Heritage of Meaning in Yeats's 'Sailing to Byzantium'." *Yeats Eliot Review* 10 (4) (Fall 1990): 85–89.

Lense, Edward. "Sailing the Seas to Nowhere." *Yeats: An Annual of Critical and Textual Studies* 5 (1987): 95–106.

Steinman, Michael. "Yeats's 'Sailing to Byzantium'." *The Explicator* 52 (2) (Winter 1994): 93–94.

ERNEST DOWSON, *"Non Sum Qualis Eram Bonae Sub Regno Cynarae"* (page 214)

Gardiner, Bruce. "Decadence: Its Construction and Contexts." *Southern Review* 18 (March 1985): 22–45.

Magill, Frank, ed. "Ernest Christopher Dowson." In *English Literature: Romanticism to 1945*. Pasadena, Calif.: Salem Press, 380–81.

Perkins, David. *A History of Modern Poetry from the 1890s to the High Modernist Mode*. Cambridge: Harvard University Press, 1976, 37–40.

EDWIN ARLINGTON ROBINSON, *"Miniver Cheevy"* (page 218)

Bloom, Harold, ed. *Edwin A. Robinson: Modern Critical Views*. New York: Chelsea House, 1988, 91–95.

Ellsworth, Barnard. *Edwin A. Robinson: A Critical Study*. New York: Octagon, 1977.

Sullivan, Winifred H. "The Double-Edged Irony of E. A. Robinson's 'Miniver Cheevy'." *Colby Library Quarterly* 22 (3) (September 1986): 185–91.

EDWIN ARLINGTON ROBINSON, *"Mr. Flood's Party"* (page 220)

Brasher, Thomas L. "Robinson's 'Mr. Flood's Party'." *The Explicator* 29 (1971): Item 45.

Davis, William V. " 'Enduring to the End': Edwin Arlington Robinson's 'Mr. Flood's Party'." *Colby Library Quarterly* 12 (1976): 50–51.

Joyner, Nancy. "An Unpublished Version of 'Mr. Flood's Party'." *English Language Notes* 7 (1969): 55–57.

WALTER DE LA MARE, *"The Listeners"* (page 225)

Bentinck, A. "De la Mare's 'The Listeners'." The Explicator 50 (1) (Fall 1991): 33–35.

Pierson, Robert M. "De la Mare's 'The Listeners'." *English Studies* 45 (1964): 373–81.

Whistler, Theresa. *Imagination of the Heart*. London: Duckworth, 1993, 203, 207 note, 269–70, 348.

ROBERT FROST, *"Stopping by Woods on a Snowy Evening"* (page 228)

Greiner, Donald J. "Robert Frost's Dark Woods and the Function of Metaphor." *Frost Centennial Essays*. Jackson: University of Mississippi Press, 1974–78, 373–88.

Poirier, Richard. *Robert Frost: The Work of Knowing*. New York: Oxford University Press, 1977, 7, 67, 74, 180–83, 235, 268.

Thompson, Lawrance. *Fire and Ice*. New York: Russell & Russell, 1961, 25–27, 84, 123, 137.

ROBERT FROST, *"Mending Wall"* (page 230)

Coulthard, A. R. "Frost's 'Mending Wall'." *The Explicator* 45 (2) (Winter 1987): 40–42.

Morrissey, L. J. " 'Mending Wall': The Structure of Gossip." *English Language Notes* 25 (3) (March 1988): 58–63.

Oehlschlaeger, Fritz. "Fences Make Neighbors: Process, Identity, and Ego in

Robert Frost's 'Mending Wall'." *Arizona Quarterly* 40 (3) (Autumn 1984): 242–54.

T. S. ELIOT, *"The Love Song of J. Alfred Prufrock"* (page 233)

Childs, Donald J. "Knowledge and Experience in 'The Love Song of J. Alfred Prufrock'." *English Literary History* 55 (3) (Fall 1988): 685–99.

Dickson, Lloyd F. "Prufrock in a Labyrinth: A Text Without Exits." *Yeats Eliot Review: A Journal of Criticism and Scholarship* 9 (4) (Summer–Fall 1988): 140–44.

Ledbetter, James H. "Eliot's 'The Love Song of J. Alfred Prufrock'." *The Explicator* 51 (1) (Fall 1992): 41–45.

WILFRED OWEN, *"Strange Meeting"* (page 240)

Kerr, Douglas. *Wilfred Owen's Voices*. New York: Oxford University Press, 1989.

Lane, Arthur E. *An Adequate Response: The War Poetry of Wilfred Owen and Siegfried Sassoon*. Detroit, Mich.: Wayne State University Press, 1972, 159–63.

Welland, Dennis. *Wilfred Owen: A Critical Study*. London: Chatto & Windus, 1978, 99–103.

W. H. AUDEN, *"Musée des Beaux Arts"* (page 243)

Dilworth, Thomas. "Auden's 'Musée des Beaux Arts'." *The Explicator* 49 (3) (Spring 1991): 181–83.

Mason, Kenneth M., Jr. "Auden's 'Musée des Beaux Arts'." *The Explicator* 48 (4) (Summer 1990): 283–84.

Willson, Robert F., Jr. "The Person and the Poem: Irony in Auden's 'Musée des Beaux Arts'." *Studies in Contemporary Satire* 3 (1976): 1–8.

THEODORE ROETHKE, *"My Papa's Waltz"* (page 246)

Balakian, Peter. *Theodore Roethke's Far Fields*. Baton Rouge: Louisiana State Press, 1989, 62.

Fong, Bobby. "Roethke's 'My Papa's Waltz'." *College Literature* 17 (1) (1990): 79–82.

Janssen, Ronald R. "Roethke's 'My Papa's Waltz'." *The Explicator* 44 (2) (Winter 1986): 43–44.

RANDALL JARRELL, *"The Death of the Ball Turret Gunner"*
(page 249)

Bassett, Patrick F. "Jarrell's 'The Death of the Ball Turret Gunner'." *The Explicator* 36 (3) (1978): 20–21.
Ferguson, Suzanne, ed. *Critical Essays on Randall Jarrell.* Boston: G. K. Hall, 1983. 2, 29, 52, 155–58, 169, 171, 172, 238–40, 244, 317.
Horner, Patrick J. "Jarrell's 'The Death of the Ball Turret Gunner'." *The Explicator* 36 (4) (1978): 9–10.

DYLAN THOMAS, *"Do Not Go Gentle into That Good Night"*
(page 251)

Kidder, Rushworth M. *Dylan Thomas: The Country of the Spirit.* Princeton: Princeton University Press, 1973, 94, 187–90, 197.
Murphy, Michael W. "Thomas' 'Do Not Go Gentle into That Good Night'." *The Explicator* 28 (1970): Item 55.
Westphal, Jonathan. "Thomas' 'Do Not Go Gentle into That Good Night'." *The Explicator* 52 (2) (Winter 1994): 113–15.

DYLAN THOMAS, *"Fern Hill"* (page 252)

Holley, Linda Tarte. "Dylan Thomas' 'Fern Hill': The Breaking of the Circles." *Concerning Poetry* 15 (2) (Fall 1982): 59–67.
Joselyn, M. " 'Green and Dying': The Drama of 'Fern Hill'." *Renascence: Essays on Value in Literature* 16 (1964): 219–21.
Viswanathan, R. "Thomas' 'Fern Hill'." *The Explicator* 48 (4) (Summer 1990): 285–86.

DYLAN THOMAS, *"A Refusal to Mourn the Death, by Fire, of a Child in London"* (page 255)

Gaston, Georg. *Critical Essays on Dylan Thomas.* Boston: G. K. Hall, 1989, 134–35.
Montgomery, Benilde. "The Function of Ambiguity in 'A Refusal to Mourn the Death, by Fire, of a Child in London'." *Concerning Poetry* 8 (2) (1971): 77–81.
Napieralski, Edmund A. "Thomas's 'A Refusal to Mourn the Death, by Fire, of a Child in London'." *The Explicator* 50 (3) (Spring 1992): 172–75.

The Poems in Order of Popularity

To Autumn
Kubla Khan
La Belle Dame sans Merci
The Passionate Shepherd to His Love
Stopping by Woods on a Snowy Evening
Death, Be Not Proud
Love III
To Lucasta, Going to the Wars
To the Virgins, to Make Much of Time
My Last Duchess
Pied Beauty
Ode to the West Wind
To His Coy Mistress
Because I Could Not Stop for Death
Dover Beach
The Tyger
Upon Julia's Clothes
Batter My Heart, Three-Personed God
A Red, Red Rose
Spring and Fall
Do Not Go Gentle into That Good Night
On First Looking into Chapman's Homer
At the Round Earth's Imagined Corners
Fear No More the Heat o' the Sun
Fern Hill
She Dwelt Among the Untrodden Ways

The Good-Morrow
So, We'll Go No More a-Roving
When to the Sessions of Sweet Silent Thought
The World Is Too Much with Us
And Did Those Feet in Ancient Time
The Lamb
Ozymandias
The Second Coming
The Solitary Reaper
Break, Break, Break
The Garden
The Listeners
Let Me Not to the Marriage of True Minds
The Lake Isle of Innisfree
Miniver Cheevy
Musée des Beaux Arts
The Retreat
Why So Pale and Wan, Fond Lover?
Jabberwocky
Mr. Flood's Party
The Nymph's Reply to the Shepherd
The Darkling Thrush
Home-Thoughts, from Abroad
I Heard a Fly Buzz
Leda and the Swan
She Walks in Beauty
Elegy Written in a Country Churchyard
Delight in Disorder
The Eagle
Mending Wall
Ode on the Death of a Favorite Cat, Drowned in a Tub of Gold Fishes
On My First Son
Sailing to Byzantium
Shall I Compare Thee to a Summer's Day?
With How Sad Steps, O Moon, Thou Climb'st the Skies
The Sun Rising
Ask Me No More Where Jove Bestows
The Death of the Ball Turret Gunner
Sir Patrick Spens
How Do I Love Thee? Let Me Count the Ways

The Expense of Spirit in a Waste of Shame
To Althea, from Prison
A Valediction: Forbidding Mourning
The Windhover
Edward, Edward
London
Song: To Celia
That Time of Year Thou Mayst in Me Behold
Still to Be Neat
When Icicles Hang by the Wall
Annabel Lee
Composed upon Westminster Bridge, September 3, 1802
The Latest Decalogue
Meeting at Night
Non Sum Qualis Eram Bonae sub Regno Cynarae
The Pulley
A Refusal to Mourn the Death, by Fire, of a Child in London
Go and Catch a Falling Star
Strange Meeting
To Helen
They Flee from Me That Sometime Did Me Seek
Western Wind
The Battle Hymn of the Republic
Go, Lovely Rose
The Love Song of J. Alfred Prufrock
Lycidas
My Papa's Waltz
A Narrow Fellow in the Grass
Ode to a Nightingale
A Slumber Did My Spirit Seal
To a Skylark
Auguries of Innocence
Ulysses
Virtue

INDEX OF POETS

INDEX OF TITLES & FIRST LINES

Acknowledgments

Doubleday. Theodore Roethke: "My Papa's Waltz," copyright © 1942 by Hearst Magazines, Inc. from *The Collected Poems of Theodore Roethke* by Theodore Roethke. Used by permission of Doubleday, a division of Bantam Doubleday Dell Publishing Group, Inc.

Faber and Faber Ltd. W. H. Auden: "Musée des Beaux Arts" from *Collected Poems* by W. H. Auden. T. S. Eliot: "The Love Song of J. Alfred Prufrock" from *Collected Poems 1909–1962* by T. S. Eliot. Randall Jarrell: "The Death of the Ball Turret Gunner" from *The Complete Poems* by Randall Jarrell. Theodore Roethke: "My Papa's Waltz" from *The Collected Poems of Theodore Roethke* by Theodore Roethke. Reprinted by permission of Faber and Faber Ltd.

Farrar, Straus & Giroux, Inc. Randall Jarrell: "The Death of the Ball Turret Gunner" from *The Complete Poems* by Randall Jarrell. Copyright © 1945, renewed 1972 by Mrs. Randall Jarrell. Reprinted by permission of Farrar, Straus & Giroux, Inc.

Harcourt Brace Jovanovich. T. S. Eliot: "The Love Song of J. Alfred Prufrock" from *Collected Poems 1909–1962* by T. S. Eliot, copyright © 1936 by Harcourt Brace Jovanovich, Inc., copyright © 1963, 1964 by T. S. Eliot, reprinted by permission of the publisher.

Harvard University Press. Emily Dickinson: "Because I Could Not Stop for Death," "I Heard a Fly Buzz," and "A Narrow Fellow in the Grass" from *The Poems of Emily Dickinson*, Thomas H. Johnson, editor. Cambridge, Mass.: The Belknap Press of Harvard University Press, copyright © 1951, 1955, 1979, 1983 by the President and Fellows of Harvard College. Poetry used by permission of the publishers and the Trustees of Amherst College.

David Higham Associates Limited. Dylan Thomas: "Do Not Go Gentle into That Good Night," "Fern Hill," and "A Refusal to Mourn the Death, by Fire, of a Child in London" from *The Poems* published by J. M. Dent. Reprinted by permission of David Higham Associates Limited.

Henry Holt & Company. Robert Frost: "Stopping by Woods on a Snowy Evening" from *The Poetry of Robert Frost*, edited by Edward Connery Lathem. Copyright © 1951 by Robert Frost, copyright 1923, 1969 by Henry Holt and Company, Inc. Reprinted by permission of Henry Holt and Company.